THE SHADES OF THE WILDERNESS
A STORY OF LEE'S GREAT STAND

By
JOSEPH A. ALTSHELER

The Shades Of The Wilderness
A Story Of Lee's Great Stand

by Joseph A. Altsheler

Copyright © 2023

All Rights reserved.
No part of this publication may be reproduced, stored in a retrieval system, or transmitted in any form or by any means, electronic, mechanical, photocopying or Otherwise, without the written permission of the publisher.

The author/editor asserts the moral right to be identified as the author/editor of this work.

ISBN: 978-93-57486-21-7

Published by

DOUBLE 9 BOOKS

2/13-B, Ansari Road, Daryaganj
New Delhi – 110002
info@double9books.com
www.double9books.com
Tel. 011-40042856

This book is under public domain

ABOUT THE AUTHOR

Joseph A. Altsheler was born on April 29, 1862, in Three Springs, Hart County, Kentucky, to Joseph and Louise Altsheler. He was a newspaper reporter, editor, and author of popular juvenile historical fiction. He wrote fifty novels and at least fifty-three short stories. Seven of his novels were in sequence. He worked as an editor at the Louisville Courier-Journal in 1885. In 1892, he started to work for New York World and then as the editor of the World's tri-weekly magazine. He wrote children's stories due to a lack of suitable stories. On May 30, 1880, Altsheler married Sarah Boles and had a son named Sidney. In 1914, during World War I Altsheler and his family were in Germany and they were forced to remain there. Altsheler died at the age of 57, on June 5, 1919, in New York. His wife, Sarah Boles died after 30 years. Their bodies are buried at the Cave Hill Cemetery in Louisville, Kentucky. Although each of the thirty-two novels constitutes an independent story, Altsheler suggested reading in sequence for each series (that is, he numbered the volumes). You can read the remaining eighteen novels in any order.

CONTENTS

CHAPTER I
THE SOUTHERN RETREAT 7

CHAPTER II
THE NORTHERN SPY 24

CHAPTER III
THE FLOODED RIVER 38

CHAPTER IV
A HERALD TO LEE 54

CHAPTER V
THE DANGEROUS ROAD 70

CHAPTER VI
TESTS OF COURAGE 85

CHAPTER VII
IN THE WAGON 99

CHAPTER VIII
THE CROSSING 109

CHAPTER IX
IN SOCIETY 123

CHAPTER X
THE MISSING PAPER 139

CHAPTER XI
    A VAIN PURSUIT 153

CHAPTER XII
    IN WINTER QUARTERS 167

CHAPTER XIII
    THE COMING OF GRANT 182

CHAPTER XIV
    THE GHOSTLY RIDE 195

CHAPTER XV
    THE WILDERNESS 208

CHAPTER XVI
    SPOTTSYLVANIA 228

CHAPTER I
THE SOUTHERN RETREAT

A train of wagons and men wound slowly over the hills in the darkness and rain toward the South. In the wagons lay fourteen or fifteen thousand wounded soldiers, but they made little noise, as the wheels sank suddenly in the mud or bumped over stones. Although the vast majority of them were young, boys or not much more, they had learned to be masters of themselves, and they suffered in silence, save when some one, lost in fever, uttered a groan.

But the chief sound was a blended note made by the turning of wheels, and the hoofs of horses sinking in the soft earth. The officers gave but few orders, and the cavalrymen who rode on either flank looked solicitously into the wagons now and then to see how their wounded friends fared, though they seldom spoke. The darkness they did not mind, because they were used to it, and the rain and the coolness were a relief, after three days of the fiercest battle the American continent had ever known, fought in the hottest days that the troops could recall.

Thus Lee's army drew its long length from the fatal field of Gettysburg, although his valiant brigades did not yet know that the clump of trees upon Cemetery Hill had marked the high tide of the Confederacy. All that memorable Fourth of July, following the close of the battle they had lain, facing Meade and challenging him to come on, confident that while the invasion of the North was over they could beat back once more the invasion of the South.

They had no word of complaint against their great commander, Lee. The faith in him, which was so high, remained unbroken, as it was destined to remain so to the last. But men began to whisper to one another, and say if only Jackson had been there. They mourned anew that terrible evening in the Wilderness when Lee had lost his mighty lieutenant, his striking arm, the invincible Stonewall. If the man in the old slouch hat had only been with Lee on Seminary Ridge it would now be the army of Meade retreating farther into the North, and they would be pursuing. That belief was destined to sink deep in the soul of the South, and remain there long after the Confederacy was but a name.

The same thought was often in the mind of Harry Kenton, as he rode near the rear of the column, whence he had been sent by Lee to observe and then to report. It was far after midnight now, and the last of the Southern army could not leave Seminary Ridge before morning. But Harry could detect no sign of pursuit. Now and then, a distant gun boomed, and the thunder muttered on the horizon, as if in answer. But there was nothing to indicate that the Army of the Potomac was moving from Gettysburg in pursuit, although the President in Washington, his heart filled with bitterness, was vainly asking why his army would not reap the fruits of a victory won so hardly. Fifty thousand men had fallen on the hills and in the valleys about Gettysburg, and it seemed, for the time, that nothing would come of such a slaughter. But the Northern army had suffered immense losses, and Lee and his men were ready to fight again if attacked. Perhaps it was wiser to remain content upon the field with their sanguinary success. At least, Meade and his generals thought so.

Harry, toward morning came upon St. Clair and Langdon riding together. Both had been wounded slightly, but their hurts had not kept them from the saddle, and they were in cheerful mood.

"You've been further back than we, Harry," said St. Clair. "Is Meade hot upon our track? We hear the throb of a cannon now and then."

"It doesn't mean anything. Meade hasn't moved. While we didn't win we struck the Yankees such a mighty blow that they'll have to rest, and breathe a while before they follow."

"And I guess we need a little resting and breathing ourselves," said Langdon frankly. "There were times when I thought the whole world had just turned itself into a volcano of fire."

"But we'll come back again," said St. Clair. "We'll make these Pennsylvania Dutchmen take notice of us a second time."

"That's the right spirit," said Langdon. "Arthur had nearly all of his fine uniform shot off him, but he's managed to fasten the pieces together, and ride on, just as if it were brand new."

But Harry was silent. The prescient spirit of his famous great grandfather, Henry Ware, had descended upon his valiant great grandson. Hope had not gone from him, but it did not enter his mind that they should invade Pennsylvania again.

"I'm glad to leave Gettysburg," he said. "More good men of ours have fallen there than anywhere else."

"That's true," said St. Clair, "but Marse Bob will win for us, anyhow. You don't think any of these Union generals here in the East can whip our Lee, do you?"

"Of course not!" said Happy Tom. "Besides, Lee has me to help him."

"How are Colonel Talbot and Lieutenant-Colonel St. Hilaire?" asked Harry.

"Sound asleep, both of 'em," replied St. Clair. "And it's a strange thing, too. They were sitting in a wagon, having resumed that game of chess which they began in the Valley of Virginia, but they were so exhausted that both fell sound asleep while playing. They are sitting upright, as they sleep, and Lieutenant-Colonel St. Hilaire's thumb and forefinger rest upon a white pawn that he intended to move."

"I hope they won't be jarred out of their rest and that they'll sleep on," said Harry. "Nobody deserves it more."

He waved a hand to his friends and continued his ride toward the rear. The column passed slowly on in silence. Now and then gusts of rain lashed across his face, but he liked the feeling. It was a fillip to his blood, and his nerves began to recover from the tremendous strain and excitement of the last four days.

Obeying his orders he rode almost directly back toward the field of Gettysburg from which the Southern forces were still marching. A friendly voice from a little wood hailed him, and he recognized it at once as that of Sherburne, who sat his horse alone among the trees.

"Come here, Harry," he said.

"Glad to find you alive, Sherburne. Where's your troop?"

"What's left of it is on ahead. I'll join the men in a few minutes. But look back there!"

Harry from the knoll, which was higher than he had thought, gazed upon a vast and dusky panorama. Once more the field of Gettysburg swam before him, not now in fire and smoke, but in vapors and misty rain. When he shut his eyes he saw again the great armies charging on the slopes, the blazing fire from hundreds of cannon and a hundred thousand rifles. There, too, went Pickett's brigades, devoted to death but never flinching. A sob burst from his throat, and he opened his eyes again.

"You feel about it as I do," said Sherburne. "We'll never come back into the North."

"It isn't merely a feeling within me, I know it."

"So do I, but we can still hold Virginia."

"I think so, too. Come, we'd better turn. There goes the field of Gettysburg. The rain and mist have blotted it out."

The panorama, the most terrible upon which Harry had ever looked, vanished in the darkness. The two rode slowly from the knoll and into the road.

"It will be daylight in an hour," said Sherburne, "and by that time the last of our men will be gone."

"And I must hasten to our commander-in-chief," said Harry.

"How is he?" asked Sherburne. "Does he seem downcast?"

"No, he holds his head as high as ever, and cheers the men. They say that Pickett's charge was a glorious mistake, but he takes all the blame for it, if there is any. He doesn't criticize any of his generals."

"Only a man of the greatest moral grandeur could act like that. It's because of such things that our people, boys, officers and all, will follow him to the death."

"Good-by, Sherburne," said Harry. "Hope I'll see you again soon."

He urged his horse into a faster gait, anxious to overtake Lee and report that all was well with the rear guard. He noticed once more, and with the greatest care that long line of the wounded and the unwounded, winding sixteen miles across the hills from Gettysburg to Chambersburg, and his mind was full of grave thoughts. More than two years in the very thick of the greatest war, then known, were sufficient to make a boy a man, at least in intellect and responsibility.

Harry saw very clearly, as he rode beside the retreating but valiant army that had failed in its great attempt, that their role would be the defensive. For a little while he was sunk in deep depression. Then invincible youth conquered anew, and hope sprang up again. The night was at the darkest, but dawn was not far away. Fugitive gusts of wind drenched him once more, but he did not mind it, nor did he pay any attention to the occasional growl of a distant gun. He was strong in the belief that Meade would not pursue—at least not yet. A general who had just lost nearly one-third of his own army was not in much condition to follow his enemy.

He urged his horse to increased speed, and pressed on toward the head of the column. The rain ceased and cool puffs of wind came out of the east. Then the blackness there turned to gray, which soon deepened into silver. Through the silver veil shot a bolt of red fire, and the sun came over the hills.

Although the green world had been touched with brown by the hot sun of July it looked fresh and beautiful to Harry. The brown in the morning sunlight was a rosy red, and the winds of dawn were charged with life. His horse, too, felt the change and it was easy now to force him into a gallop toward a fire on a low hill, which Harry felt sure had been built to cook breakfast for their great commander.

As he approached he saw Lee and his generals standing before the blaze, some eating, and others drinking. An orderly, near by, held the commander's famous horse, Traveller, and two or three horses belonging to the other generals were trying to find a little grass between the stony outcrops of the hills. Harry felt an overwhelming curiosity, but he kept it in restraint, dismounting at a little distance, and approaching on foot.

He could not observe much change in the general's appearance. His handsome gray suit was as neat as ever, and the three stars, the only marks of his rank that he wore, shone untarnished upon his collar. The dignified and cheerful manner that marked him before Gettysburg marked him also afterward. To Harry, so young and so thoroughly charged with the emotions of his time and section, he was a figure to be approached with veneration.

He saw the stalwart and bearded Longstreet and other generals whom he knew, among them the brilliant Stuart in his brilliant plumage, but rather quiet and subdued in manner now, since he had not come to Gettysburg as soon as he was needed. Harry hung back a little, fearing lest he might be regarded as thrusting himself into a company so much his superior in rank, but Lee saw him and beckoned to him.

"I sent you back toward Gettysburg to report on our withdrawal, Lieutenant Kenton," he said.

"Yes, sir. I returned all the way to the field. The last of our troops should be leaving there just about now. The Northern army had made no preparation for immediate pursuit."

"Your report agrees with all the others that I have received. How long have you been without sleep?"

"I don't know, sir," he said at last. "I can't remember. Maybe it has been two or three days."

Stuart, who held a cup of coffee in his hand, laughed. "The times have been such that there are generals as well as lieutenants," he said, "who can't remember when they've slept."

"You're exhausted, my lad," said Lee gravely and kindly, "and there's nothing more you can do for us just now. Take some breakfast with us, and then you must sleep in one of the wagons. An orderly will look after your horse."

Lee handed him a cup of coffee with his own hand, and Harry, thanking him, withdrew to the outer fringe of the little group, where he took his breakfast, amazed to find how hungry he was, although he had not thought of food before. Then without a word, as he saw that the generals were engrossed in a conference, he withdrew.

"You'll find Lieutenant Dalton of the staff in the covered wagon over there," said the orderly who had taken his horse. "The general sent him to it more'n two hours ago."

"Then I'll be inside it in less than two minutes," said Harry.

But with rest in sight he collapsed suddenly. His head fell forward of its own weight. His feet became lead. Everything swam before his eyes. He felt that he must sleep or die. But he managed to drag himself to the wagon and climbed inside. Dalton lay in the center of it so sound asleep that he was like one dead. Harry rolled him to one side, making room for himself, and lay down beside him. Then his eyes closed, and he, too, slept so soundly that he also looked like one dead.

He was awakened by Dalton pulling at him. The young Virginian was sitting up and looking at Harry with curiosity. He clapped his hands when the Kentuckian opened his eyes.

"Now I know that you're not dead," he said. "When I woke up and found you lying beside me I thought they had just put your body in here for safekeeping. As that's not the case, kindly explain to me and at once what you're doing in my wagon."

"I'm waking up just at present, but for an hour or two before that I was sleeping."

"Hour or two? Hour or two? Hear him! An orderly who I know is no liar told me that you got in here just after dawn. Now kindly lift that canvasflap, look out and tell me what you see."

Harry did as he was told, and was amazed. The same rolling landscape still met his eyes, and the sun was just about as high in the sky as it was when he had climbed into the wagon. But it was in the west now instead of the east.

"See and know, young man!" said Dalton, paternally. "The entire day has elapsed and here you have lain in ignorant slumber, careless of everything, reckless of what might happen to the army. For twelve hours General Lee has been without your advice, and how, lacking it, he has got this far, Heaven alone knows."

"It seems that he's pulled through, and, since I'm now awake, you can hurry to him and tell him I'm ready to furnish the right plans to stop the forthcoming Yankee invasion."

"They'll keep another day, but we've certainly had a good sleep, Harry."

"Yes, a provision or ammunition wagon isn't a bad place for a wornout soldier. I remember I slept in another such as this in the Valley of Virginia, when we were with Jackson."

He stopped suddenly and choked. He could not mention the name of Jackson, until long afterward, without something rising in his throat.

The driver obscured a good deal of the front view, but he suddenly turned a rubicund and smiling face upon them.

"Waked up, hev ye?" he exclaimed. "Wa'al it's about time. I've looked back from time to time an' I wuzn't at all shore whether you two gen'rals wuz alive or dead. Sometimes when the wagon slanted a lot you would roll over each other, but it didn't seem to make no diffunce. Pow'ful good sleepers you are."

"Yes," said Harry. "We're two of the original Seven Sleepers."

"I don't doubt that you are two, but they wuz more'n seven."

"How do you know?"

"'Cause at least seven thousand in this train have been sleepin' as hard as you wuz. I guess you mean the 'rig'nal Seventy Thousand Sleepers."

Harry's spirits had returned after his long sleep. He was a lad again. The weight of Gettysburg no longer rested upon him. The Army of Northern Virginia had merely made a single failure. It would strike again and again, as hard as ever.

"It's true that we've been slumbering," he said, "but we're as wide awake now as ever, Mr. Driver."

"My name ain't Driver," said the man.

"Then what is it?"

"Jones, Dick Jones, which I hold to be a right proper name."

"Not romantic, but short, simple and satisfying."

"I reckon so. Leastways, I've never wanted to change it. I'm from No'th Calliny, an' I've been followin' Bobby Lee a pow'ful long distance from home. Fine country up here in Pennsylvany, but I'd rather be back in them No'th Calliny mountains. You two young gen'rals may think it's an easy an' safe job drivin' a wagon loaded with ammunition. But s'pose you have to drive it right under fire, as you most often have to do, an' then if a shell or somethin' like it hits your wagon the whole thing goes off kerplunk, an' whar are you?"

"It's a sudden an' easy death," said Dalton, philosophically.

"Too sudden an' too easy. I don't mind tellin' you that seein' men killed an' wounded is a spo't that's beginnin' to pall on me. Reckon I've had enough of it to last me for the next thousand years. I've forgot, if I ever knowed, what this war wuz started about. Say, young fellers, I've got a wife back thar, a high-steppin', fine-lookin' gal not more'n twenty years old—I'm just twenty-five myself, an' we've got a year-old baby the cutest that wuz ever born. Now, when I wuz lookin' at that charge of Pickett's men, an' the whole world wuz blazin' with fire, an' all the skies wuz rainin' steel and lead, an' whar grass growed before, nothin' but bayonets wuz growin' then, do you know what I seed sometimes?"

"What was it?" asked Harry.

"Fur a secon' all that hell of fire an' smoke an' killin' would float away, an' I seed our mountain, with the cove, an' the trees, an' the green grass growin' in it, an' the branch, with the water so clear you could see your face in it, runnin' down the center, an' thar at the head of the cove my cabin, not much uv a buildin' to look at, no towerin' mansion, but just a stout two-room log cabin that the snows an' hails of winter can't break into, an' in the door wuz standin' Mary with the hair flyin' about her face, an' her eyes shinin', with the little feller in her arms, lookin' at me 'way off as I come walkin' fast down the cove toward 'em, returnin' from the big war."

There was a moment's silence, and Dalton said gruffly to hide his feelings:

"Dick Jones, by the time this war is over, and you go walking down the cove toward your home, a man with mustache and side whiskers will come forward to meet you, and he'll be that son of yours."

But Dick Jones cheerfully shook his head.

"The war ain't goin' to last that long," he said confidently, "an' I ain't goin' to git killed. What I saw will come true, 'cause I feel it so strong."

"There ought to be a general law forbidding a man with a young wife and baby to go to a war," said Harry.

"But they ain't no sich law," said Dick Jones, in his optimistic tone, "an' so we needn't worry 'bout it. But if you two gen'rals should happen along through the mountains uv western No'th Calliny after the war I'd like fur you to come to my cabin, an' see Mary an' the baby an' me. Our cove is named Jones' Cove, after my father, an' the branch that runs through it runs into Jones' Creek, an' Jones' Creek runs into the Yadkin River an' our county is Yadkin. Oh, you could find it plumb easy, if two sich great gen'rals as you wuzn't ashamed to eat sweet pertaters an' ham an' turkey an' co'n pone with a wagon driver like me."

Harry saw, despite his playful method of calling them generals, that he was thoroughly in earnest, and he was more moved than he would have been willing to confess.

"Too proud!" he said. "Why, we'd be glad!"

"Mebbe your road will lead that way," said Jones. "An' ef you do, jest remember that the skillet's on the fire, an' the latch string is hangin' outside the do'."

The allusion to the mountains made Harry's mind travel far back, over an almost interminable space of time now, it seemed, when he was yet a novice in war, to the home of Sam Jarvis, deep in the Kentucky mountains, and the old, old woman who had said to him as he left: "You will come again, and you will be thin and pale, and in rags, and you will fall at the door. I see you coming with these two eyes of mine."

A little shiver passed over him. He knew that no one could penetrate the future, but he shivered nevertheless, and he found himself saying mechanically:

"It's likely that I'll return through the mountains, and if so I'll look you up at that home in the cove on the brook that runs into Jones' Creek."

"That bein' settled," said Jones, "what do you gen'rals reckon to do jest now, after havin' finished your big sleep?"

"Your wagon is about to lose the first two passengers it has ever carried," replied Harry. "Orderlies have our horses somewhere. We belong on the staff of General Lee."

"An' you see him an' hear him talk every day? Some people are pow'ful lucky. I guess you'll say a lot about it when you're old men."

"We're going to say a lot about it while we're young men. Good-by, Mr. Jones. We've been in some good hotels, but we never slept better in any of them than we have in this moving one of yours."

"Good-by, you're always welcome to it. I think Marse Bob is on ahead."

The two left the wagon and took to a path beside the road, which was muddy and rutted deeply by innumerable hoofs and wheels. But grass and foliage were now dry after the heavy rains that followed the Battle of Gettysburg, and the sun was shining in late splendor. The army, taking the lack of pursuit and attack as proof that the enemy had suffered as much as they, if not more, was in good spirits, and many of the men sang their marching songs. A band ahead of them suddenly began to play mellow music, "Partant Pour La Syrie," and other old French songs. The airs became gay, festive, uplifting to the soul, and they tickled the feet of the young men.

"The Cajun band!" exclaimed Harry. "It never occurred to me that they weren't all dead, and here they are, playing us into happiness!"

"And the Invincibles, or what's left of them, won't be far away," said Dalton.

They walked on a little more briskly and beside them the vast length of the unsuccessful army still trailed its slow way back into the South. The sun was setting in uncommon magnificence, clothing everything in a shower of gold, through which the lilting notes of the music came to Harry and Dalton's ears. Presently the two saw them, the short, dark men from far Louisiana, not so many as they had been, but playing with all the fervor of old, putting their Latin souls into their music.

"And there are the Invincibles just ahead of them!" exclaimed Dalton. "The two colonels have left the wagon and are riding with their men. See, how erect they sit."

"I do see them, and they're a good sight to see," said Harry. "I hope they'll live to finish that chess game."

"And fifty years afterward, too."

A shout of joy burst from the road, and a tall young man, slender, dark and handsome, rushed out, and, seizing the hands of first one and then the other, shook them eagerly, his dark eyes glittering with happy surprise.

"Kenton! Dalton!" he exclaimed. "Both alive! Both well!"

It was young Julien de Langeais, the kinsman of Lieutenant-Colonel Hector St. Hilaire, and he too was unhurt. The lads returned his grasp warmly. They could not have kept from liking him had they tried, and they certainly did not wish to try.

"You don't know how it rejoices me to see you," said Julien, speaking very fast. "I was sad! very sad! Some of my best friends have perished back there in those inhospitable Pennsylvania hills, and while the band was playing it made me think of the homes they will never see any more! Don't think I'm effusive and that I show grief too much, but my heart has been very heavy! Alas, for the brave lads!"

"Come, come, de Langeais," said Harry, putting his hand on his shoulder. "You've no need to apologize for sorrow. God knows we all have enough of it, but a lot of us are still alive and here's an army ready to fight again, whenever the enemy says the word."

"True! True!" exclaimed de Langeais, changing at once from shadow to sunshine. "And when we're back in Virginia we'll turn our faces once more to our foe!"

He took a step or two on the grass in time to the music which was now that of a dance, and the brilliant beams of the setting sun showed a face without a care. Invincible youth and the invincible gayety of the part of the South that was French were supreme again. Dalton, looking at him, shook his Presbyterian head. Yet his eyes expressed admiration.

"I know your feelings," said Harry to the Virginian.

"Well, what are they?"

"You don't approve of de Langeais' lightness, which in your stern code you would call levity, and yet you envy him possession of it. You don't think it's right to be joyous, without a care, and yet you know it would be mighty pleasant. You criticize de Langeais a little, but you feel it would be a gorgeous thing to have that joyous spirit of his."

Dalton laughed.

"You're pretty near the truth," he said. "I haven't known de Langeais so very long, but if he were to get killed I'd feel that I had lost a younger brother."

"So would I."

Two immaculate youths, riding excellent horses, approached them, and favored them with a long and supercilious stare.

"Can the large fair person be Lieutenant Kenton of the staff of the commander-in-chief?" asked St. Clair.

"It can be and it is, although we did not think to see him again so soon," replied Happy Tom Langdon, "and the other—I do not allude to de Langeais—is that spruce and devout young man, Lieutenant George Dalton, also of the staff of the commander-in-chief."

"Why do we find them in such humble plight, walking on weary feet in a path beside the road?"

"For the most excellent reason in the world, Arthur."

"And what may that reason be, Tom?"

"Because at last they have come down to their proper station in life, just as surely as water finds its level."

"But we'll not treat them too sternly. We must remember that they also serve who walk and wait."

But St. Clair and Langdon, their chaff over, gave them happy greeting, and told them that the two colonels would be rejoiced to see them again, if they could spare a few minutes before rejoining their commander.

"And here is an orderly with both your horses," said St. Clair, "so, under the circumstances, we'll sink our pride and let you ride with us."

De Langeais, with a cheerful farewell until the next day, returned to his command, and Harry and Dalton, mounting, were in a few minutes beside the Invincibles. Colonel Leonidas Talbot and Lieutenant-Colonel Hector St. Hilaire turned their horses from the road into the path and saluted them with warmth.

"We caught a glimpse of you just after our departure, Harry," said Colonel Talbot, "but we did not know what had happened since. There is always a certain amount of risk attending the removal of a great army."

"I am glad, Leonidas, that you used the word 'removal' to describe our operations after our great victory at Gettysburg," said Lieutenant-Colonel St. Hilaire. "I have been feeling about for the right word or phrase myself, but you have found it first."

"Do you think it was a victory, sir?" asked Harry.

"Undoubtedly. We have won several vast and brilliant triumphs, but this is the greatest of them all. We have gone far into the enemy's country, where we have struck him a terrible blow, and now, of our own choice—understand it is of our own choice—we withdraw and challenge him to come and repeat on our own soil our exploit if he can. It is like a skilled and daring prize fighter who leaps back and laughingly bids his foe come on. Am I not right, Leonidas?"

"Neither Aristotle nor Plato was ever more right, Hector, old friend. Usually there is more to a grave affair than appears upon the surface. We could have gone on, after the battle, to Philadelphia, had we chosen, but it was not alone a question of military might that General Lee had to decide. He was bound to give weight to some very subtle considerations. You boys remember your Roman history, do you not?"

"Fragments of it, sir," replied Harry.

"Then you will recall that Hannibal, a fine general, to be named worthily with our great Lee so far as military movements are concerned, after famous victories over greatly superior numbers of Romans, went into camp at Capua, crowded with beauty, wine and games, and the soldiers became enervated. Their fiber was weakened and their bodies softened. They were quicker to heed the call to a banquet than the call to arms."

"Unless it was the arms of beauty, Leonidas."

"Well spoken, Hector. The correction is most important, and I accept it. But to take up again the main thread of my discourse. General Lee undoubtedly had the example of the Carthaginian army and Capua in mind when he left Gettysburg and returned toward the South. Philadelphia is a great city, far larger and richer than any in our section. It is filled with magnificent houses, beautiful women, luxury of every description, ease and softness. Our brave lads, crowned with mighty exploits and arriving there as conquerors, would have been received with immense admiration, although we are official enemies. And the head of youth is easily turned. The Army of Northern Virginia, emerging from Philadelphia, to achieve the conquest of New York and Boston would not be the army that it is to-day. It would lack some of that fire and dash, some of the extraordinary courage and tenacity which have enabled it to surpass the deeds of the veterans of Hannibal and Napoleon."

"But, sir, I've heard that the people of Philadelphia are mostly Quakers, very sober in dress and manner."

"Harry, my lad, when you've lived as long as I have you will know that a merry heart may beat beneath a plain brown dress, and that an ugly hood cannot wholly hide a sweet and saucy face. The girls—God bless 'em—have been the same in all lands since the world began, and will continue so to the end. While this war is on you boys cannot go a-courting, either in the North or South. Am I not right, Hector, old friend?"

"Right, as always, Leonidas. I perceive, though, that the sun is about to set; not a new thing, I admit, but we must not delay our young friends, when the general perhaps needs them."

"Well spoken again, Hector. You are an unfailing fount of wisdom. Good night, my brave lads. Not many of the Invincibles are left, but every one of them is a true friend of you both."

As they rode across the darkening fields Harry and Dalton knew that the colonel spoke the truth about the Invincibles.

"I like a faith such as theirs," said Dalton.

"Yes, it can often turn defeat into real victory."

They quickly found the general's headquarters, and as usual, whenever the weather permitted, he had made arrangements to sleep in the open air, his blankets spread upon soft boughs. Harry and Dalton, having slept all day, would be on night duty, and after supper they sat at a little distance, awaiting orders.

Coolness had come with the dark. A good moon and swarms of bright stars rode in the heavens, turning the skies to misty silver, and softening the scars of the army, which now lay encamped over a great space. Lee was talking with Stuart, who evidently had just arrived from a swift ride, as an orderly near by was holding his horse, covered with foam. The famous cavalryman was clothed in his gorgeous best. His hat was heavy with gold braid, and the broad sash about his waist was heavy with gold, also. Dandy he was, but brilliant cavalryman and great soldier too! Both friend and foe had said so.

Harry, sitting on the grass, with his back against a tree, watched the two generals as they talked long and earnestly. Now and then Stuart nervously switched the tops of his own high riding boots with the little whip that he carried, but the face of Lee, revealed clearly in the near twilight, remained grave and impassive.

After a long while Stuart mounted and rode away, and Sherburne, who had been sitting among the trees on the far side of the fire, came over and joined Harry and Dalton. He too was very grave.

"Do you know what has happened?" he said in a low tone to the two lads.

"Yes, there was a big battle at Gettysburg, and as we failed to win it we're now retreating," replied Harry.

"That's true as far as it goes, but it's not all. We've heard—and the news is correct beyond a doubt—that Grant has taken Vicksburg and Pemberton's army with it."

"Good God, Sherburne, it can't be so!"

"It shouldn't be so, but it is! Oh, why did Pemberton let himself be trapped in such a way! A whole army of ours lost and our greatest fortress in the West taken! Why, the Yankee men-of-war can steam up the Mississippi untouched, all the way from the Gulf to Minnesota."

Harry and Dalton were appalled, and, for a little while, were silent.

"I knew that man Grant would do something terrible to us," Harry said at last. "I've heard from my people in Kentucky what sort of a general he is. My father was at Shiloh, where we had a great victory on, but Grant wouldn't admit it, and held on, until another Union army came up and turned our victory into defeat. My cousin, Dick Mason, has been with Grant a lot, and I used to get a letter from him now and then, even if he is in the Yankee army. He says that when Grant takes hold of a thing he never lets go, and that he'll win the war for his side."

"Your cousin may be right about Grant's hanging on," said Dalton with sudden angry emphasis, "but neither he nor anybody else will win this war for the Yankees. We've lost Vicksburg, and an army with it, and we've retreated from Gettysburg, with enough men fallen there to make another army, but they'll never break through the iron front of Lee and his veterans."

"Hope you're right," said Sherburne, "but I'm off now. I'm in the saddle all night with my troop. We've got to watch the Yankee cavalry. Custer and Pleasanton and the rest of them have learned to ride in a way that won't let Jeb Stuart himself do any nodding."

He cantered off and the lads sat under the trees, ready for possible orders. They saw the fire die. They heard the murmur of the camp sink. Lee lay down on his bed of boughs, other generals withdrew to similar beds or to tents, and the two boys still sat under the trees, waiting and watching, and never knowing at what moment they would be needed.

CHAPTER II
THE NORTHERN SPY

But the night remained very quiet. Harry and Dalton, growing tired of sitting, walked about the camp, and looked again to their horses, which, saddled and bridled, were nevertheless allowed to nip the grass as best they could at the end of their lariats. The last embers of the fire went out, but the moon and stars remained bright, and they saw dimly the sleeping forms of Lee and his generals. Harry, who had seen nothing strange in Meade's lack of pursuit, now wondered at it. Surely when the news of Vicksburg came the exultant Army of the Potomac would follow, and try to deliver a crushing blow.

It was revealed to him as he stood silent in the moonlight that a gulf had suddenly yawned before the South. The slash of Grant's sword in the West had been terrible, and the wound that it made could not be cured easily. And the Army of Northern Virginia had not only failed in its supreme attempt, but a great river now flowed between it and Virginia. If the Northern leaders, gathering courage anew, should hurl their masses upon Lee's retreating force, neither skill nor courage might avail to save them. He suddenly beheld the situation in all its desperation; he shivered from head to foot.

Dalton saw the muscles of Harry's face quivering, and he noticed a pallor that came for an instant.

"I understand," he said. "I had thought of it already. If a Northern general like Lee or Stonewall Jackson were behind us we might never get back across the Potomac. It's somewhat the same position that we were in after Antietam."

"But we've no Stonewall Jackson now to help us."

Again that lump rose in Harry's throat. The vision of the sober figure on Little Sorrel, leading his brigades to victory, came before him, but it was a vision only.

"It's strange that we've not come in contact with their scouts or cavalry," he said. "In that fight with Pleasanton we saw what horsemen they've become, and a force of some kind must be hanging on our rear."

"If it's there, Sherburne and his troop will find it."

"I think I can detect signs of the enemy now," said Harry, putting his glasses to his eyes. "See that hill far behind us. Can't you catch the gleam of lights on it?"

"I think I can," replied Dalton, also using glasses. "Four lights are there, and they are winking, doubtless to lights on another hill too far away for us to see."

"It shows that the enemy at least is watching, and that while we may retreat unattacked it will not be unobserved. Hark! do you hear that, George? It's rifle shots, isn't it?"

"Yes, and a lot of 'em, but they're a long distance away. I don't think we could hear 'em at all if it were not night time."

"But it means something! There they go again! I believe it's a heavy skirmish and it's in the direction in which Sherburne rode."

"The general's up. It's likely that one of us will be sent to see what it's all about."

General Lee and his whole staff had risen and were listening attentively. The faint sound of many shots still came, and then a sharper, more penetrating crash, as if light field guns were at work. The commander beckoned to Harry.

"Ride toward it," he said briefly, "and return with a report as soon as you can."

Harry touched his cap, sprang upon his horse and galloped away. He knew that other messengers would be dispatched also, but, as he had been sent first, he wished to arrive first. He found a path among the trees along which he could make good speed, and, keeping his mind fixed on the firing, he sped forward.

Thousands of soldiers lay asleep in the woods and fields on either side of him, but the thud of the horse's hoofs awakened few of them. Nor did the firing disturb them. They had fought a great battle three days long, and then after a tense day of waiting under arms, they had marched hard. What to them was the noise made by an affair of outposts, when they had heard so long the firing of a hundred and fifty thousand rifles and three or four hundred big guns? Not one in a hundred stood up to see.

The country grew rougher, and Harry was compelled to draw his horse down to a walk. But the firing, a half-mile or more ahead, maintained its volume, and as he approached through thick underbrush, being able to find no other way, he dismounted and led his horse. Presently he saw beads of flame appearing among the bushes, seen a moment, then gone like a firefly, and as he went further he heard voices. He had no doubt that it was the Southern pickets in the undergrowth, and, calling softly, he received confirmatory replies.

A rifleman, a tall, slender fellow in ragged butternut, appeared beside him, and, recognizing Harry's near-gray uniform as that of an officer, said:

"They're dismounted cavalry on the other side of a creek that runs along over there among the bushes. I don't think they mean any real attack. They expect to sting us a little an' find out what we're about."

"Seems likely to me too. They aren't strong enough, of course, for an attempt at rushing us. What troops are in here in the woods on our side?"

"Captain Sherburne's cavalry, sir. They're a bit to our right, an' they're dismounted too. You'll find the captain himself on a little knoll about a hundred yards away."

"Thanks," said Harry, and leading his horse he reached the knoll, to find the rifleman's statement correct. Sherburne was kneeling behind some bushes, trying with the aid of glasses and moonlight to pick out the enemy.

"That you, Harry?" he said, glancing back.

"Yes, Captain. The general has sent me to see what you and the rest of you noisy fellows are doing."

"Shooting across a creek at an enemy who first shot at us. It's only under provocation that we've roused the general and his staff from sleep. Use your glasses and see what you can make out in those bushes on the other side! Keep down, Harry! For Heaven's sake keep down! That bullet didn't miss you more than three inches. You wouldn't be much loss to the army, of course, but you're my personal friend."

"Thanks for your advice. I intend to stay so far down that I'll lie almost flat."

He meant to keep his word, too. The warning had been a stern one. Evidently the sharpshooters who lay in the thickets on the Union side of the creek were of the first quality.

"There's considerable moonlight," whispered Sherburne, "and you mustn't expose an inch of your face. I take it that we have Custer's cavalry over there, mixed with a lot of scouts and skirmishers from the Northwest, Michigan and Wisconsin, most likely. They're the boys who can use the rifles in the woods. Had to do it before they came here, and they're a bad lot to go up against."

"It's a pretty heavy fire for a mere scouting party. If they want to discover our location they can do it without wasting so much powder and lead."

"I think it's more than a scout. They must have discovered long since just where we are. I imagine they mean to shake our nerve by constant buzzing and stinging. I fancy that Meade and his generals after deciding not to pursue us have changed their minds, perhaps under pressure from Washington, and mean to cut us off if they can."

"A little late."

"But not too late. We're still in the enemy's country. The whole population is dead against us, and we can't make a move that isn't known within an hour to the Union leaders. I tell you, Harry, that if we didn't have a Lee to lead I'd be afraid that we'd never get out of Pennsylvania."

"But we have a Lee and the question is settled. What a volley that was! Didn't you feel the twigs and leaves falling on your face?"

"Yes, it went directly over our heads. It's a good thing we're lying so close. Perhaps they intend to force a passage of the creek and stampede at least a portion of our camp."

"And you're here to prevent it."

"I am. They can't cross that creek in face of our fire. We're good night-hawks. Every boy in the South knows the night and the woods, and here in the bush we're something like Indians."

"I'm the descendant of a famous Indian fighter myself," said Harry. And there, surrounded by deep gloom and danger, the spirit of his mighty ancestor, the great Henry Ware, descended upon him once more. An orderly had taken their horses to the rear, where they would be out of range of the bullets, and, as they crouched low in the bushes, Sherburne looked curiously at him.

Harry's face as he turned from the soldier to the Indian fighter of old had changed. To Sherburne's fascinated gaze the eyes seemed amazingly vivid and bright, like those of one who has learned to see in the dark. The complexion was redder—Henry Ware had always burned red instead of brown—like that of one who sleeps oftener in the open air than in a house. His whole look was dominant, compelling and fierce, as he leaned on his elbows and studied the opposing thickets through his glasses.

The glasses even did not destroy the illusion. To Sherburne, who had learned Harry's family history, the great Henry Ware was alive, and in the flesh before him. He felt with all the certainty of truth that the Union skirmishers in the thicket could not escape the keen eyes that sought them out.

"I can see at least twenty men creeping about among the bushes, and seeking chances for shots," whispered Harry.

"I knew that you would see them."

It was Harry's turn to give a look of curiosity.

"What do you mean, Captain?" he asked.

"I knew that you had good eyes and I believed that with the aid of the glasses you would be able to trace figures, despite the shelter of the bushes. Study the undergrowth again, will you, Harry, and tell me what more you can see there?"

"I don't need to study it. I can tell at one look that they're gathering a force. Maybe they mean to rush the creek at a shallow place."

"Is that force moving in any direction?"

"Yes, it's going down the creek."

"Then we'll go down the creek with it. We mustn't be lacking in hospitality."

Sherburne drew a whistle from his pocket and blew a low call upon it. Scores of shadowy figures rose from the undergrowth, and followed his lead down the stream. Harry was still able to see that the force on the other side was increasing largely in numbers, but

Sherburne reminded him that his duties, as far as the coming skirmish was concerned, were over.

"General Lee didn't send you here to get killed," he said. "He wants you instead to report how many of us get killed. You know that while the general is a kind man he can be stern, too, and you're not to take the risk. The orderly is behind that hill with your horse and mine."

Harry, with a sigh, fell back toward the hill. But he did not yet go behind it, where the orderly stood. Instead he lay down among the trees on the slope, where he could watch what was going forward, and once more his face turned to the likeness of the great Indian fighter.

He saw Sherburne's dismounted troop and others, perhaps five hundred in all, moving slowly among the bushes parallel with the stream, and he saw a force which he surmised to be of about equal size, creeping along in the undergrowth on the other side. He followed both bodies with his glasses. With long looking everything became clearer and clearer. The moonlight had to him almost the brilliancy of day.

His eyes followed the Union force, until it came to a point where the creek ran shallow over pebbles. Then the Union leader raised his sword, uttered a cry of command, and the whole force dashed at the ford. The cry met its response in an order from Sherburne, and the thickets flamed with the Southern rifles.

The advantage was wholly with the South, standing on the defense in dark undergrowth, and the Union troop, despite its desperate attempts at the ford, was beaten back with great loss.

Harry waited until the result was sure, and then he walked slowly over the hill toward the point, where the orderly was waiting with the horses. The man, who knew him, handed him the reins of his mount, saying at the same time:

"I've a note for you, sir."

"For me?"

"Yes, sir. It was handed to me about fifteen minutes ago by a large man in our uniform, whom I didn't know."

"Probably a dispatch that I'm to carry to General Lee."

"No, sir. It's addressed to you."

The note was written in pencil on a piece of coarse gray paper, folded several times, but with a face large enough to show Harry's name upon it. He wondered, but said nothing to the sentinel, and did not look at the note again, until he had ridden some distance.

He stopped in a little glade where the moonlight fell clearly. He still heard scattered firing behind him, but he knew that the skirmish was in reality over, and he concluded that no further attempt by Union detachments to advance would be made in the face of such vigilance. He could report to General Lee that the rear of his army was safe. So he would delay and look at the letter that had come to him out of the mysterious darkness.

The superscription was in a large, bold hand, and read:

LIEUTENANT HARRY KENTON,
    STAFF OF GENERAL ROBERT E. LEE, C. S. A.,
        COMMANDER-IN-CHIEF,
            ARMY OF NORTHERN VIRGINIA.

He felt instinctively that something uncommon was coming, and, as most people do when they are puzzled at the appearance of a letter, he looked at it some seconds before opening it. Then he read:

MR. KENTON:

I have warned you twice before, once when Jefferson Davis was inaugurated at Montgomery, and once again in Virginia. I told you that the South could never win. I told you that she might achieve brilliant victories, and she may achieve them even yet, but they will avail her nothing. Victories permit her to maintain her position for the time being, but they do not enable her to advance. A single defeat causes her to lose ground that she can never regain.

I tell you this as a warning. Although your enemy, I have seen you more than once and talked with you. I like you and would save your life if I could. I would induce you, if I could, to leave the army and return to your home, but that I know to be impossible. So, I merely tell you that you are fighting for a cause now lost. Perhaps it is pride on my part to remind you that my early predictions have come true, and perhaps it is a wish that the thought I may plant in your mind will spread to others. You have lost at

Gettysburg a hope and an offensive that you can never regain, and Grant at Vicksburg has given a death blow to the Western half of the Confederacy.

As for you, I wish you well.

WILLIAM J. SHEPARD.

Harry stared in amazement at this extraordinary communication, and read it over two or three times. He was not surprised that Shepard should be near, and that he should have been inside the Confederate lines, but that he should leave a letter, and such a letter, for him was uncanny. His first feeling, wonder, was succeeded by anger. Did Shepard really think that he could influence him in such a way, that he could plant in his mind a thought that would spread to others of his age and rank and weaken the cause for which he fought? It was a singular idea, but Shepard was a singular man.

But perhaps pride in recalling the prediction that he had made long ago was Shepard's stronger motive, and Harry took fire at that also. The Confederacy was not beaten. A single defeat — no, it was not a defeat, merely a failure to win — was not mortal, and as for the West, the Confederacy would gather itself together there and overwhelm Grant!

Then came a new emotion, a kind of gratitude to Shepard. The man was really a friend, and would do him a service, if it could be done, without injuring his own cause! He could not feel any doubt of it, else the spy would not have taken the risk to send him such a letter. He read it for the last time, then tore it into little pieces which he entrusted to the winds.

The firing behind him had died completely, and there was no sound but the rustle of dry leaves in the light wind, nothing to tell that there had been sharp fighting along the creek, and that men lay dead in the forest. The moon and the stars clothed everything in a whitish light, that seemed surcharged with a powerful essence, and this essence was danger.

The spirit of the great forest ranger descended upon him once more, and he read the omens, all of which were sinister. He foresaw terrible campaigns, mighty battles in the forest, and a roll of the dead so long that it seemed to stretch away into infinity.

Then he shook himself violently, cast off the spell, and rode rapidly back with his report. Lee had risen and was standing under a tree. He was fully dressed and his uniform was trim and unwrinkled. Harry thought anew as he rode up, what a magnificent figure he was. He was the only great man he ever saw who really looked his greatness. Nothing could stir that calm. Nothing could break down that loftiness of manner. Harry was destined to feel then, as he felt many times afterward, that without him the South had never a chance. And the choking came in his throat again, as he thought of him who was gone, of him who had been the right arm of victory, the hammer of Thor.

But he hid all these feelings as he quickly dismounted and saluted the commander-in-chief.

"What have you seen, Lieutenant Kenton?" asked Lee.

"A considerable detachment of the enemy tried to force the passage of the creek in our right rear. They were met by Captain Sherburne's troop dismounted, and three companies of infantry, and were driven back after a sharp fight."

"Very good. Captain Sherburne is an alert officer."

He turned away, and Harry, giving his horse to an orderly, again resumed his old position under a tree, out of hearing of the generals, but in sight. Dalton was not there, but he knew that skirmishing had occurred in other directions, and doubtless the Virginian had been sent on an errand like his own.

He had a sense of rest and realization as he leaned back against the tree. But it was mental tension, not physical, for which relief came, and Shepard, much more than the battle at the creek, was in his thoughts.

The strong personality of the spy and his seeming omniscience oppressed him again. Apparently he was able to go anywhere, and nothing could be hidden from him. He might be somewhere in the circling shadows at that very moment, watching Lee and his lieutenants. His pulses leaped. Shepard had achieved an extraordinary influence over him, and he was prepared to believe the impossible.

He stood up and stared into the bushes, but sentinels stood there, and no human being could pass their ring unseen. Presently Dalton came, made a brief report to General Lee and joined his comrade. Harry was glad of his arrival. The presence of a comrade brought him back to earth and earth's realities. The sinister shadows that oppressed him melted away and he saw only the ordinary darkness of a summer night.

The two sat side by side. Dalton perhaps drew as much strength as Harry from the comradeship, and they watched other messengers arrive with dispatches, some of whom rolled themselves in their blankets at once, and went to sleep, although three, who had evidently slept in the day, joined Harry and Dalton in their vigil.

Harry saw that the commander-in-chief was holding a council at that hour, nearer morning than midnight. A general kicked some of the pieces of burned wood together and fanned them into a light flame, enough to take away the slight chill that was coming with the morning. The men stood around it, and talked a long time, although it seemed to Harry that Lee said least. Nevertheless his tall figure dominated them all. Now and then Harry saw his face in the starshine, and it bore its habitual grave and impassive look.

The youth did not hear a word that was said, but his imaginative power enabled him to put himself in the place of the commander-in-chief. He knew that no man, however great his courage, could fail to appreciate his position in the heart of a hostile country, with a lost field behind him, and with superior numbers hovering somewhere in his rear or on his flank. He realized then to the full the critical nature of their position and what a mighty task Lee had to save the army.

One of his young comrades whispered to him that the Potomac, the barrier between North and South, was rising, flooded by heavy rains in both mountains and lowlands, and that a body of Northern cavalry had already destroyed a pontoon bridge built by the South across it. They might be hemmed in, with their backs to an unfordable river, and an enemy two or three times as numerous in front.

"Don't you worry," whispered Dalton, with sublime confidence. "The general will take us to Virginia."

Harry projected his imagination once more. He sought to put himself in the place of Lee, receiving all the reports and studying them, trying to measure space that could not be measured, and to weigh a total that could not be weighed. Greatness and responsibility were compelled to pay thrice over for themselves, and he was glad that he was only a young lieutenant, the chief business of whom was to fetch and carry orders.

Shafts of sunlight were piercing the eastern foliage when the council broke up, and shortly after daylight the Southern army was again on the march, with Northern cavalry and riflemen hanging on its flanks and rear. Harry was permitted to rejoin, for a while, his friends of the Invincibles and he found Colonel Leonidas Talbot and Lieutenant-Colonel Hector St. Hilaire riding very erect, a fine color in their faces.

"You come from headquarters, Harry, and therefore you are omniscient," said Colonel Talbot. "We heard firing in the night. What did it mean?"

"Only skirmishers, Colonel. I think they wanted to annoy us, but they paid the price."

"Inevitably. Our general is as dangerous in retreat as in advance. I fancy that General Meade will not bring up his lagging forces until we near the Potomac."

"They say it's rising, sir, and that it will be very hard to cross."

"That creates a difficulty but not an impossibility. Ordinary men yield to difficulties, men like our commander-in-chief are overcome only by impossibilities. But the further we go, Harry, the more reconciled I grow to our withdrawal. I have seen scarcely a friendly face among the population. I would not have us thrust ourselves upon people who do not like us. It would go very hard with our kindly Southern nature to have to rule by force over people who are in fact our brethren. Defensive wars are the just wars, and perhaps it will be really better for us to retire to Virginia and protect its sacred soil from the tread of the invader. Eh, Hector?"

"Right, as usual, Leonidas. The reasons for our retirement are most excellent. We have already spoken of the fact that Philadelphia might prove a Capua for our young troops, and now we are relieved from the chance of appearing as oppressors. It can never be said of us by the people of Pennsylvania that we were tyrants. It's an invidious task to rule over the unwilling, even when one rules with justice and wisdom. It's strange, perhaps, Leonidas, but it's a universal truth, that people would rather be ruled by themselves in a second rate manner than by the foreigner in a first rate manner. Now, the government of our states is attacked by Northern critics, but such as it is, it is ours and it's our first choice. Do we bore you, Harry?"

"Not at all, sir. I never listen to either you or Colonel Talbot without learning something."

The two colonels bowed politely.

"I have wished for some time to speak to you about a certain matter, Hector," said Colonel Talbot.

"What is it, Leonidas?"

"During the height of that tremendous artillery fire from Little Round Top I was at a spot where I could see the artillerymen very well whenever the smoke lifted. Several times, I noticed an officer directing the fire of the guns, and I don't think I could have been mistaken in his identity."

"No, Leonidas, you were not. I too observed him, and we could not possibly be mistaken. It was John Carrington, of course."

"Dear old John Carrington, who was with us at West Point, the greatest artilleryman in the world. And he was facing us, when the fortunes of the South were turning on a hair. If any other man had been there, directing those guns, we might have taken Cemetery Hill."

"That's true, Leonidas, but it was not possible for any other man to be in such a place at such a time. Granting that such a crisis should arise and that it should arise at Gettysburg you and I would have known long before that John would be there with the guns to stop us. Why, we saw that quality in him all the years we were with him at West Point. The world has never seen and never will see another such artilleryman as John Carrington."

"Good old John. I hope he wasn't killed."

"And I hope so too, from the bottom of my heart. But we'll know before many days."

"How will you find out?" asked Harry curiously.

Both colonels laughed genially.

"Because he will send us signs, unmistakable signs," replied Colonel Talbot.

"I don't understand, sir."

"His signs will be shells, shrapnel and solid shot. We may not have a battle this week or next week, but a big one is bound to come some time or other and then if any section of the Northern artillery shows uncommon deadliness and precision we'll know that Carrington is there. Why, we can recognize his presence as readily as the deer scents the hunter. We'll have many notes to compare with him when the war is over."

Harry sincerely hoped that the three would meet in friendship around some festive table, and he was moved by the affection and admiration the two colonels held for Carrington. Doubtless the great artilleryman's feelings toward them were the same.

They went into camp once more that night in a pleasant rolling country of high hills, rich valleys, scattered forests, and swift streams of clear water. Harry liked this Northern land, which was yet not so far from the South. It was not more beautiful than his own Kentucky, but it was much trimmer and neater than the states toward the Gulf. He saw all about him the evidences of free labor, the proof that man worked more readily, and with better results, when success or failure were all his own.

He was too young to spend much time in concentrated thinking, but as he looked upon the neat Pennsylvania houses and farms and the cultivated fields he felt the curse of black slavery in the South, but he felt also that it was for the South itself to abolish it, and not for the armed hand of the outsider, an outsider to whom its removal meant no financial loss and dislocation.

Despite himself his mind dwelt upon these things longer than before. He disliked slavery, his father disliked it, and nearly all their friends and relatives, and here they were fighting for it, as one of the two great reasons of the Civil War. He felt anew how strangely things come about, and that even the wisest cannot always choose their own courses as they wish them.

A fire, chiefly for cooking purposes, had been built for the general and his staff in a cove surrounded by trees. A small cold spring gushed from the side of a hill, flowed down the center of the cove, and then made its way through the trees into the wider world beyond. It was a fine little spring, and before the general came, the younger members of the staff knelt and drank deeply at it. It brought thoughts of home to all these young rovers of the woods, who had drunk a thousand times before at just such springs as this.

Soon Lee and his generals sat there on the stones or on the moss. Longstreet, Stuart, Pickett, Alexander, Ewell, Early, Hill and many others, some suffering from wounds, were with their commander, while the young officers who were to fetch and carry sat on the fringe in the woods, or stretched themselves on the turf.

Harry was in the group, but except in extreme emergency he would not be on duty that night, as he had already been twenty-four hours in the saddle. Nevertheless he was not yet sleepy, and lying on his blanket, he watched the leaders confer, as they had conferred every other night since the Battle of Gettysburg. He was aware, too, that the air was heavy with suspense and anxiety. He breathed it in at every breath. Cruel doubt was not shown by words or actions, but it was an atmosphere which one could not mistake.

Word had been brought in the afternoon by hard riders of Stuart that the Potomac was still rising. It could not be forded and the active Northern cavalry was in between, keeping advanced parties of the Southern army from laying pontoons. Every day made the situation more desperate, and it could not be hidden from the soldiers, who, nevertheless, marched cheerfully on, in the sublime faith that Lee would carry them through.

Harry knew that if the Army of the Potomac was not active in pursuit its cavalrymen and skirmishers were. As on the night before, he heard the faint report of shots, and he knew that rough work was going forward along the doubtful line, where the fringes of the two armies almost met. But hardened so much was he that he fell asleep while the generals were still in anxious council, and the fitful firing continued in the distant dark.

CHAPTER III
THE FLOODED RIVER

Harry and Dalton were aroused before daylight by Colonel Peyton of Lee's staff, with instructions to mount at once, and join a strong detachment, ready to go ahead and clear a way. Sherburne's troop would lead. The Invincibles, for whom mounts had been obtained, would follow. There were fragments of other regiments, the whole force amounting to about fifteen hundred men, under the command of Sherburne, who had been raised the preceding afternoon to the rank of Colonel, and whose skill and valor were so well known that such veterans as Colonel Talbot and Lieutenant Colonel St. Hilaire were glad to serve under him. Harry and Dalton would represent the commander-in-chief, and would return whenever Colonel Sherburne thought fit to report to him.

Harry was glad to go. While he had his periods of intense thought, and his character was serious, he was like his great ancestor, essentially a creature of action. His blood flowed more swiftly with the beat of his horse's hoofs, and his spirits rose as the free air of the fields and forests rushed past him. Moreover he was extremely anxious to see what lay ahead. If barriers were there he wanted to look upon them. If the Union cavalry were trying to keep them from laying bridges across the Potomac he wanted to help drive them away.

Harry and Dalton had a right as aides and messengers of Lee to ride with Sherburne, but before they joined him they rode among the Invincibles, who were in great feather, because they too, for the time being, rode, and toiled in neither dust nor mud.

"Colonel Sherburne may think a good deal of his own immediate troop," said St. Clair to Harry, "but if the men of the Invincibles could achieve so much on foot they'll truly deserve their name on horseback. Where is this enemy of ours? Lead us to him."

"You'll find him soon enough," said Harry. "You South Carolina talkers have learned many times that the Yankees will fight."

"Yes, Harry, I admit it freely. But you must admit on your part that the South Carolinians will fight as well as talk, although at present most of the South Carolinians in this regiment are Virginians."

"But not our colonel and lieutenant-colonel," said Happy Tom. "Real old South Carolina still leads."

"May they always lead!" said Harry heartily, looking at the two gray figures.

"Tell Colonel Sherburne," said Happy Tom, who was in splendid spirits, "that we congratulate him on his promotion and are ready to obey him without question."

"All right. He'll be glad to know that he has your approval."

"He might have the approval of worse men. I feel surging within me the talents of a great general, but I'm too young to get 'em recognized."

"You'll have to wait until the sections are not fighting each other, but are united against a common foe. But meanwhile I'll tell Colonel Sherburne that if he gets into a tight pinch not to lose heart as you are here."

Saluting Colonel Talbot and Lieutenant-Colonel St. Hilaire, Harry and Dalton rode to the head of the column, where Sherburne led. They ate their breakfast on horseback, and went swiftly down a valley in the general direction of the Potomac. The dawn had broadened into full morning, clear and bright, save for a small cloud that hung low in the southwest, which Sherburne noticed with a frown.

"That's a little cloud and it looks innocent," he said to Harry, "but I don't like it."

"Why not?"

"Because in the ten minutes that I've been watching it I've been able to notice growth. I'm weather-wise and we may have more rain. More rain means a higher Potomac. A higher Potomac means more difficulty in crossing it. More difficulty in crossing it means more danger of our destruction, and our destruction would mean the end of the Confederacy."

He spoke with deadly earnestness as he continued to look at the tiny dusky spot on the western sky. Harry had a feeling of awe. Again he realized that such mighty issues could turn upon a single hair. The increase or decrease of that black splotch might mean the death or life of the Confederacy. As he rode he watched it.

His heart sank slowly. The little baby cloud, looking so harmless, was growing. He said to himself in anger that it was not, but he knew that it was. Black at the center, it radiated in every direction until it became pale gray at the edges, and by and by, as it still spread, it gave to the southwest an aspect that was distinctly sinister.

Sherburne shook his head and the gravity of his face increased. As the cloud grew alarm grew with it in his mind.

"Maybe it will pass," said Harry hopefully.

"I don't think so. It's not moving away. It just hangs there and grows and grows. You're a woodsman, Harry, and you ought to feel it. Don't you think the atmosphere has changed?"

"I didn't have the courage to say so until you asked me, but it's damper. If I were posing as a prophet I should say that we're going to have rain."

"And so should I. Usually at this period of the year in our country we want rain, but now we dread it like a pestilence. At any other time the Potomac could rise or fall, whenever it pleased, for all I cared, but now it's life and death."

"Our doubts are decided and we've lost. Look, sir the whole southwest is dark now!"

"And here come the first drops!"

Sherburne sent hurried orders among the men to keep their ammunition and weapons dry, and then they bent their heads to the storm which would beat almost directly in their faces. Soon it came without much preliminary thunder and lightning. The morning that had been warm turned cold and the rain poured hard upon them. Most of the horsemen were wet through in a short time, and they shivered in their sodden uniforms, but it was a condition to which they were used, and they thought little of themselves but nearly all the while of the Potomac.

Few words were spoken. The only sounds were the driving of the rain and the thud of many hoofs in the mud. Harry often saw misty figures among the trees on the hills, and he knew that they were watched by hostile eyes as the Northern armies in Virginia, were always watched with the same hostility. It was impossible for Lee's men to make any secret march. The population, intensely loyal to the Union, promptly carried news of it to Meade or his generals.

Twice he pointed out the watchers to Sherburne who merely shrugged his shoulders.

"I might send out men and cut off a few of them," he said, "but for what good? Hundreds more would be left and we'd merely be burdened with useless prisoners. Here's a creek ahead, Harry, and look how muddy and foamy it is! It's probably raining harder higher up in the hills than it is here, and all these creeks and brooks go to swell the Potomac."

The swift water rose beyond their stirrups and there was a vast splashing as fifteen hundred men rode through the creek. It was a land of many streams, and a few miles farther on they crossed another, equally swollen and swift.

They had hoped that the rain, like the sudden violence of a summer shower, would pass soon, but the skies remained a solid gray and it settled into a steady solemn pour, cold and threatening, and promising to continue all day long. They could see that every stream they crossed was far above its normal mark, and the last hope that they might find the Potomac low enough for fording disappeared.

The watchers on the hills were still there, despite the rain, but they did no sharpshooting. Nor did the Southern force do damage to anybody or anything, as it passed. Near noon Sherburne resolved to build a fire in a cove protected by cliffs and heavy timber, and give his men warm food lest they become dispirited.

It was a task to set the wet wood, but the men of his command, used to forest life, soon mastered it. Then they threw on boughs and whole tree trunks, until a great bonfire blazed and roared merrily, thrusting out innumerable tongues of red and friendly flame.

"Is there anything more beautiful than a fine fire at such a time?" said St. Clair to Harry. "As it blazes and eats into the wood it crackles and those crackling sounds are words."

"What do the words say?"

"They say, 'Come here and stand before me. So long as you respect me and don't come too close I'll do you nothing but good. I'll warm you and I'll dry you. I'll drive the wet from your skin and your clothes, and I'll chase the cold out of your body and bones. I'll take hold of your depressed and sunken heart and lift it up again. Where you saw only gray and black I'll make you see gold and red. I'll warm and cook your food for you, giving you fresh life and strength. With my crackling coals and my leaping flames I'll change your world of despair into a world of hope.'"

"Hear! Hear!" said Happy Tom. "Arthur has turned from a sodden soldier into a giddy poet! Is any more poetry left in the barrel, Arthur?"

"Plenty, but I won't turn on the tap again to-day. I've translated for you. I've shown you where beauty and happiness lie, and you must do the rest for yourself."

They crowded about the huge fire which ran the entire length of the cove, and watched the cooks who had brought their supplies on horseback. Great quantities of coffee were made, and they had bacon and hard biscuits.

Although the rain still reached them in the cove they forgot it as they ate the good food — any food was good to them — and drank cup after cup of hot coffee. Youthful spirits rose once more. It wasn't such a bad day after all! It had rained many times before and people still lived. Also, the Potomac had risen many times before, but it always fell again. They were riding to clear the way for Lee's invincible army which could go wherever it wanted to go.

"Men on horseback looking at us!" hailed Happy Tom. "About fifty on a low hill on our right. Look like Yankee cavalrymen. Wonder what they take us for anyway!"

Harry, St. Clair, Langdon and Dalton walked to the edge of the cove, every one holding a cup of hot coffee in his hand. Sherburne was already there and with his glasses was examining the strange group, as well as he could through the sweeping rain.

"A scouting party undoubtedly," he said, "but weather has made their uniforms and ours look just about alike. It's equally certain though that they're Yankees. No troop of ours so small would be found here."

Harry was also watching them through glasses, and he took particular note of one stalwart figure mounted upon a powerful horse. The distance was too great to recognize the face, but he knew the swing of the broad shoulders. It was Shepard and once more he had the uneasy feeling winch the man always inspired in him. He appeared and reappeared with such facility, and he was so absolutely trackless that he had begun to appear to him as omniscient. Of course the man knew all about Sherburne's advance and could readily surmise its purpose.

"They're an impudent lot to sit there staring at us in that supercilious manner," said Colonel Talbot. "Shall I take the Invincibles, sir, and teach them a lesson?"

Sherburne smiled and shook his head.

"No, Colonel," he said, "although I thank you for the offer. They'd melt away before you and we'd merely waste our energies. Let them look as much as they please, and now that the boys have eaten their bread and bacon and drunk their coffee, and are giants again, we'll ride on toward the Potomac."

"Do we reach it to-day, sir?" asked Colonel Talbot.

"Not before to-morrow afternoon, even if we should not be interrupted. This is the enemy's country and we may run at any time into a force as large as our own if not larger."

"Thank you for the information, Colonel Sherburne. My ignorance of geography may appear astonishing to you, although we had to study it very hard at West Point. But I admit my weakness and I add, as perhaps some excuse, that I have lately devoted very little attention to the Northern states. It did not seem worth my time to spend much study on the rivers, and creeks and mountains of what is to be a foreign country—although I may never be able to think of John Carrington and many other of my old friends in the army as the foreigners they're sure to become. Has the thought ever occurred to you, Colonel, that by our victories we're making a tremendous lot of foreigners in America?"

"It has, Colonel Talbot, but I can't say that the thought has ever been a particularly happy one."

"It's the Yankees who are being made into foreigners," said Lieutenant-Colonel St. Hilaire. "The gallant Southern people, of course, remain what they are."

"They're going," said Harry. "They've seen enough of us."

The distant troop disappeared over the crest of the hill. Harry had noticed that Shepard led the way as if he were the ruling spirit, but he did not consider it necessary to say anything to the others about him. The trumpet blew and Sherburne's force, mounting, rode away from the cove. Harry cast one regretful glance back at the splendid fire which still glowed there, and then resigned himself to the cold and rain.

They did not stop again until far in the night. The rain ceased, but the whole earth was sodden and the trees on the low ridge, on which Sherburne camped, dripped with water. Spies might be all around them, but for the sake of physical comfort and the courage that he knew would come with it, he ordered another big fire built. Vigilant riflemen took turns in beating up the forests and fields for possible enemies, but the young officers once more enjoyed the luxury of the fire. Their clothing was dried thoroughly, and their tough and sinewy frames recovered all their strength and elasticity.

"To enjoy being dry it is well to have been wet," said Dalton sententiously.

"That's just like you, you old Presbyterian," said Happy Tom. "I suppose you'll argue next that you can't enjoy Heaven unless you've first burned in the other place for a thousand years."

"There may be something in that," said Dalton gravely, "although the test, of course, would be an extremely severe one."

"I know which way you're headed, George."

"Then tell me, because I don't know myself."

"As soon as this war is over you'll enter the ministry, and no sin will get by you, not even those nice little ones that all of us like to forgive."

"Maybe you're right, Happy, and if I do go into the ministry I shall at once begin long and earnest preparation for the task which would necessarily be the most difficult of my life."

"And may I make so bold as to inquire what it is, George?"

"Your conversion, Happy."

Langdon grinned.

"But why do you want to convert me, George? I'm perfectly happy as I am."

"For your own well being, Tom. Your happiness is nothing to me, but I want to make you good."

Both laughed the easy laugh of youth, but Harry looked long at Dalton. He thought that he detected in him much of the spirit of Stonewall Jackson, and that here was one who had in him the makings of a great minister. The thought lingered with him.

St. Clair was carefully smoothing out his uniform and brushing from it the least particle of mud. His first preoccupation always asserted itself at the earliest opportunity, and in a very short time he was the neatest looking man in the entire force. Harry, although he often jested with him about it, secretly admired this characteristic of St. Clair's.

"You boys sleep while you can," said Sherburne, "because we can't afford to linger in this region. Our safety lies in rapid marching, giving the enemy no chance to gather a large force and trap us. Make the best of your time because we're up and away an hour after midnight."

The young officers were asleep within ten minutes, but the vigilant riflemen patrolled the country in a wide circuit about them. Sherburne himself, although worn by hard riding, slept but little. Anxiety kept his eyes open. He knew that his task to find a passage for the army across the swollen Potomac was of the utmost importance and he meant to achieve it. He understood to the full the dangerous position in which the chief army of the Confederacy stood. His own force might be attacked at any moment by overwhelming numbers and be cut off and destroyed or captured, but he also knew the quality of the men he led, and he believed they were equal to any task.

As he sat by the fire thinking somberly, a figure in the brush no great distance away was watching him. Shepard, the spy, in the darkness had passed with ease between the sentinels, using the skill of an Indian in stalking or approaching, and now, lying well hidden, almost flat upon his stomach, he surveyed the camp. He looked at Sherburne, sitting on a log and brooding, and he made out Harry's figure wrapped in a blanket and lying with his feet to the fire.

Shepard's mind was powerfully affected. An intense patriot, something remote and solitary in his nature had caused him to undertake this most dangerous of all trades, to which he brought an intellectual power and comprehension that few spies possess. As Harry had discovered long since, he was a most uncommon man.

Now Shepard as he gazed at this little group felt no hatred for them or their men. He had devoted his life to the task of keeping the Union intact. His work must be carried out in obscure ways. He could never hope for material reward, and if he perished it would be in some out-of-the-way corner, perhaps at the end of a rope, a man known to so few that there would be none to forget him. And yet his patriotism was so great and of such a fine quality that he viewed his enemies around the fire as his brethren. He felt confident that the armies of the North would bring them back into the Union, and when that occurred they must come as Americans on an equal footing with other Americans. They could not be in the Union and not of it.

But Shepard's feeling for his official enemies would not keep him from acting against them with all the skill, courage and daring that he possessed in such supreme measure. He knew that it was Sherburne's task to open a way for the Army of Northern Virginia to the Potomac and to find a ford, or, in cooperation with some other force, to build a bridge. It was for him to defeat the plan if he could.

While the rain all the day before had brought gloom to the hearts of Sherburne and his men it had filled his with joy, as he thought of the innumerable brooks and creeks that were pouring their swollen waters into the Potomac, already swollen too. He meant now to follow Sherburne's force, see what plan it would attempt, what point, perhaps, it would select for the bridge, and then bring the Union brigades in haste to defeat it.

It is said that men often feel when they are watched, although the watcher is invisible, but it was not so in Sherburne's case. He did not in the least suspect the presence of Shepard or of any foe, and the spy, after he had seen all he wished, withdrew, with the same stealth that had marked his coming.

An hour after midnight all were awakened and they rode away. The next day they reached the Potomac near Williamsport, where their pontoon bridge had been destroyed, and looked upon the wide stream of the Potomac, far too deep for fording.

"If General Lee is attacked on the banks of this river by greatly superior forces," said Sherburne, "he'll have no time to build bridges. If we didn't happen to be victorious our forces would have to scatter into the mountains, where they could be hunted down, man by man."

"But such a thing as that is unthinkable, sir," said Harry. "We may not win always, but here in the East we never lose. Remember Antietam and the river at our back."

"Right you are, Harry," said Sherburne more cheerfully. "The general will get us out of this, and here is where we must cross. The river may run down enough in two or three days to permit of fording. God grant that it will!"

"And so say I!" repeated Harry with emphasis.

"I mean to hold this place for our army," continued Sherburne.

"A reserved seat, so to speak."

"Yes, that's it. We must keep the country cleared until our main force comes up. It shouldn't be difficult. I haven't heard of any considerable body of Union troops between us and the river."

They made camp rapidly in a strong position, built their fires for cooking, set their horses to grazing and awaited what would come. It was a dry, clear night, and Harry, who had no duties, save to ride with a message at the vital moment, looked at once for his friends, the Invincibles.

St. Clair met him and held up a warning hand, while Happy touched his lip with his finger. Before the double injunction of silence and caution, Harry whispered:

"What's happened?"

"A tragedy," replied St. Clair.

"And a victory, too," said Happy Tom.

"I don't understand," said Harry.

"Then look and you will," said St. Clair.

He pointed to a small clear space in which Colonel Leonidas Talbot and Lieutenant-Colonel Hector St. Hilaire sat on their blankets facing each other with an empty cracker box between them, upon which their chess men were spread. The firelight plainly revealed a look of dismay upon the face of Colonel Talbot, and with equal plainness a triumphant expression upon that of Lieutenant-Colonel St. Hilaire.

"Colonel Talbot has lost his remaining knight," whispered St. Clair. "I don't know how it came about, but when the event occurred we heard them both utter a cry. Listen!"

"I fail even yet, Hector, to see just how it occurred." said Colonel Talbot.

"But it has occurred, Leonidas, and that's the main thing. A general in battle does not always know how he is whipped, but the whipping hurts just as much."

"You should not show too much elation over your triumph, Hector. Remember that he laughs best who laughs last."

"I take my laugh whenever I can, Leonidas, because no one knows who is going to laugh last. It may be that he who laughs in the present will also laugh at the end. What do you mean by that move, Leonidas?"

"That to you is a mystery, Hector. It's like one of Stonewall Jackson's flanking marches, and in due time the secret will be revealed with terrible results."

"Pshaw, Leonidas, you can't frighten a veteran like me. That for your move, and here's mine in reply."

The two gray heads bent lower over the board as the colonels made move after move. The youths standing in the shadow of the trees watched until the second time that night the two uttered a simultaneous cry. But they were very different in quality. Now Colonel Talbot's expressed victory and Lieutenant-Colonel St. Hilaire's consternation.

"Your bishop, Hector!" exclaimed Colonel Talbot. "Pious and able gentleman as he is, an honor to his cloth, he is nevertheless my captive."

"I admit that it was most unexpected, Leonidas. You have matched my victory with one of yours. It was indeed most skillful and I don't yet see what led to it."

"Did I not warn you a little while ago that you couldn't frighten me? I prepared a trap for you, and thus I rise from defeat to victory."

"At any rate we are about even on the evening's work, Leonidas, and we have made more progress than for the whole six months preceding. It seems likely now that we can finish our game soon."

A sudden crash of rifle fire toward the east and from a point not distant told them no. They rose to their feet, but they put the chessmen away very deliberately, while the young officers hastened to their posts. The fire continued and spread about them in a half circle, accompanied now and then by the deeper note of a light field gun. Sherburne made his dispositions rapidly. All the men remained on foot, but a certain number were told off to hold the horses in the center of the camp.

"We're attacked by a large force," said Sherburne, "Our scouts gave us warning in time. Evidently they wish to drive us away from here because this will be the ford in case the river falls in time."

"Then you look for a sharp fight?"

"Without question. And remember that you're to avoid all risk if you can. It's not your business to get shot here, but it is your business, and your highly important business, to ride back to General Lee with the news of what's happening. In order to do that it's necessary for you to remain alive."

"I obey orders," said Harry reluctantly.

"Of course you do. Keep back with the men who are holding the horses. That fire is growing fast! I'm glad we were able to find a camp so defensible as this hill."

He hurried away to watch his lines and Harry remained at his station near the horses, where Dalton was compelled by the same responsibility to stay with him. It was the first time that Harry had been forced to remain a mere spectator of a battle raging around him, and while not one who sought danger for danger's sake, it was hard work to control himself and remain quiet and unmoved.

"I suspect they're trying to cut us off completely from our own army," he said to Dalton.

"Seems likely to me, too," said Dalton. "Wipe us out here, and hold the river for themselves. Our scouts assured us that there was no large force of the enemy in this region. It must have been gathered in great haste."

"In whatever way it was gathered, it's here, that's sure."

There was a good moon now, and, using his glasses, Harry saw many details of the battle. The attack was being pressed with great vigor and courage. He saw in a valley numerous bodies of cavalry, firing their carbines, and he saw two batteries, of eight light guns each, move forward for a better range. Soon their shells were exploding near the hill on which Harry stood, and the fire of the rifles, unbroken now, grew rapidly in volume.

But the men under Sherburne, youthful though most of them might be, were veterans. They knew every trick of war, and columns of infantry swept forward to meet the attack, preceded by the skirmishers, who took heavy toll of the foe.

"If they'd been able to make it a surprise they might have rushed us," said Harry.

"Nobody catches Sherburne sleeping," said Dalton.

"That's true, and because they can't they won't be able to overcome him here. Now there go our rifles! Listen to that crash. I fancy that about a thousand were fired together, and they weren't fired for nothing."

"No," said Dalton, "but the Yankees don't give way. You can see by their line of fire that they're still coming. Look there! A powerful body of horse is charging!"

It was unusual to see cavalry attack at night, and the spectacle was remarkable, as the moonlight fell on the raised sabers. But the defiant rebel yell, long and fierce, rose from the thicket, and, as the rifles crashed, the entire front of the charging column was burned away, as if by a stroke of lightning. But after a moment of hesitation they came on, only to ride deeper into a rifle fire which emptied saddles so fast that they were at last compelled to turn and gallop away.

"Brave men," said Harry. "A gallant charge, but it had to meet too many Southern rifles, aimed by men who know how to shoot."

"But their infantry are advancing through that wood," said Dalton. "Hear them cheering above the rifle fire!"

The Northern shout rang through the forest, and the rebel yell, again full of defiance, replied. The cavalry had been driven off, but the infantry and artillery were far from beaten. The sixteen guns of the two batteries were massed on a hill and they began to sweep the Southern lines with a storm of shells and shrapnel. The forest and the dark were no protection, because the guns searched every point of the Southern line with their fire. Sherburne's men were forced to give ground, before cannon served with such deadly effect.

"What will the colonel do?" asked Dalton. "The big guns give the Yankees the advantage."

"He'll go straight to the heart of the trouble," said Harry. "He'll attack the guns themselves."

He did not know actually in what manner Sherburne would proceed, but he was quite sure that such would be his course. The wary Southern leader instantly detailed a swarm of his best riflemen to creep through the woods toward the cannon. In a few minutes the gunners themselves were under the fire of hidden marksmen who shot surpassingly well. The gunners, the cannoneers, the spongers, the rammers and the ammunition passers were cut down with deadly certainty.

The captain of the guns, knowing that the terrible rifle fire was coming from the thickets, deluged the woods and bushes with shells and shrapnel, but the riflemen lay close, hugging the ground, and although a few were killed and more wounded, the vast majority crept closer and closer, shooting straight and true in the moonlight. The fire from the batteries became scattered and wild. Their crews were cut down so fast that not enough men were left to work the guns, and their commander reluctantly gave the order to withdraw to a less exposed position.

"Rifles triumphant over artillery," said Harry, who studied everything through his glasses; "but of course the dusk helped the riflemen."

"That's true," said Dalton, "but it takes good men like Sherburne to use the favoring chances. Now our boys are charging!"

The tremendous rebel yell swelled through the forest, and the Southern infantry rushed to the attack. Harry saw that the charge was successful, and his ears told him so too. The firing moved further and further away, and soon declined in volume.

"They've been beaten off," said Harry.

"At least for the time," said Dalton, "but I've an idea they'll hang on our front and may attack again in a day or so."

"How then are you and I to get through and tell General Lee that this is the place to bridge the Potomac, if it's to be bridged at all?"

Dalton shook his head.

"I don't know," he replied, "and I won't think about it until Colonel Sherburne gives his orders."

The sounds of battle died in the distant woods. The last shot, whether from cannon or rifle, was fired, and the Southern troops returned to their positions, which they began to fortify strongly. Sherburne appeared presently, his uniform cut by bullets in two or three places, but his body untouched. He drew Harry and Dalton aside, where their words could not be heard by anybody else.

"You two," he said, "were to report to General Lee when I thought fit. Well, the time has come; Harry, you go first, and, at a suitable moment, George will follow. We have news of surpassing importance. We took a number of prisoners in that battle and we were also lucky enough to rescue several of our men who had been held as captives. We've learned from them that General Meade, after making up his mind to pursue, followed straight behind us for a while, but he has now turned and gone southward in the direction of Frederick. He will cross South Mountain, advance toward Sharpsburg, and attempt to smash us here, with our backs to this swollen river. Why, some of the Federal leaders consider the Army of Northern Virginia as good as destroyed already!"

He spoke with angry emphasis.

"But it isn't," said Harry.

"No, it isn't. Doubtless General Lee will learn from scouts of his own of General Meade's flanking movement, but we mustn't take the chance. Moreover, we must tell him that this is the place for our army to cross. If the river runs down in two or three days we'll have a ford here."

"I'm ready to go at any moment," said Harry. "Night helping me, I may be able to ride through the lines of our enemies out there."

"No, Harry, you must not go that way. They're so vigilant that you would not have any possible chance. Nor can you ride. You must leave your horse behind."

"What way then must I go, sir?"

"By the river. We have gathered up a few small boats, used at the crossing here. You can row, can't you?"

"Fairly well, sir."

"'Twill do, because you're not to stay in the boat long. I want you to drop down the stream until you're well beyond the Federal lines. Then leave the boat and strike out across the country for General Lee. You know the way. You can buy or seize a horse, and you must not fail."

"I will not fail," said Harry confidently.

"You'll succeed if anybody will, and now you must be off. Your pistols are loaded, Harry? You may have to use them."

They did not delay a minute, going down the shelving shore to the Potomac, where a man held a small boat against the bank.

"Get in, Harry," said Sherburne. "You'd better drop down three or four miles, at least. Good-by and good luck."

He shook hands with his colonel and Dalton, took the oars and pulled far out into the stream.

CHAPTER IV
A HERALD TO LEE

When he swept out upon the sullen bosom of the Potomac, Harry looked back only once. He saw two dim figures going up the bank, and, at its crest, a line of lights that showed the presence of the Southern force. There was no sound of firing, and he judged that the enemy had withdrawn to a distance of two or three miles.

The night had turned darker since the battle ceased, and not many stars were out. Clouds indicated that flurries of rain might come, but he did not view them now with apprehension. Darkness and rain would help a herald to Lee. The current was strong, and he did not have to pull hard, but, observing presently that the far shore was fringed with bushes, he sent the boat into their shadow.

He did not anticipate any danger from the southern shore, but the old inherited caution of the forest runners was strong within him. Under the hanging bushes he was well hidden, but, in some places, the flood in the river had turned the current back upon itself, and he was compelled to pull with vigor on the oars.

The clouds that had threatened did not develop much, and while the forests were dark, the surface of the river showed clearly in the faint moonlight. Any object upon it could be seen from either bank, and Harry was glad that he had sought the shelter of the overhanging bushes. He realized now that in this region, which was really the theater of war, many scouts and skirmishers must be about.

The bank above him was rather high and quite steep, for which he was glad, as it afforded protection. A half mile farther down he came to the mouth of a creek coming in from the South, and just as he passed it he heard voices on the bank. He held his boat among the bushes on the cliff and listened. Several men were talking, but he judged them to be farmers, not soldiers. Yet they talked of the battle that night, and Harry surmised that they were looking at the lights in the Southern camp which might yet be visible from the high point on which they stood. He could not gather from their words whether they were Northern or Southern sympathizers, but it did not matter, as he had no intention of speaking to them, hoping only that they would go away in a few minutes and let him continue his journey unseen.

His hope speedily came to pass. He heard their voices sinking in the distance, and leaving the shelter of the bushes he pulled down the stream once more. Then he found that he had deceived himself about the clouds. If they had retired, they had merely recoiled, to use the French phrase, in order to gather again with greater force.

During his short stay among the bushes at the foot of the cliff the whole heavens had blackened and the air was surcharged with the heavy damp and tensity that betoken a coming storm. The lightning blazed across the river thrice, and he heard a mutter which was not that of cannon. Then came rain and a rushing wind and the surface of the river was troubled grievously. It rose up in waves like those of a lake, and Harry's boat rocked and tumbled so badly that in a few minutes it was half-full of water.

Fearing he might sink, carrying with him his great message, he pulled again, but fiercely now, for the southern bank and the shelter of the bushes, which, fortunately for him, grew here in the water's edge. He shoved his boat with all his might among them, as their tops snapped and crackled in the hurricane. But he knew he was safe there, and he continued to push until it reached the edge of the land.

The river would be swollen by another storm, but for the present it did not bother him greatly. He was more immediately concerned with his wish to get back to Lee as soon as possible, and he was grateful for that dense clump of bushes, growing in the very water's edge, because the wind was blowing like a hurricane and the waves were chasing one another on the Potomac, like the billows on a lake. He was a fair oarsman, but it would have taken greater skill than his to have kept his boat afloat in the tempestuous river.

The bushes formed an absolute protection. His boat swayed with them, which saved it from being damaged, and the overhanging lee of the cliff kept most of the rain from him. He also wrapped about his body the pair of blankets that he always carried, and he sat there not only in safety, but with a certain physical pleasure.

Once more amid surroundings with the like of which Henry Ware had been so familiar, the soul of his great ancestor seemed to have descended upon him. Most young officers, no matter how brave or how skilled in war, would have been awed and alarmed. He had no comrades at his elbow. There was no light, no friendly sound to encourage him, he was as truly alone, so far as his present situation was concerned, as any pioneer had ever been in the heart of the wilderness. But for him there was pleasure at that moment in being alone. He did not quiver when the thunder rolled and crashed above his head, and the lightning blazed in one Titanic sword slash after another across the surface of the river. Rather, the wilderness and majesty of the scene appealed to him. Leaning well back in his boat with his blankets closely wrapped about him, he watched it, and his soul rose with the storm.

Harry knew from its sudden violence that the rain would soon pass, and if the waves abated a little he would certainly take his boat into the river and try his fortunes again. Yet a precious hour was lost, and nothing could replace it. The thunder ceased by and by and there was only dim lightning on the far horizon. The waves began to abate, and, taking off his blankets, he pushed his boat once more into the stream.

It rocked prodigiously and shipped water, but by strenuous effort he kept it afloat, and as the wind sank still further he decided that he would seek the northern shore and disembark as soon as possible. It would be easier to steal through the thickets than to navigate what amounted to a wild sea. But the banks were yet too high and steep for a landing, and he continued to row, keeping now near the middle of the stream.

Wind and rain were dying fast, and he heard a sound behind uncommonly like the distant swish of oars. It sent an unpleasant thrill through him, because he wished to be alone on the river at that particular time, but his eyes, tracing a course through all the dusk and gloom, rested upon another boat, about two hundred yards away, containing a single occupant.

A farmer or a riverman, Harry thought, but to his great astonishment the man suddenly raised himself up a little and shouted to him in a tremendous voice to halt. Harry had not the least idea of stopping for anybody. He bent to his oars and rowed swiftly on.

Again came that shout to halt, and it seemed more insolent to him than before. He put a few more ounces of strength into his arms and shoulders and increased his speed.

The pursuer, suddenly drawing in his oars, raised a rifle from the bottom of his boat, and fired point blank at the fugitive. The bullet whistled so near Harry that he felt his ear burn, and at first thought he was hit. He would have been glad to fire back, but his pistols could not carry like his enemy's rifle, and there was nothing to do but flee. Once again he sought to draw a few more ounces of energy from his body. But the man behind him was a much greater oarsman than he and gained rapidly. The stranger, shouting another command to halt, to which no attention was paid, fired a second time, and the bullet went through the side of Harry's boat, barely scraping his knee as it passed.

His rage became intense. He had been shot at many times in battle, and many times he had fired his pistols into the opposing masses, but here upon this river a man sought his life, as the savages of old sought the hunter. Another glance showed him that pursuer had closed up half the distance between them, and, snatching one of the pistols from his belt, he fired. He knew that he had missed, as he saw the water spurt up beside the boat, but he thought that his bullet and the probability of more might delay the pursuit. Nevertheless the man came on as boldly and as fast as ever. If he fired a third time he could scarcely miss at such short range.

It seemed to Harry the gift of Heaven, that a whole pack of clouds should drift above them at that moment, deepening the obscurity and making the pursuing boat, although it was so near, a shapeless form in the mist. He could not see the features of the man, but he was able to discern his large and powerful figure, and he noticed the rhythmic manner in which his arms and shoulders worked at the oars. Obviously he had no chance to escape him by flight, and drawing his second pistol he fired. The bullet struck the boat but did no damage. The man came on faster than ever. Harry took a desperate resolution, and, whirling his boat about, he rowed it straight at his pursuer, who was now almost level with him. He intended to ram and take his chances. His movement was so quick and unexpected that it succeeded. The bow of his boat, helped perhaps by a wave, struck the other with such violence that both were shattered and sank instantly.

Harry went down with his craft, but in a few seconds came up again, his mouth and eyes full of muddy water. He was a splendid swimmer, and his eyes clearing in a moment he looked toward the northern shore, seeking an easy place for landing. They encountered ten feet away a large sun-browned face and two burning eyes.

"Shepard!" Harry gasped.

"And so it was you, Lieutenant Kenton. Perhaps if I had known it was you I wouldn't have fired upon you."

"Don't let that deter you. We're enemies."

"I merely said 'perhaps!' I like you, but that wouldn't keep me from stopping you by any method I could from reaching Lee."

"I'm sure it wouldn't. I like you, too, Mr. Shepard, but we're enemies here in this river, deadly enemies, and I mean to beat you off."

"One may mean to do a thing and yet not do it. I'm the larger and the more powerful. Besides, I'm toughened by superior age. You'd better surrender, Mr. Kenton. I don't want to do you any bodily harm."

"I admit that you're larger and stronger, but on land only. I'm the better swimmer. We're both floating now, but if you'll make a comparison, Mr. Shepard, you'll find that I'm doing it with the greatest ease. Take my advice, and swim to the southern bank of the river while I go to the northern. I say it in all good faith."

"I've no doubt of that, but the young are likely to over-estimate their powers. I'm a good swimmer, and you can't escape me."

"The important point is not whether I can escape you, but whether you can escape me. Since you have lost your boat and your rifle and we're in such a treacherous and unstable element as water, I occupy the superior position. The young may indeed over-estimate their powers, but in swimming at least I'm a competent critic. For instance, you're holding your shoulders too high, and you kick too much. You're splashing water, a useless waste of energy. Now observe me. The surface of this river is rough. Little waves are yet running upon it, but I float as easily as a fish, come up to see by the moon what time it is. It is not egotism on my part, merely a recognition of the facts, but I warn you, Mr. Shepard, to swim to the other shore and let me alone."

The two were not ten feet apart, and, despite the lightness of their talk, their eyes burned with eagerness and intensity. Harry knew that Shepard would not dream of turning back. Yet in the water he awaited the result with a confidence that he would not have felt on land.

"It's your move, Mr. Shepard," he said.

The intensity of Shepard's gaze increased, and Harry never took his eyes from those of his enemy. He intended like a prize fighter to read there what the man's next effort would be.

"I don't see that it's my move," said Shepard, as he floated calmly.

"You're following me for the purpose of capturing me."

"To capture you, or delay you. Meanwhile, it seems to me that I'm delaying you very successfully. I can't see that you're making much progress towards Lee."

"That depends upon which way this river is flowing. You note that we float gently with the stream."

"It's a poor argument. The Potomac flows directly by Washington, and if we were to float on we'd float into the heart of great Northern fortresses instead of Lee's camp."

"That's true as far as it goes, but it doesn't go far enough. I'm leaving the river soon. You can have it all then."

"Thanks, but I think I'll go with you, Lieutenant Kenton."

"Then come to the bottom!" exclaimed Harry, as he dived forward like a flash, seized Shepard by the ankles and headed for the bottom of the river with him. The water gurgled in his eyes and ears and nose, but he held on for many seconds, despite the man's desperate struggles. Then he was forced to let go and rise.

As his head shot above the stream he saw another shooting up in the same manner about fifteen feet away. Both were choked and gasping, but Harry managed to say:

"I didn't intend for you to come up so soon."

"I suppose not, but perhaps you didn't pause to think that when you rose I'd rise with you."

"Yes, that's true. It seems to me that matters grow complicated. Can't you persuade yourself, Mr. Shepard, to go and leave me alone? I really have no use for you here."

"I'd like to oblige you, Lieutenant Kenton, but I intend to see that you don't reach General Lee."

"Still harping upon that? It seems to me that you're a stupidly stubborn man. Don't you know that I'm going anyhow?"

Harry had never ceased to watch his eyes, and he saw there the signal of a coming movement. Shepard dived suddenly for him, intending to repeat his own trick, but the youth was like a fish in the water, and he darted to the right. The man came up grasping nothing. Harry laughed. The chagrin of Shepard compelled his amusement, although he liked the man.

"I wish you'd go away, Mr. Shepard," he said. "On land you could, perhaps, overpower me, but in the water I think I'm your master. All through my boyhood I devoted a great deal of my time to swimming. Dr. Russell of the Pendleton Academy—but you never knew him—used to say that if I would swim less and study more I could make greater pretensions to scholarship."

Shepard, swimming rather easily, regarded him thoughtfully.

"While we talk to each other in this more or less polite manner, Mr. Kenton," he said, "we must not forget that we're in deadly earnest. I mean to take you, and our scouts mean to take every other messenger who goes out from Colonel Sherburne's camp. You know, and I know, that if the Army of Northern Virginia does not reach in a few days that camp, where there is a ford in ordinary weather, it will be driven up against the Potomac and we can accumulate such great forces against it that it cannot possibly escape. Even at Sherburne's place its escape is more than doubtful, if it has to linger long."

"Yes, I know these things quite well, Mr. Shepard. I know also, as you do, that General Meade's army is not in direct pursuit, and, that in a flanking movement, he is advancing across South Mountain and toward Sharpsburg. It is a march well calculated and extremely dangerous to General Lee, if he does not hear of it in time. But he will hear of it soon enough. A comrade of mine, George Dalton, will tell him. Others from Colonel Sherburne's camp will tell him, and I mean to tell him too. I hope to be the first to do so."

Harry never deceived himself for a moment. He knew that although Shepard liked him, he would go to the uttermost to stop him, and as for himself, while he had a friendly feeling for the spy, he meant to use every weapon he could against him. Realizing that he could not linger much longer, as the chill of the water was already entering his body, he swam closer to Shepard, still staring directly into his eyes. How thankful he was now for those innumerable swimmings in the little river that ran near Pendleton! Everything learned well justifies itself some day.

Although there was but little moonlight they were so close together that they could see the eyes of each other clearly, and Harry detected a trace of uneasiness in those of Shepard. A good swimmer, the water nevertheless was not his element, and although a man of great physique and extraordinary powers, he longed for the solid earth under his feet.

Harry drew himself together as if he were going to dive, but instead of doing so suddenly raised himself in the water and shot forth his clenched tight fist with all his might. Shepard was taken completely by surprise and he sank back under the water, leaving a blood stain on its surface. Harry watched anxiously, but Shepard came up again in a moment or two, gasping and swimming wildly. The point of his jaw was presented fairly and Harry struck again as hard as he could in the water. Shepard with a choked cry went under and Harry, diving forward, seized his body, bringing it to the surface.

Shepard was senseless, but getting an arm under his shoulders Harry was able to swim with him to the northern shore, although it took nearly all his strength. Then he dragged him out upon the bank, and sank down, panting, beside him.

The great Civil War in America, the greatest of all wars until nearly all the nations of Europe joined in a common slaughter, was a humane war compared with other wars approaching it in magnitude. It did not occur to Harry to let Shepard drown, nor did he leave him senseless on the bank. As soon as his own strength returned he dragged him into a half-sitting position, and rubbed the palms of his hands. The spy opened his eyes.

"Good-by, Mr. Shepard," said Harry. "I'm bound to leave before you recover fully because then I wouldn't be your match. I'm sorry I had to hit you so hard, but there was nothing else to do."

"I don't blame you. It was man against man."

"The water was in my favor. I'm bound to admit that on land you'd have won."

"At any rate I thank you for dragging me out of the river."

"You'd have done as much for me."

"So I would, but our personal debts of gratitude can't be allowed to interfere with our military duty."

"I know it. Therefore I take a running start. Good-by."

"We'll meet again."

"But not on this side of the Potomac. It may happen when the Army of Northern Virginia and the Army of the Potomac go into battle on the other side of the river."

Harry darted into the forest, and ran for a half-hour. He meant to put as much distance as possible between Shepard and himself before the latter's full strength returned. He knew that Shepard would follow, if he could, but it was not possible to trail one who had a long start through dark and wet woods.

He came through the forest and into a meadow surrounded by a rail fence, on which he sat until his breath came back again. He had forgotten all about his wet uniform, but the run was really beneficial to him as it sent the blood leaping through his veins and warmed his body.

"So far have I come," said Harry, "but the omens promise a hard march."

He had his course fixed very clearly, and a veteran now in experience, he could guide himself easily by the moon and stars. The clouds were clearing away and a warm wind promised him dry clothing, soon. Long afterward he thought it a strange coincidence that his cousin, Dick Mason, in the far South should have been engaged upon an errand very similar in nature, but different in incident.

He crossed the meadow, entered an orchard and then came to a narrow road. The presence of the orchard indicated the proximity of a farmhouse, and it occurred to Harry that he might buy a horse there. The farmer was likely to be hostile, but risks must be taken. He drew his pistols. He knew that neither could be fired after the thorough wetting in the river, but the farmer would not know that. He saw the house presently, a comfortable two-story frame building, standing among fine shade trees. Without hesitation he knocked heavily on the door with the butt of a pistol.

He was so anxious to hasten that his blows would have aroused the best sleeper who ever slept, and the door was quickly opened by an elderly man, not yet fully awake.

"I want to buy a horse."

"Buy a horse? At this time of the night?"

He was about to slam the door, but Harry put his foot over the sill and the muzzle of his pistol within six inches of the man's nose.

"I want to buy a horse," he repeated, "and you want to sell one to me. I think you realize that fact, don't you?"

"Yes, I do," replied the man, looking down the muzzle of the big horse pistol.

"Come outside and close the door behind you. I know you haven't on many clothes, but the night's warm, and you need fresh air."

The man with the muzzle of the pistol still near his nose, obeyed. But as he looked at the weapon he also had a comprehensive view of the one who held it.

"Wet ain't you?" he said.

"Do you think it necessary to put it in the form of a question?"

"I don't like to say, unless I'm shore."

"Where do you keep your horses?"

"In the barn here to the left. What kind of a horse did you think you'd keer fur most, stranger?"

"The biggest, the strongest and fastest you've got"

"I thought mebbe you'd want one with wings, you 'pear to be in such a pow'ful hurry. I wish you wouldn't keep that pistol so near to my nose. 'Sides, you've gethered so much mud an' water 'bout you that you ain't so very purty to look at!"

"It's your own mud and water. I didn't bring it into this country with me."

"Which means that you don't belong in these parts. I reckon lookin' at you that you wuz one o' them rebels that went to Gettysburg and then come back ag'in."

"Exactly right, Mr. Farmer. I'm an officer in General Lee's army."

"Then I wuz right 'bout you needin' a horse with wings. An' I guess all the men in your army need horses with wings. Don't be in such a tarnal hurry. You're goin' to stay right up here with us, boarders, so to speak, till the war is over."

Harry laughed.

"Kind of you," he said, "but here is the stable and do you open the stall doors one by one, and let me see the horses. At the first sign of any trick I pull the trigger."

"Well, as I don't like violence I'll show you the horses. Here's the gray mare, five years old, swift but can't last long. This is old Rube, nigh onto ten, mighty strong, but as balky as a Johnny Reb hisself. Don't want him! No? Then I think that's about all."

"No it's not! You open that last stall door at once!"

The farmer made a wry face, and threw back the door with a slam. Harry still covering the man with the pistol that couldn't go off, saw a splendid bay horse about four years old.

"Holding out on me, were you?" he said. "Did you think a Confederate officer could be fooled in that manner?"

"I reckon I oughtn't to have thought so. I've always heard that the rebels had mighty good eyes for Yankee horseflesh."

"I'll let that pass, because maybe it's true. Now, saddle and bridle him quicker than ever before in your life."

The farmer did so, and Harry took care to see that the girth was secure.

"At how much did you value this horse?" he asked.

"I did put him down at two hundred dollars, but I reckon he's worth nothin' to me now."

"Here's your money. When General Lee goes through the enemy's country he pays for what he takes."

He thrust a roll of good United States bills into the astonished man's hand, and sprang upon the horse. Then he turned from the stable and rode swiftly up the road, but not so swiftly that he did not hear a bullet singing past his ears. A backward glance showed him an elderly farmer in his night clothes standing on his porch and reloading his rifle.

"Well, I can't blame you, I suppose," said Harry. "You can guess pretty well what I am, and it's your business to stop me."

But he rode fast enough to be far beyond the range of a second bullet, and maintained a good pace for a long time, through hilly and wooded country. His uniform dried upon him, and his hardy form felt no ill result from the struggle in the river. The horse was strong and spirited, and Harry knew that he could carry him without weariness to Lee. He looked upon his mission as already accomplished, but his ambition to reach the commander-in-chief first was yet strong.

He rode throughout the rest of the night and dawn and the pangs of hunger came together. But he decided that he would not turn from his path to seek food. He would go on straight for Lee and let hunger have its way. He had a splendid horse under him and he was faring quite as well as he had a right to expect. He thought of Shepard, and felt pity for him. The man had only striven to do his duty, and while he had used force he had been very courteous and polite about it. Harry was bound to acknowledge that his had been a very chivalrous enemy and only his superiority in swimming had enabled him to win over Shepard. He was glad that he had saved him and had left him on the bank, so to speak, to dry.

Then Shepard faded away with the mists and vapors that were retreating before a brilliant dawn. The country was high, rolling, and the foliage, although much browned by the July sun, which was unusually hot that year, was still dense. Most of the hills were heavy with forest, but all the valleys between were fertile and well cultivated. With the dew of the morning fresh upon it the whole region was refreshing and soothing to the eye with a look of peace, where in reality there was no peace. Many thin columns of smoke lying blue against the silver sky told where farmhouses stood, and hunger suddenly seized upon Harry again.

Hunger is natural to youth, and his severe exertions all through the night had greatly increased it. It became both a pain and a weakness. His shoulders drooped with fatigue, and he felt that he must have food or faint by the way.

He was ashamed of his physical weakness, but he knew that unless he found food his faintness would increase, and hunger alone would stop him, where so able a man as Shepard could not. His uniform, faded anyhow, was so permeated with the dried mud of the river that it would take a keen eye to tell whether it was Federal or Confederate, and he need not disclose his identity in this region, which was so strongly for the Union. He made up his mind quickly and rode for the nearest farmhouse.

Harry knew that he was inviting risks. His pistols were still useless but they would be handy for threats, and he should be able to take care of himself at a farmhouse.

The house that he had chosen was only a few hundred yards away, its white walls visible among trees, and the clatter of his horse's hoofs brought a man from a barn in the rear. Harry noted him keenly. He was youngish, stalwart and the look out of his blue eyes was fearless. He came forward slowly, examining his visitor, and his manner was not altogether hospitable. Harry decided that he had to deal with a difficult customer but he had no idea of turning back.

"Good morning," he said politely.

"Good morning."

"I wish some breakfast and I will pay. I've ridden all night in our service."

"You've so much dried mud on you that you look as if you'd been passin' through a river."

"Correct. That's exactly what happened."

"But there's none on your horse."

"He didn't pass with me. I'm willing to answer any reasonable number of questions, but, as I told you before, I ride on an important service. I must have breakfast at once, and I'll pay."

"Whose service? Ours or Reb's?"

"A military messenger can't answer the chance questions of those by the roadside. I tell you I want breakfast at once."

"Fine horse you ride, stranger. How long have you had him?"

"All this year."

"Funny. When I saw him last week he belonged to Jim Kendall down by the Potomac, an' livin' on this very road, too."

"It isn't half as funny as you think. Hands up! Now call to your wife as loud as you can to bring me coffee and food at the gate! I know they're ready in the kitchen. I can smell 'em here. Out with it, call as fast as and as loud as you can, or off goes the top of your head!"

Although a horse pistol held in a firm hand was thrust under his nose, the man's blue eyes glared hate and defiance, and his mouth did not open. Harry, in his excitement and anger, forgot that the charge in his weapon was ruined and hence it was no acting with him when his own eyes blazed down at the other and he fairly shouted:

"I give you until I can count ten to call your wife! One! two! three! four! five! six! seven! eight! nine! — "

"Sophy! Sophy!" cried the farmer, who saw death flaming in the eyes that looked into his, "Come! Come a-runnin'!"

A good looking young woman threw open a door and ran, frightened, toward the gate, where she saw her husband under the pistol muzzle of a wild and savage looking man on horseback.

"Sophy," said the farmer, "bring this infernal rebel a cup of coffee and a plate of bread and meat. If it weren't for his pistol I'd drag him off his horse and carry him to General Meade, but he's got the drop on me!"

"And Sophy," said Harry, who was growing cooler, "you make it a big tin cup of coffee and you see that the plate is piled high with meat and bread. Now don't you make one mistake. Don't you come back with any weapon in your hand in place of food, and don't you fire on me from the house with the family rifle. You're young and you're good looking, and, doubtless the widow of our friend here with the upraised hands, wouldn't have to wait long for another husband just as good as he is."

The woman paled a little, and Harry knew that some thought of the family rifle had been in her mind. The husband's glare became ferocious.

"You can take your hands down," said Harry. "I've no wish to torture you, and I'm satisfied now that you're not armed."

The man dropped his arms and the woman hurried to the kitchen. Harry did not watch her, but kept his eyes continually upon the man, who he knew would take advantage of his first careless moment, and spring for him like a tiger. A pistol that he couldn't fire wouldn't be of much use to him then.

But the woman returned with a big tin cup of smoking coffee and a plate piled high with bread and bacon and beefsteak. It was a welcome sight. The aspect of the whole world became brighter at once, and the pulse of hope beat high. But happiness did not make him relax caution.

"Stand back about ten feet more," he said to the man, "I don't like your looks."

"What's the matter with my looks?"

"It's not exactly your looks I mean, though they're scarcely worthy of the lady, your wife, but it's rather your attitude or position which reminds me of a lion or a tiger about to spring upon something it hates."

The man, with a savage growl, withdrew a little.

"I'd like to put a bullet through you," he said.

"I've no doubt of it, your eyes show it, but before I take a polite leave of you I want to tell you that I did not steal this horse from your friend, Jim Kendall. I paid for it at his own valuation."

"Confederate money that won't be worth a dollar a bale before long."

"Oh, no, bills that were made and stamped at Washington, and I pay for this breakfast in silver."

He dropped it into the hand of the woman, as he took the huge cup of coffee from her. Then he drank deep and long, and again and again, draining the last drop of the brown liquid.

"I hope it's burnt the lining out of your throat," said the man savagely.

"It was warm, but I like it that way. It was good indeed, and I'm sorry, Madame, that you have such a violent and ill-tempered husband. Maybe your next will be a much better man."

"John is neither violent nor ill-tempered. He's never said a harsh word to me since we were married. But he hates the rebels dreadfully."

"That's too bad. I don't hate him and I'm glad you can give him a good character. A man's own wife knows best. Now, I'm going to eat this breakfast as I ride on. You'll find the plate on the fence a quarter of a mile ahead."

He bowed to both, and still keeping a wary eye on the man, thrust his pistol into his belt, and as his horse moved forward at a swift and easy gait he began to eat with a ravenous appetite.

A backward glance showed husband and wife still gazing at him. But it was only for a moment. They ran into the house and a little further on Harry looked back again. They had reappeared and he almost expected to hear again the whistle of a rifle shot, fired from a window. But the distance was much too great, and he devoted renewed attention to the demands of hunger.

When he had finished his breakfast he put the plate upon the fence as he had promised, and, looking back for the last time, he saw an American flag wave to and fro on the roof of the house. He felt a thrill of alarm. It must be a signal concerning him and it could be made only to his enemies. Speaking sharply to his horse, he urged him into a gallop.

CHAPTER V
THE DANGEROUS ROAD

The road led in the general direction of Lee's army and Harry knew that if he followed it long enough he was bound to reach his commander, but the two words "long enough" might defeat everything. Undoubtedly a Federal force was near, or the farmer and his wife would not be signaling from the roof of their house.

A plucky couple they were and he gave them all credit, but he was aware that while he had secured breakfast from them they had put the wolves upon his trail. There were high hills on both the right and left of the road, and, as he galloped along he examined them through his glasses for flags answering the signal on the house. But he saw nothing and the thickness of the forest indicated that even if the signals were made there it was not likely he could see them.

Now he wisely restrained the speed of his horse, so full of strength and spirit that it seemed willing to run on forever, and brought him down to a walk. He had an idea that he would soon be pursued, and then a fresh horse would be worth a dozen tired ones.

The road continued to run between high, forested hills, splendid for ambush, and Harry saw what a danger it was not to have knowledge of the country. He understood how the Union forces in the South were so often at a loss on ground that was strange to them.

The road now curved a little to the left, and a few hundred yards ahead another from the east merged with it. Along this road the forest was thinner, and upon it, but some distance away, he saw bobbing heads in caps, twenty, perhaps, in number. He knew at once that they were the enemy, called by the signal, and leaning forward he spoke in the ear of his good horse.

"You and I haven't known each other long," he said, "but we're good friends. I paid honest and sufficient money for you, when I could have ridden away on you without paying a cent. I know you have a powerful frame and that your speed is great. I really believe you're the fastest runner in all this part of the state. Now, prove it!"

The horse stretched out his neck, and the road flew behind him, his body working like a mighty machine perfectly attuned, even to its minutest part. Harry's words had met a true response. He heard a cry on the cross road, and the bobbing heads came forward much faster. Either they had seen him or they had heard the swift beat of his horse's hoofs. Loud shouts arose, but he saw the uniforms of the men, and he knew that they belonged to the Northern army.

He went past the junction of the roads, as if he were flying, but he was not a bit too soon, as he heard the crack of rifles, and bullets struck in the earth behind him. He knew that they would follow, hang on persistently, but he had supreme confidence in the speed and strength of his horse, and youth rode triumphant. It was youth more than anything else that made him raise himself a little in his saddle, look back to his pursuers and fling to them a long, taunting cry, just as Henry Ware more than once had taunted his Indian pursuers before disappearing in a flight that their swiftest warriors could not match.

But the little band of Union troopers clung to the chase. They too had good horses, and they knew that the man before them was a Southern messenger, and in those hot July days of 1863 all military messages carried on the roads north of the Potomac were important. The fate of an army or a nation might turn upon any one of them, and the lieutenant who led the little Union troop was aware of it. He was a man of intelligence and a consuming desire to overtake the lone horseman lay hold of him. He knew, as well as any general, that since Gettysburg the fate of the South was verily trembling in the balance, and the slightest weight somewhere might decide the scales. So he resolved to hang on through everything and the chances were in his favor. It was his own country. The Federal troops were everywhere, and any moment he might have aid in cutting off the fugitive.

When Harry eased his horse's flight he saw the troop, very distant but still pursuing, and he read the mind of the Union leader. He was saving his mounts, trailing merely, in the hope that Harry would exhaust his own horse, after which he and his men would come on at great speed.

Harry looked down at his horse and saw that he was heaving with his great effort. He knew that he had made a mistake in driving him so hard at first, and with the courage of which only a young veteran would have been capable he brought the animal almost to a walk, and resolutely kept him there, while the enemy gained. When they were almost within rifle shot he increased his speed again, but he did not seek for the present to increase his gain.

As long as their bullets could not reach him his horse should merely go stride for stride with theirs, and when the last stretch was reached, he would send forward the brave animal at his utmost speed. His were the true racing tactics drawn from his native state. He had no doubt of his ability to leave his pursuers far behind when the time came, but his true danger was from interference. He too knew that many Union cavalry troops were abroad, and he watched on either flank for them as he rode on. At the crest of every little hill he swept the whole country, but as yet he saw nothing but peaceful farmhouses.

The day was clear and bright, not so warm as its predecessors, and he calculated by the sun that he was going straight toward Lee. He knew that a great army always marched slowly, and he was able to reckon with accuracy just how far the Army of Northern Virginia had come since Gettysburg. He should reach it in the morning, with full information about the Potomac, and the best place for a crossing.

He arrived at the crest of a hill higher than the others, and saw the Union troop, about a quarter of a mile behind, stop beside a clump of tall trees. Their action surprised Harry, who had thought they would never quit as long as they could find his trail. To his further surprise he saw one of the men dismount and begin to climb the tallest of the trees. Then he brought his glasses into play.

He saw the climber go up, up, until he had reached the last bough that would support him. Then he drew some thing from his pocket which he unrolled and began to wave rapidly. It was a flag and through his powerful glasses Harry clearly saw the Stars and Stripes. It was evident that they were signaling, but when one signals one usually signals to somebody. His breath shortened for a moment. He believed that the man in the tree was talking with his flag about the fugitive. Where was the one to whom he was talking?

He looked to both left and right, searching the fields and the forests, and saw nothing. Then, as he was sweeping his glasses again in a half curve he caught a glimpse of something straight ahead that made the great pulse in his throat beat hard. About a mile in front of him another man in a tree was waving a flag and beneath the tree were horsemen.

Harry knew now that the two flags were talking about the Confederate messenger between. The one behind said: "Look out! He's young, riding a bay horse and he's coming directly toward you," to which the one in front replied, "We're waiting. He can't escape us. There are fields with high fences on either side of the road and if he manages to break through the fence he's an easy capture in the soft and muddy ground there."

Harry thought hard and fast, while the two flags talked so contemptuously about him. The fields were unquestionably deep with mud from the heavy rains, but he must try them. It was lucky that he had seen the flags while both forces were out of rifle shot. He decided for the western side, sprang from his horse and threw down a few rails. In a half minute he was back on his horse, leaped him over the fence, and struck across the field.

It had been lately plowed and the going was uncommonly heavy. It would be just as heavy however for his pursuers, and his luck in seeing their signals would put him out of range before they reached the field. But it was a wide field and his horse's feet sank so deep in the mud that he dismounted and led him. When he was two-thirds of the way across a shout told him that the two forces had met, and had discovered the ruse of the fugitive. It did not take much intelligence to understand what he had done, because he was yet in plain sight, and a few of the cavalrymen took pot shots at him, their bullets falling far short. Harry in his excited condition laughed at these attempts. Almost anything was a triumph now. He shook his fist at them and regretted that he could not send back a defiant shot.

The cavalrymen conferred a little. Then a part pursued across the field, and two detachments rode along its side, one to the north and the other to the south. Harry understood. If the mud held him back sufficiently they might pass around the field and catch him on the other side. He continued to lead his horse, encouraging him with words of entreaty and praise.

"Come on!" he cried. "You won't let a little mud bother you. You wouldn't let yourself be overtaken by a lot of half-bred horses not fit to associate with you?"

The brave animal responded nobly, and what had been the far edge of the field was rapidly coming nearer. Beyond it lay woods. But the flanking movement threatened. The two detachments were passing around the field on firm ground, and Harry knew that he and his good horse must hasten. He talked to him continually, boasting about him, and together they reached the fence, which he threw down in all haste. Then he led his weary horse out of the mud, sprang upon his back and galloped into the bushes.

He knew that the horses passing around the field on firm ground would be fresh, and that he must find temporary hiding, at least as soon as he could. He was in deep thickets now and he galloped on, careless how the bushes scratched him and tore his uniform. The Union cavalry would surely follow, but he wanted a little breathing time for his horse, and in eight or ten minutes he stopped in the dense undergrowth. The horse panted so hard that any one near would have heard him, but there was no other sound in the thicket. The rest was valuable for both. Harry was able to concentrate his mind and consider, while the panting of the horse gradually ceased, and he breathed with regularity. The young lieutenant patted him on the nose and whispered to him consolingly.

"Good, old boy," he said, "you've brought me safely so far. I knew that I could trust you."

Then he stood quite still, with his hand stroking the horse's nose to keep him silent. He had heard the first sounds of search. To his right was the distant beat of hoofs and men's voices. Evidently they were going to make a thorough search for him, and he decided to resume his flight, even at the risk of being heard.

He led the horse again, because the forest was so dense that one could scarcely ride in it, and he thought, for a while, that he had thrown off the pursuit, but the voices came again, and now on his left. They had never relaxed the hunt for an instant. They had a good leader, and Harry admitted that in his place he would have done the same.

The country grew rougher, being so steep and hilly that it was not easy of cultivation, and hence remained clothed in dense forest and undergrowth. Twice more Harry heard the sound of pursuing voices and hoofs, and then the noise of running water came to his ears. Twenty yards farther and he came to a creek flowing between high banks, on which the forest grew so densely that the sun was scarcely able to reach the water below.

The creek at first seemed to be a bar to his advance, but thinking it over he led his horse carefully down into the stream, mounted him and rode with the current, which was not more than a foot deep. Fortunately the creek had a soft bottom and there was no ringing of hoofs on stones.

He went slowly, lest the water splash too much, and kept a wary watch on the banks above, which were growing higher. He did not know where the creek led, but it offered both a road and concealment, and it seemed that Providence had put it there for his especial help.

He rode in the bed of the stream fully an hour, and then emerged from the hills into a level and comparatively bare country. It was a region utterly unknown to him, but with his splendid idea of direction and the sun to guide him he knew his straight course to Lee. The country before him seemed to be given up wholly to grass, as he noticed neither corn nor wheat. He saw several farm hands, but decided to keep away from them. That was no country for the practice of horsemanship by a lone Confederate soldier, nor did he like to be the fox in a fox hunt.

Yet the fox he was. He chose a narrow road leading between cedars, and when he had advanced upon it a few hundred yards he heard the sound of a trumpet behind him, and at the edge of the woods that he had left. He saw horsemen in blue emerging and he had no doubt that they were the same men whom he had eluded in the thickets.

"Their pursuit of me is getting to be a habit," he said to himself with the most intense annoyance. "It's a good thing, my brave horse, that you've had a long rest."

He shook up the reins and began to gallop. He heard a faint shout in the distance and saw the troopers in pursuit. But he did not fear them now. Numerous fences would prevent them from flanking him, and he saw that the road led on, straight and level. He shook the reins again and the horse lengthened his stride.

He felt so exultant that he laughed. It would be easy enough now to distance this Union troop. Then the laugh died suddenly on his lips. A bullet whistled so near his face that it almost took away his breath. An elderly farmer standing in his own door had fired it, and Harry snatched one of the pistols from his own belt, remembering then with rage that it could not be fired. He shouted to his horse and made him run faster.

A bullet struck the pommel of his saddle and glanced off. A boy in an orchard had fired it. A load of bird-shot, a handful it seemed to Harry, flew about his ears. A bent old man who ought to have been sitting on a porch in a rocking chair had discharged it from the edge of a wood. A squirrel hunter on a hill took a pot shot at him and missed.

Harry was furious with anger. Decidedly this was no place for a visitor from the South. He did not detect the faintest sign of hospitality. Men and women alike seemed to dislike him. A powerful virago hurled a stone at his head, which would have struck him senseless had it not missed, and a farmer standing by a fence had a shotgun cocked and ready to be fired as he passed, but Harry, snatching one of the useless pistols from his belt, hurled it at him with all his might. It struck the man a glancing blow on the head, felling him as if he had been shot, and then Harry, thinking quickly, acted with equal quickness.

He reined in his horse with such suddenness that he nearly shot from the saddle. Then he leaped down, seized the shotgun from under the hands of the fallen man, sprang on his horse and was away again, sending back a cry of defiance.

Harry had never before in his life been so furious. To be hunted thus by a whole countryside, as if he were a mad dog, was intolerable. It was not only a threat to one's life, it was also an insult to one's dignity to be treated as an animal. Although he was armed now the insult continued. The call of the trumpet sounded almost without ceasing, and the Union troopers uttered many shouts as do those who chase the fox, although Harry knew that their cries were intended to rouse the farmers who might head him off.

The chase grew hotter, but he felt better with the shotgun. It was a fine double-barreled weapon of the latest make, and he hoped that it was loaded with buckshot. He was a sharpshooter, and he could give a good account of any one who came too near.

Yet with the trumpet shrilling continually behind him the huntsmen gathered fast on either flank. It was yet the day when nearly every house in America, outside a town, contained a rifle, and bullets fired from a distance began to patter around Harry and his horse. The riflemen were too far away to be reached with the shotgun, and it seemed inevitable to him that in time a bullet would strike him. He was truly the fox, and he knew that nothing could save him but forest.

It was in his favor that the country was so broken and wooded so heavily, and fixing his eyes on trees a half-mile ahead he raced for them. If none of this yelling pack dragged him down he felt sure that he might escape again in the forest. The trees swiftly came nearer, but the shots on either flank increased. More than ever he felt like the fox with the hounds all about him, and just one slender chance to reach the burrow ahead.

He felt his horse shake and knew that he had been hit. Yet the brave animal ran on as well as ever, despite the triumphant shout behind, which showed that he must be leaving a trail of blood. But the woods, thick and inviting, were near, and he believed that he would reach them. The horse shook again, much more violently than before, and then fell to his knees. Harry leaped off, still clutching the shotgun, just as the brave animal fell over on his side and began to breathe out his life.

He heard again that shout of triumph, but he was one who never gave up. He had alighted easily on his feet. The trees were not more than fifteen yards away and he disappeared among them as bullets clipped bark and twigs about him.

He breathed a deep sigh of thankfulness when he entered the forest. It was so dense, and there was so much undergrowth that the horsemen could not follow him there. If they came on foot, and spread out, as they must, to hunt him, he had the double-barreled shotgun and it was a deadly weapon. The fox had suddenly become the panther, alert, powerful, armed with claws that killed.

Harry went deep into the thickets before he sat down. He had no doubt that they would follow him, but at present he was out of their sight and hearing. He felt a mixture of elation and sadness, elation over his temporary escape, and sadness over the loss of his gallant horse. But one could not dwell long on regrets at such a time, and, advancing a little farther, he sat down among the densest bushes that he could find with the shotgun across his knees.

Now Harry saw that the horse had really done all that it was possible for him to do. He had brought him to the wood, and within he would have been a drawback. A man on foot could conceal himself far more easily. Everything favored him. There were bushes and vines everywhere and he could be hidden like a deer in its covert.

He looked up at the sun shining through the tops of the trees and saw that he had kept to his true course. His flight had taken him directly toward Lee at a much faster pace than he would have come otherwise. The enemy had driven him on his errand at double speed. He felt that he could spare a little time now, while he waited to see what the pursuit would do.

His feeling of exultation was now unalloyed. Deep in the forest with his foes looking for him in vain, the spirit of Henry Ware was once more strong within him. He was the reincarnation of the great hunter. He lay so still, clasping the shotgun, that the little creatures of the woods were deceived. A squirrel ran up the trunk of an oak six feet away, and stood fearlessly in a fork with his bushy tail curved over his back. A small gray bird perched on a bough just over Harry's head and poured out a volume of song. Farther away sounded the tap tap of a woodpecker on the bark of a dead tree.

Harry, although he did not move, was watching and listening with intense concentration, but his ears now would be his surest signals. He could not see deep in the thickets, but he could hear any movement in the underbrush a hundred yards away. So far there was nothing but the hopping of a rabbit. The bird over his head sang on. There was no wind among the branches, not even the flutter of leaves to distract his attention from anything that might come on the ground.

He rejoiced in this period of rest, of the nerves, rather than purely physical. He had been keyed so high that now he relaxed entirely, and soon lay perfectly flat, but with the shotgun still clasped in his arms. He had a soft couch. Under him were the dead leaves of last year, and over him was the pleasant gloom of thick foliage, already turning brown. The bird sang on. His clear and beautiful note came from a point directly over his head, but Harry could not see his tiny body among the leaves. He became, for a little while, more interested in trying to see him than in hearing his pursuers.

It was annoying that such a volume of sound should come from a body that could be hidden by a leaf. If a man could shout in proportion to his own size he might be heard eight to ten miles away. It was an interesting speculation and he pursued it. While he was pursuing it his mind relaxed more and more and traveled farther and farther away from his flight and hiding. Then his heavy eyelids pulled down, and, while his pursuers yet searched the thickets for him, he slept.

But his other self, which men had thought of as far back as Socrates, kept guard. When he had slept an hour a tiny voice in his ear, no louder than the ticking of a watch, told him to awake, that danger was near. He obeyed the call, sleep was lifted from him and he opened his eyes. But with inherited caution he did not move. He still lay flat in his covert, trusting to his ears, and did not make a leaf move about him.

His ears told him that leaves were rustling not very far away, not more than a hundred feet. His power of hearing was great, and the forest seemed to make it uncommonly sensitive and delicate.

He knew that the rustling of the leaves was made by a man walking. By and by he heard his footfalls, and he knew that he wore heavy boots, or his feet would not have crushed down in such a decisive manner. He was looking for something, too, because the footfalls did not go straight on, but veered about.

Harry was well aware that it was a Union soldier, and that he was the object of his search. He was a clumsy man, not used to forests, because Harry heard him stumble twice, when his feet caught on vines. Nor was any comrade near, or he would have called to him for the sake of companionship. Harry judged that he was originally a mill hand, and he did not feel the least alarm about him, laughing a little at his clumsiness and awkwardness, as he trod heavily among the bushes, tripped again on the vines, and came so near falling that he could hear the rifle rattle when it struck a tree. He did not have the slightest fear of the man, and at last, raising his head, he took a look.

All his surmises were justified. He saw a great hulking youth of heavy and dull countenance, carrying a rifle awkwardly, his place obviously around some town and not in the depths of a forest, looking for a wary enemy, who knew more of the wilderness than he could ever learn in all his life. Harry saw that he was perspiring freely and that he looked more like the hunted than the hunter. His eyes expressed bewilderment. He was obviously lonely and apprehensive, not because he was a coward, but because the situation was so strange to him.

Besides his rifle he carried a large knapsack, so much distended that Harry knew it to be full of food. It was this that decided him. A soldier, like an army, must travel on his stomach, and he wanted that knapsack. Moreover he meant to get it. He leveled his shotgun and called in a low tone, but a tone so sharp that it could be heard distinctly by the one to whom it was addressed:

"Throw up your hands at once!"

The man threw them up so abruptly that the rifle fell from his shoulder into the bushes, and he turned around, staring face toward the point from which the command had come. Harry saw at once that he was of foreign birth, probably. The features inclined to the Slav type, although Slavs were not then common in this country, even in the mill towns of the North.

"Are you an American?" asked Harry, standing up.

"All but two years of my life."

"The first two years then, as I see you speak good English. What's your name?"

"Michael Stanislav."

"Do you think that anybody named Michael Stanislav has the right to interfere in the quarrel of the Northern and Southern states? Don't the Stanislavs have trouble enough in the country where the Stanislavs grow?"

The big youth stared at him without understanding.

"Do you know who I am?" asked Harry, severely.

"The running rebel that we all look for."

"Rebels don't run. Besides, there are no rebels. Anyway I'm not the man you're looking for. My name is Robin Hood."

"Robin Hood?"

"Yes, Robin Hood! Didn't you ever hear of him?"

"Never."

"Then you have the honor of hearing of him and meeting him at the same time. As I said, my name is Robin Hood and my trade is that of a benevolent robber. I lie around in the greenwood, and I don't work. I've a lot of followers, Friar Tuck and others, but they're away for a while. They're as much opposed to work as I am. That's why they're my followers. We're the friends of the poor, because they have nothing we want, and we're the enemies of the rich because they have a lot we do want and that we often take. Still, we couldn't get along very well, if there were no rich for us to rob. It's like taking sugar water from a maple tree. We won't take too much, because it would kill the tree and we want to take its sugar water again, and many times. Do you understand?"

"Yes," replied the big youth, but Harry knew he didn't. Harry meanwhile was listening keenly to all that was passing in the forest, and he was sure that no other soldier had wandered near. It was perhaps partly a feeling of loneliness on his own part that caused him to linger in his talk with Michael Stanislav.

"Michael," he continued, "you appreciate our respective positions, don't you?"

"Ah!" said Michael, in a puzzled voice.

"I've explained carefully to you that I'm Robin Hood, and you at the present moment represent the rich."

"I am not rich. Before I turn soldier I work in a mill at Bridgeport."

"That's all very well, but you can't get out of it by referring to your past. Just now you are a proxy of the rich, and it's my duty to rob you."

The mouth of the big fellow expanded into a wide grin.

"You won't rob me," he said. "I have not a cent."

"But I'm going to rob you just the same. Don't you dare to drop a hand toward the pistols in your belt. If you do I'll blow your head off. I'm covering you with a double-barreled shotgun. Each barrel contains about twenty buckshot, and at close range their blast would be so terrific that you'd make an awful looking corpse."

"I hold up my hands a long time. Don't want to be any kind of a corpse."

"That's the good boy. Steady now. Don't move a muscle. I'm going to rob you. It's a brief and painless operation, much easier than pulling a tooth."

He deftly removed the two pistols and the accompanying ammunition from the man's belt, placing them in his own. His belt of cartridges he put on the ground beside the fallen rifle, and then as he felt a glow of triumph he passed the well-filled knapsack from the stalwart shoulders of the other to his own shoulders, equally stalwart.

"Is everything in it first class, Michael?" he demanded with much severity.

"The best. Our army feeds well."

"It's a good thing for you that it's so. Robin Hood is never satisfied with anything second class, and he's likely to be offended if you offer it to him. On the whole, Michael, I think I like you and I'm glad you came this way. But do you care for good advice?"

"Yes, sir."

"That's right. Say 'sir' to me. It pleases my robber's heart. Then, my advice to you is never again to go into the woods alone. All the forest looks alike to those who don't know it, and you're lost in a minute. Besides, it's filled with strange and terrible creatures, Robin Hood—that's me, though I have some redeeming qualities—the Erymanthean boar, the Hydra-headed monster, Medusa of the snaky locks, Cyclops, Polyphemus with one awful eye, the deceitful Sirens, the Old Man of the Mountain, Wodin and Osiris, and, last and most terrible of all, the Baron Munchausen."

A flicker of fear appeared in the eyes of the captive.

"But I'll see that none of these monsters hurt you," said Harry consolingly. "The open is directly behind you, about a mile. Right about! Wheel! Well done! Now, you won't see me again, but you'll hear me giving commands. Forward, march! Quit stumbling! No true forester ever does! Nor is it necessary for you to run into more than three trees! Keep going! No, don't curve! Go straight ahead, and remember that if you look back I shoot!"

Michael walked swiftly enough. He deemed that on the whole he had fared well. The great brigand, Robin Hood, had spared his life and he had lost nothing. The army would replace his weapons and ammunition and he was glad enough to escape from that terrible forest, even if he were driven out of it.

Harry watched him until he was out of sight, and then picking up the rifle and belt of cartridges he fled on soundless feet deeper into the forest. Two or three hundred yards away he stopped and heard a great shouting. Michael, no longer covered by a gun, had realized that something untoward had happened to him, and he was calling to his comrades. Harry did not know whether Michael would still call the man who had held him up, Robin Hood, nor did he care. He had secured an excellent rifle which would be much more useful to him than a shotgun, and his course still led straight toward the point where he should find Lee's army on the march. He felt that he ought to throw away the shotgun, as two weapons were heavy, but he could not make up his mind to do so.

A hundred yards farther and he heard replies to Michael's shouts, and then several shots, undoubtedly fired by the Union troops themselves, as signals of alarm. He laughed to himself. Could such men as these overtake one who was born to the woods, the great grandson of Henry Ware, the most gifted of the borderers, who in the woods had not only a sixth sense, but a seventh as well? And his great grandson had inherited many of his qualities.

Harry, in the forest, felt only contempt for these youths of Central Europe who could not tell one point of the compass from another. He guided his own course by the sun, and continued at a good pace until he could hear shouts and shots no longer. Then in the dense woods, where the shadows made a twilight, he came to a tiny stream flowing from under a rock. He knelt and drank of the cool water, and then he opened Michael's knapsack. It was truly well filled, and he ate with deep content. Then he drank again and rested by the side of the pool.

As he reflected over his journey Harry concluded that Providence had watched over him so far, but there was much yet to do before he reached Lee. Providence had a strange way of watching over a man for a while, and then letting him go. He would neglect no precaution. The forest would not continue forever and then he must take his chances in the open.

Still burning with the desire to be the first to reach Lee, he put the rifle and the shotgun on either shoulder, and set off at as rapid a pace as the thickets would permit. But he soon stopped because a sound almost like that of a wind, but not a wind, came to his ears. There was a breeze blowing directly toward him, but he paid no attention to it, because to him most breezes were pleasant and friendly. But the other sound had in it a quality that was distinctly sinister like the hissing of a snake.

Harry paused in wonder and alarm. All his instincts warned him that a new danger was at hand. The breath of the wind suddenly grew hot, and sparks carried by it blew past him. He knew, in an instant, that the forest was on fire behind him and that tinder dry, it would burn fast and furious. Changing from a walk to a run, he sped forward as swiftly as he could, while the flames suddenly sprang high, waved and leaped forward in chase.

CHAPTER VI
TESTS OF COURAGE

Harry did not know how the woods had been set on fire, and he never knew. He did not credit it to the intent of Michael and his comrades, but he thought it likely that some of these men, ignorant of the forest, had built a campfire. His first thought was of himself, and his second was regret that so fine a stretch of timber should be burned over for nothing.

But he knew that he must hurry. Nor could he choose his way. He must get out of that forest even if he ran directly into the middle of a Union brigade. The wind was bringing the fire fast. It leaped from one tree to another, despite the recent rains, gathering volume and power as it came. Sparks flew in showers, and fragments of burned twigs rained down. Twice Harry's face was scorched lightly and he had a fear that one of the blazing twigs would set his hair on fire. He made another effort, and ran a little faster, knowing full well that his life was at stake.

The fire was like a huge beast, and it reached out threatening red claws to catch him. He was like primeval man, fleeing from one of the vast monsters, now happily gone from the earth. He was conscious soon that another not far from him was running in the same way, a man in a faded blue uniform who had dropped his rifle in the rapidity of his flight.

Harry kept one eye on him but the stranger did not see him until they were nearly out of the wood. Then Harry, with a clear purpose in view, veered toward him. He saw that they would escape from the fire. Open fields showed not far ahead, and while the sparks were numerous and sometimes scorched, the roaring red monster behind them would soon be at the end of his race. He could not follow them into the open fields.

When the two emerged from the forest Harry was not more than fifteen feet from the stranger, who evidently took him for a friend and who was glad to have a comrade at such a time. They raced across fields in which the wheat had been cut, and then sank down four or five hundred yards from the fire, which was crackling and roaring in the woods with great violence, and sending up leaping flames.

"I was glad enough to get out of that. Do you think the rebels set it on fire?"

"I don't think so, but I was as pleased as you to escape from it, Mr. Haskell."

"Why, how did you know my name?" exclaimed the man in wonder.

"Why should I forget you? I've seen you often enough. Your name is John Haskell and you belong to the Fifth Pennsylvania."

"That's right, but I don't seem to recall you."

"It takes a lot of us some time to clear up our minds wholly after such a battle as Gettysburg. In some ways I've been in a sort of confused state myself. I dare say you've seen me often enough."

"That's likely."

"Pity you had your horse shot under you, Mr. Haskell. A man who is carrying important messages at a time like this can't do very well without his horse."

"How did you know I'd lost my horse?"

"Oh, I'm a mind reader. I can tell you a lot now. You carry your dispatch in the left-hand pocket of your waistcoat, just over your heart. And it hasn't been long, either, since you lost your horse, perhaps not more than an hour."

Haskell stared at him, but Harry's face was innocent. Nevertheless he had read Haskell's name and regiment on his canteen, cut there with his own knife. It was a mere guess that he was a dispatch bearer, but he had located the dispatch, because at the mention of the word "message" the man's hand had involuntarily gone to his left breast to see if the dispatch were still there. Boots with little dirt on them indicated that he had been riding.

"A mind reader!" said Haskell, with suspicion. "What business has a mind reader in this war?"

"He could be of enormous value. If he were a real mind reader he could tell his general exactly what the opposing general intended to do. I'm employed at a gigantic salary for that particular purpose."

"I guess you're trying to be funny. Why do you carry both a rifle and a shotgun?"

"In order to hit the target with one, if the other misses. I always use the rifle first, because if the bullet doesn't get home the shotgun, spreading its charge over a much wider area, is likely to do something."

"Now I know you're trying to be funny. As I'm going about my business as fast as I can, I'll leave you here."

"I like you so well that I can't bear to see you go. Don't move. My rifle covers your heart exactly and you are not more than ten feet away. I shall have no possible need of the shotgun. Keep your hands away from your belt. You're in a dangerous position, Mr. Haskell."

"I believe you're an infernal rebel."

"Take out the objectionable adjective 'infernal' and you're right. Keep those hands still, I tell you."

"What do you want?"

"Your dispatches! Oh, I must have 'em. Unbutton your coat and waistcoat and hand 'em to me at once. I hate to take human life, but war demands a terrible service, and I mean what I say!"

His voice rang with determination. The man slowly unbuttoned his waistcoat and took out a folded dispatch.

"Put it on the ground in front of you. That's right, and don't you reach for it again. Now, lay your canteen beside it!"

"What in thunder do you want with my canteen? It's empty!"

"I can fill it again. This is a well watered country. That's right; put it beside the dispatch. Now you walk about one hundred yards to the right with your back to me. If you look around at all I fire, and I'm a good marksman. Stand there ten minutes, and then you can move on! That's right! Now march!"

The man walked away slowly and when he had gone about half the distance Harry, picking up the dispatch, took flight again across the fields. Climbing a fence, he looked back and saw the figure of John Haskell, standing motionless on a hill. He knew that the man was not likely to remain in that position more than half the allotted time. It was certain that he would soon turn, despite the risk, but Harry was already beyond his reach.

He leaped from the fence, crossed another field and entered a wood. There he paused among the trees and saw Haskell returning. But when he had come a little distance, he shook his head doubtfully, and then walked toward the north.

"A counsel of wisdom," chuckled Harry, who was going in quite another direction. "I think I'll read my dispatch now."

He opened it and blessed his luck. It was from Meade to Pleasanton, directing him to cut in with all the cavalry he could gather on the enemy's flank. The Potomac was in great flood and the Army of Northern Virginia could not possibly cross. If it were harried to the utmost by the Union cavalry the task of destroying it would be much easier.

"So it would," said Harry to himself. "But Pleasanton won't get this dispatch. Providence has not deserted me yet; and it's true that fortune favors the brave. I'm John Haskell of the Fifth Pennsylvania and I can prove it."

He had put the canteen over his shoulder and the name upon it was a powerful witness in his favor. The dispatch itself was another, and his faded uniform told nothing.

Harry had passed through so much that a reckless spirit was growing upon him, and he had succeeded in so much that he believed he would continue to succeed. Regretfully he threw the shotgun away, as it would not appear natural for a messenger to carry it and a rifle too.

He went forward boldly now, and, when an hour later he saw a detachment of Union cavalry in a road, he took no measures to avoid them. Instead he went directly toward the horsemen and hailed them in a loud voice. They stopped and their leader, a captain, looked inquiringly at Harry, who was approaching rapidly.

Harry held up both hands as a sign that he was a friend, and called in a loud voice:

"I want a horse! And at once, if you please, sir!"

He had noticed that three led horses with empty saddles, probably the result of a brush with the enemy, and he meant to be astride one of them within a few minutes.

"You're a cool one," said the captain. "You come walking across the field, and without a word of explanation you say you want a horse. Don't you want a carriage too?"

"I don't need it. But I must have a horse, Captain. I ride with a message and it must be of great importance because I was told to go with it at all speed and risk my life for it. I've risked my life already. My horse was shot by a band of rebels, but luckily it was in the woods and I escaped on foot."

As he spoke he craftily moved the canteen around until the inscription showed clearly in the bright sunlight. The quick eyes of the captain caught it at once.

"You do belong to the Fifth Pennsylvania," he said. "Well, you're a long way from your regiment. It's back of that low mountain over there, a full forty miles from here, I should say."

Harry felt a throb of relief. It was his only fear that these men themselves should belong to the Fifth Pennsylvania, a long chance, but if it should happen to go against him, fatal to all his plans.

"I don't want to join my regiment," he said. "I'm looking for General Pleasanton."

"General Pleasanton! What can you happen to want with him?"

Harry gave the officer a wary and suspicious look, and then his eyes brightened as if he were satisfied.

"I told you I was riding with a message," he said, "and that message is for General Pleasanton. It's from General Meade himself and it's no harm for me to show it to so good a patriot as you."

"No, I think not," said the captain, flattered by the proof of respect and confidence.

Harry took the letter from his pocket. It had been sealed at first, but the warmth of the original bearer's body with a little help from Harry later had caused it to come open.

"Look at that," said Harry proudly as he took out the paper.

The captain read it, and was mightily impressed. He was, as Harry had surmised, a thoroughly staunch supporter of the Union. He would not only furnish this valiant messenger with a good horse, but he would help him otherwise on his way.

"Dexter," he called to an orderly, "bring the sorrel mare. She was ridden by a good man, Mr. Haskell, but he met a sharpshooter's bullet. Jump up."

Harry sprang into the saddle, and, astride such a fine piece of horseflesh, he foresaw a speedy arrival in the camp of General Lee.

"I'll not only mount you," said the captain, "but we'll see you on the way. General Pleasanton is on Lee's left flank and, as our course is in that direction, we'll ride with you, and protect you from stray rebel sharpshooters."

Harry could have shouted aloud in anger and disappointment. While the captain trusted him fully, he would not be much more than a prisoner, nevertheless.

"Thank you very much, Captain," he said, "but you needn't trouble yourself about me. Perhaps I'd better go on ahead. One rides faster alone."

"Don't be afraid that we'll hold you back," said the captain, smiling. "We're one of the hardest riding detachments in General Pleasanton's whole cavalry corps, and we won't delay you a second. On the contrary, we know the road so well that we'll save you wandering about and losing time."

Harry did not dare to say more. And so Providence, which had been watching over him so well, had decided now to leave him and watch over the other fellow. But he had at least one consolation. Pleasanton was on Lee's flank and their ride did not turn him from the line of his true objective. Every beat of his horse's hoofs would bring him nearer to Lee. Invincible youth was invincibly in the saddle again, and he said confidently to the captain:

"Let's start."

"All right. You keep by my side, Haskell. You appear to be brave and intelligent and I want to ask you questions."

The tone, though well meant, was patronizing, but Harry did not resent it.

"This troop is made up of Massachusetts men, and I'm from Massachusetts too," continued the captain. "My name is Lester, and I had just graduated from Harvard when the war began."

"Good stock up there in Massachusetts," said Harry boldly, "but I've one objection to you."

"What's that?"

"Everything wonderful in our history was done by you. No chance was left for anybody else."

"Well, not everything, but almost everything. Good old Massachusetts! As Webster said, 'There she stands!'"

"It was mostly New York and Pennsylvania that stood at Gettysburg."

"Yes, you did very well there."

"Don't you think, Captain, that a nation or a state is often lucky in its possession of writers?"

"I don't catch your drift exactly."

"I'll make an illustration. I've often wondered what were the Persian accounts of Marathon and Thermopylae, of Salamis and Plataea. Now most of our history has been written by Massachusetts men."

"And you insinuate that they have glorified my state unduly?"

"The expression is a trifle severe. Let's say that they have dwelled rather long upon the achievements of Massachusetts and not so long upon those of New York and Pennsylvania."

"Then let New York and Pennsylvania go get great writers. No state can be truly great without them. There's another detachment of ours just ahead, but we'll talk to them only a minute or two."

The second detachment reported that Pleasanton, with a heavy cavalry force, was about six miles farther west and that there was a fair road all the way. They should overtake him in an hour.

Harry's heart beat hard. Unless something happened within that hour he would never reach Lee, and his brain began to work with extraordinary activity. Plans passed in review before it as rapidly as pictures on a film, but all were rejected. He was in despair. They were trotting rapidly down a smooth road. A quarter of an hour passed and then a half-hour. A low bare hill appeared immediately on their right, and Harry saw beyond it the tops of trees.

"Captain Lester," he said, "suppose that you and I ride to the crest of the hill. You have strong glasses, so have I, and we may see something worth while. The men will ride on, but we can easily overtake them."

"Not a bad idea, Haskell," said the captain, still in that slightly patronizing tone. "I judge by your speech that you're a well educated man, and you appear to think."

They rode quickly to the summit, and Lester, putting his glasses to his eyes, gazed westward over a vast expanse of cultivated country. But Harry looking immediately down the slope, saw the forest that he wished.

Lester swept the glasses in a wide circle, looking for Union troops. His own troop was about a hundred yards ahead and the hoofbeats were growing fainter. Then Harry's courage almost failed him, but necessity was instant and cruel. Still he modified the blow, nor did he use any weapon, save one that nature had given him.

"Look out!" he cried, and as Lester turned in astonishment he struck him on the point of the jaw. Even as his fist flashed forward he held back a little and his full strength was not in the blow.

Nevertheless it was sufficient to strike Lester senseless, and he slid from his horse. Harry caught him by the shoulder and eased him in his fall. Then he lay stretched on his back in the grass like one asleep, with his horse staring at him. Harry knew that he would revive in a minute or two, and with a "Farewell, Captain Lester," he galloped down the slope and into the covering woods.

He knew that Lester's men, finding that they did not follow, would quickly come back, and he raced his horse among the trees as fast as he dared. A couple of miles between him and the hill and he felt safe, at least so far as the troop of Captain Lester was concerned. Fortune seemed to have made him a favorite again, but he knew that dangers were still as thick around him as leaves in Vallombrosa.

He tied his horse, climbed a tree, and used his glasses. Two miles to the west the bright sun flashed on long lines of mounted men, obviously the horsemen of Pleasanton. How was he to get through that cavalry screen and reach Lee? He did not see a way, but he knew that to find, one must seek. His desire to get through, intense as it always had been, was now doubled. He not only carried the news to Lee about the possible ford, but he also bore Meade's dispatch to Pleasanton, directing a movement which, if successful, must be most dangerous to the Army of Northern Virginia.

He descended the tree and waited a while in the forest. He found a spring at which he drank, and he filled the canteen. It was a precious canteen with the name of John Haskell engraved upon it, and he meant that it should carry him through all dangers into his camp. But he did not mean to use it yet. If he rode into Pleasanton's ranks they would merely take his letter to the general, and that would be the failure of his real mission.

Night was now not far distant, and, concluding that he had a much better chance to run the gantlet under its cover, he still waited in the wood until the twilight came.

Wrapped in a coil of dangers he was ready to risk anything. Quickness, resource and boldness, of which the last had been most valuable, had brought him so far, and, encouraged by success, he rode forward full of confidence.

On his right was a small house standing among the usual shade trees, and, approaching it without hesitation, he spoke to a man who stood in the yard.

"Which way is General Pleasanton?" he asked.

The man hesitated.

"I belong to the Fifth Pennsylvania," said Harry, pointing to the name on the canteen, still visible in the twilight. The man's eyes brightened and he replied:

"Down there," pointing toward the southwest.

"I've a message for him and I don't want to run into any of the rebel raiders."

"Then you keep away from there," he said, pointing due west.

"What's the trouble in that direction?"

"Jim Hurley was here about an hour ago. The whole country is terribly excited about these big armies marching over it, and he said that our cavalry was riding on fast. A lot of it was ahead of the rebel army, but straight there in the west some of the rebel horsemen had spread out on their own flank. If you went that way in the night you'd be sure to run right into a nest of 'em."

"So the Johnnies are west of us, your friend Hurley said. Tell me again what particular point I have to watch in order to keep away from them."

"Almost as straight west as you can make it. A valley running east and west cuts in there and it's full of the rebels. It's the only place all along here where they are."

"And consequently the only place for me to avoid. Thanks. Your information may save me from capture. Good night."

"Good night and good luck."

Harry rode toward the southwest until a dip in the valley hid him from possible view of the man at the house. Then he turned and rode due west, determined to reach as soon as possible those "rebel raiders" in the valley, but fully aware that he must yet use every resource of skill, courage and patience.

The twilight turned into night, clear, dry and bright. Unless it was raining in the mountains the flood in the Potomac could not be increasing. Here, at last, the conditions were all that he wished. The captured haversack still contained plenty of food, and, as he rode, he ate. He had learned long ago that food was as necessary as weapons to a soldier, and that one should eat when one could. Moreover, he was always hungry.

He kept among trees wherever possible, and, as the night grew, and the stars came out in the dusky blue, he enjoyed the peace. Even though he searched with his glasses he could not see soldiers anywhere, although he knew they were in the hollows and the forests. A pleasant breeze blew, and an owl, reckless of armies, sent forth its lonesome hoot.

But he kept his horse's head straight for the narrow valley where the "rebel raiders" rode. He met presently a small detachment of Connecticut men, but the sight of his canteen and letter was sufficient for them. Again he rode southwest, merely to turn due west once more, after he had passed from their sight, and near the head of the valley he encountered two men in blue on horseback watching. They were alert, well-built fellows and examined Harry closely, a process to which long usage had reconciled him.

"I hear that the rebels are down in that valley, comrade," he said.

"So they are," replied the elder and larger of the men. "We've got to ask you who you are and which way you're going."

"John Haskell, Fifth Pennsylvania, with dispatches from General Meade to General Pleasanton. They're tremendously important, too, and I've got to be in a hurry."

"More haste less speed. You know the old saying. In a time like this it's sometimes better for a man to know where he's going than it is to get there, 'cause he may arrive at the wrong place."

"Good logic, comrade, but I must hurry just the same. Which is my best way to find General Pleasanton?"

"Southwest. But I'm bound to tell you a few things first."

"All right. What are they?"

"You and I must be kinsfolk."

"How do you make that out?"

"Because my name is William Haskell, and I belong to the Fifth Pennsylvania, the same regiment that you do."

"Is that so? It's strange that we haven't met before. But funny things happen in war."

"So they do. Awfully funny. Now my brother's name is John Haskell, and you happen to be carrying his canteen, but you've changed looks a lot in the last few days, Brother John."

Haskell's voice had been growing more menacing, and Harry, with native quickness, was ready to act. When he saw the man's pistol flash from his belt he went over the side of his horse and the bullet whistled where his body had been. His own rifle cracked in reply, but Haskell's horse, not he, took the bullet, and, screaming with pain and fright, ran into the woods as the rider slipped from his back.

Harry, realizing that his peril was imminent and deadly, fired one of his pistols at the second man, who fell from his horse, too badly wounded in the shoulder to take any further part in the fight.

But Harry found in Haskell an opponent worthy of all his skill and courage. The Union soldier threw himself upon the ground and fired at Harry's horse, which instantly jerked the bridle from his hand and fled as the other had done. Harry dropped flat in the grass and leaves and listened, his heart thumping.

But luck had favored him again. He lay in a slight depression and any bullet fired at him would be sure to go over him unless he raised his head. He could not see his enemies, but he could depend upon his wonderful power of hearing, inherited and cultivated, which gave him an advantage over his opponents.

He heard the wounded man groan ever so lightly, and then the other whisper to him, "Are you much hurt, Bill?" The reply came in a moment: "My right shoulder is put out for the time, and I can't help you now." Presently he heard the slight sound of the other crawling toward him. Evidently this Haskell was a fearless fellow, bound to get him, and he called from the shadow in which he lay.

"You'd better stop, Haskell! I've got the best pair of ears in all this region, and I hear you coming! Crawl another step and you meet a bullet! But I want to tell you first that your interesting brother John is all right. I didn't kill him. I merely robbed him."

"Robbed him of what?"

"Oh, of several things."

"What things?"

"They don't concern you, Haskell. These are matters somewhat above you."

"They are, are they? Well, maybe they are, but I'm going to see that you don't get away with the proceeds of your robbery."

Harry didn't like his tone. It was fierce and resolute, and he realized once more that he had a man of quality before him. If Haskell had behaved properly he would have withdrawn with his wounded comrade. But then he was an obstinate Yankee.

He raised up ever so little and glanced across the intervening space, seeing the muzzle of a rifle not many yards away. There could be no doubt that Haskell was watchful and would continue watching. He drew his head back again and said:

"Let's call it a draw. You go back to your army, Mr. Haskell, and I'll go back to mine."

"Couldn't think of it. As a matter of fact, I'm with my army now; that is, I'm in its lines, while you can't reach yours. All I've got to do is to hold you here, and in the course of time some of our people will come along and take you."

"Do you think I'm worth so much trouble?"

"In a way it's a sort of personal affair with me. You admit having robbed my brother, and I feel that I must avenge him. He has been acting as a dispatch rider, and I can make a pretty shrewd guess about what you took from him. So I think I'll stay here."

Harry blamed himself bitterly for his careless and unfortunate expressions. He did not fear the result of a duel with this man, being the master of woodcraft that he was, but he was losing time, valuable time, time more precious than gold and diamonds, time heavy with the fate of armies and a nation. He grew furiously angry at everything, and angriest at Haskell.

"Mr. Haskell," he called, "I'm getting tired of your society, and I make you a polite request to go away."

"Oh, no, you're not tired. You merely think you are, and I couldn't consider conceding to your request. It's for your good more than mine. My society is elevating to any Johnny Reb."

"Then I warn you that I may have to hurt you."

"How about getting hurt yourself?"

Harry was silent. His acute ears brought him the sound of Haskell moving a little in his own particular hollow. The lonesome owl hooted twice more, but there was no sound to betoken the approach of Union troops in the forest. The duel of weapons and wits would have to be fought out alone by Haskell and himself.

He went over everything again and again and he concluded that he must rely upon his superior keenness of ear. He could hear Haskell, but Haskell could not hear him, and there was Providence once more taking him into favor. Summer clouds began to drift before the moon, and many of the stars were veiled. It was possible that Haskell's eyes also were not as keen as his own.

When the darkness increased, he began to crawl from the little shallow. Despite extreme precautions he made a slight noise. A pistol flashed and a bullet passed over him. It made his muscles quiver, but he called in a calm voice:

"Why did you do such a foolish thing as that? You wasted a perfectly good bullet."

"Weren't you trying to escape? I thought I heard a movement in the grass."

"Wasn't thinking of such a thing. I'm just waiting here to see what you'll do. Why don't you come on and attack?"

"I'm satisfied with things as they are. I'll hold you until morning and then our men will be sure to come and pick you up."

"Maybe it will be our men who will come and pick you up."

"Oh, no; they're too busy leaving Gettysburg behind 'em."

Harry nevertheless had succeeded in leaving the shallow and was now lying on its farther bank. Then he resumed the task of crawling forward on his face, and without making any noise, one of the most difficult feats that a human being is ever called upon to do.

At the end of a dozen feet, he paused both to rest and to listen. His acute ears told him that Haskell had not moved from his own place, and his eyes showed him that the darkness was increasing. Those wonderful, kindly clouds were thickening before the moon, and the stars in troops were going out of sight.

But he did not relax his caution. He knew that he could not afford to make any sound that would arouse the suspicions of Haskell, and it was a quarter of an hour before he felt himself absolutely safe. Then he passed around a big tree and arose behind its trunk, appreciating what a tremendous luxury it was to be a man and to stand upon one's own feet.

He had triumphed again! The stars surely were with him. They might play little tricks upon him now and then to tantalize him, but in the more important matters they were on his side. He stretched himself again and again to relieve the terrible stiffness caused by such long and painful crawling, and then, unable to resist an exultant impulse, he called loudly:

"Good-by, Haskell!"

There was a startled exclamation and a bullet fired at random cut the leaves twenty yards away. Harry, making no reply, fled swiftly through the forest toward the valley where the rebel raiders rode.

CHAPTER VII
IN THE WAGON

He ran at first, reckless of impediments, and there was a sound of crashing as he sped through the bushes. He was not in the least afraid of Haskell. He had his rifle and pistols and in the woods he was infinitely the superior. He did not even believe that Haskell would pursue, but he wanted to get far beyond any possible Federal sentinels as soon as possible.

After a flight of a few hundred yards he slackened speed, and began to go silently. The old instincts and skill of the forester returned to him. He knew that he was safe from immediate pursuit and now he would approach his own lines carefully. He was grateful for the chance or series of chances that always took him toward Lee. It seemed now that his enemies had merely succeeded in driving him at an increased pace in the way he wanted to go.

He was descending a slope, thickly clothed with undergrowth. A few hundred yards farther his knees suddenly crumpled under him and he sank down, seized at the same time with a fit of nervous trembling. He had passed through so many ordeals that strong and seasoned as he was and high though his spirits, the collapse came all at once. He knew what was the matter and, quietly stretching himself out, he lay still that the spell might pass.

The lonesome owl, probably the same one that he had heard earlier, began to hoot, and now it was near by. Harry thought he could make out its dim figure on a branch and he was sure that the red eyes, closed by day, were watching him, doubtless with a certain contempt at his weakness.

"Old man, if you had been chased by the fowler as often as I have," were the words behind his teeth, addressed to the dim and fluffy figure, "you wouldn't be sitting up there so calm and cocky.

Your tired head would sink down between your legs, your feathers would be wet with perspiration and you'd be so tired you'd hardly be able to hang on to the tree."

Came again the lonesome hoot of the owl, spreading like a sinister omen through the forest. It made Harry angry, and, raising himself up a little, he shook his fist again at the figure on the branch, now growing clearer in outline.

"'Bird or devil?'" he quoted.

The owl hooted once more, the strange ominous cry carrying far in the silence of the night.

"Devil it is," said Harry, "and quoth your evil majesty 'never more.' I won't be scared by a big owl playing the part of the raven. It's not 'nevermore' with me. I've many a good day ahead and don't you dare tell me I haven't."

Came the solemn and changeless hoot of the owl in reply.

Harry's exertions and excitement had brought too much blood to his head and he was seeing red. He raised himself upon his elbows and stared at the owl which stared back from red rimmed eyes, cold, emotionless, implacable. He had been terribly shaken, and now a superstitious fright overcame him. The raven and the albatross were in his mind and he murmured under his breath passages from their ominous poems. The scholar had his raven, the mariner had his albatross and now he alone in the forest had his owl, to his mind the most terrible bird of the three.

Came again that solemn and warning cry, the most depressing of all in the wilderness, while the changeless and sinister eyes stared steadily at him. Then Harry remembered that he had a rifle, and he sat up. He would slay this winged monster. There was light enough for him to draw a bead, and he was too good a marksman to miss.

He dropped the muzzle of the rifle in a sudden access of fear as he remembered the albatross. A shiver ran through every nerve and muscle, and so heavily was he oppressed that he felt as if he had just escaped committing murder. He rubbed his hand across his damp forehead and the act brought him out of that dim world in which he had been living for the last ten or fifteen minutes.

"Bird of whatever omen you may be, I'll not shoot you. That's certain," he said, "but I'll leave you to your melancholy predictions just as soon as I can."

He stood up somewhat unsteadily, and renewed the descent of the slope. Near its foot he came to a brook and bathing his face plentifully in the cool water he felt wonderfully refreshed. All his strength was flowing back swiftly.

Then he entered the valley, pressing straight toward the west, and soon heard the tread of horses. He knew that they must be the cavalry of his own army, but he withdrew into the bushes until he was assured. A dozen men riding slowly and warily came into view, and though the moonlight was wan he recognized them at once. When they were opposite him he stepped from his ambush and said:

"A happy night to you, Colonel Talbot."

Colonel Leonidas Talbot was a brave man, but seldom in his life had he been so shaken.

"Good God, Hector!" he cried. "It's Harry Kenton's ghost!"

Lieutenant-Colonel Hector St. Hilaire turned pale.

"I don't believe in ghosts, Leonidas," he said, "but this one certainly looks like that of Harry Kenton."

"Colonel Talbot," called Harry, "I'm not a ghost. I'm the real Harry Kenton, hunting for our army."

"Pale but substantial," said St. Clair, who rode just behind the two colonels. "He's our old Harry himself, and I'd know him anywhere."

"No ghost at all and the Yankee bullets can't make him one," said Happy Tom.

A weakness seized Harry and a blackness came before his eyes. When he recovered St. Clair was holding him up, and Colonel Talbot was trying to pour strong waters down his throat.

"How long have I been this way?" he asked anxiously.

"About sixty seconds," replied Colonel Talbot, "but what difference does it make?"

"Because I'm in a big hurry to get to General Lee! Oh! Colonel! Colonel! You must speed me on my way! I've got a message from Colonel Sherburne to General Lee that means everything, and on the road I captured another from General Meade to General Pleasanton. Put me on a horse, won't you, and gallop me to the commander-in-chief!"

"Are you strong enough to ride alone?"

"I'm strong enough to do anything now."

"Then up with you! Here, on Carter's horse! Carter can ride behind Hubbell! St. Clair, you and Langdon ride on either side of him! You should reach the commander-in-chief in three-quarters of an hour, Harry!"

"And there is no Yankee cavalry in between?"

"No, they're thick on the slopes above us! You knew that, but here you're inside our own lines. Judging by your looks you've had quite a time, Harry. Now hurry on with him, boys!"

"So I have had, Colonel, but the appearance of you, Lieutenant-Colonel St. Hilaire and the boys was like a light from Heaven. Good-by!"

"Good-by!" the two colonels called back, but their voices were already dying in the distance as Harry and his comrades were now riding rapidly down the valley, knee to knee, because St. Clair and Langdon meant to keep very close to him. They saw that he was a little unsteady, and that his eyes were unnaturally bright. They knew, too, that if he said he had great news for General Lee he told the truth, and they meant that he should get there with it in the least time possible.

The valley opened out before them, broadening considerably as they advanced. The night was far gone, there was not much moonlight, but their eyes had grown used to the dark, and they could see well. They passed sentinels and small detachments of cavalry, to whom St. Clair and Langdon gave the quick password. They saw fields of wheat stubble and pastures and crossed two brooks. The curiosity of Langdon and St. Clair was overwhelming but they restrained it for a long time. They could tell by his appearance that he had passed through unimaginable hardships, but they were loath to ask questions.

An owl on their right hooted, and both of them saw Harry shiver.

"What makes an owl's cry disturb you so, Harry?" asked Langdon.

"Because one of them tried to put the hoodoo on me as they say down in your country, Happy. I was lying back there in the forest on the hill and the biggest and reddest-eyed owl that was ever born sat on a bough over head, and kept telling me that I was finished, right at the end of my rope. But he was a liar, because here I am, with you fellows on either side of me, inside our lines and riding to the camp of the commander-in-chief."

"I think you're a bit shaky, Harry," said St. Clair, "and I don't wonder at it. If I had been through all I think you've been through I'd tumble off that horse into the road and die."

"Has any messenger come from Colonel Sherburne at the river to General Lee?"

"Not that I've heard of. No, I'm sure that none's come," replied St. Clair.

"Then I'll get to him first. Don't think, Arthur, it's just a foolish ambition of mine to lead, but the sooner some one reaches the general the better."

"We'll see that you're first old man," said Langdon. "It's not more than a half-hour now."

But Harry reeled in his saddle. The singular weakness that he had felt a while back returned, and the road grew dark before him. With a mighty effort he steadied himself in the saddle and St. Clair heard him say in a fierce undertone: "I will go through with it!" St. Clair looked across at Langdon and the signaling look of Happy Tom replied. They drew in just a little closer. Now and then they talked to him sharply and briskly, rousing him again and again from the lethargy into which he was fast sinking.

"Look! In the woods over there, Harry!" exclaimed St. Clair. "See the men stretched asleep on the grass! They're the survivors of Pickett's brigades that charged at Gettysburg."

"And I was there!" said Harry. "I saw the greatest charge ever made in the history of the world!"

He reeled a little toward St. Clair, who caught him by the shoulder and straightened him in the saddle.

"Of course you had a pleasant, easy ride from the Potomac," said Happy Tom, "but I don't understand how as good a horseman as you lost your horse. I suppose he ran away while you were picking berries by the roadside."

"Me pick berries by the roadside, while I'm on such a mission!" exclaimed Harry indignantly, rousing himself up until his eyes flashed, which was just what Happy wished. "I didn't see any berries! Besides I didn't start on a horse. I left in a boat."

"A boat? Now, Harry, I know you've turned romancer. I guess your mystic troubles with the owl—if you really saw an owl—have been a sort of spur to your fancy."

"Do you mean to say, Tom Langdon, that I didn't see an owl and talk with him? I tell you I did, and his conversation was a lot more intelligent than yours, even if it was unpleasant."

"Of course it was," said St. Clair. "Happy's chief joy in life is talking. You know how he chatters away, Harry. He hates to sleep, because then he loses good time that he might use in talk. I'll wager you anything against anything, Harry, that when the Angel Gabriel blows his horn Happy will rise out of his grave, shaking his shroud and furious with anger. He'll hold up the whole resurrection while he argues with Gabriel that he blew his horn either too late or too early, or that it was a mighty poor sort of a horn anyhow."

"I may do all that, Harry," said Happy, "but Arthur is sure to be the one who will raise the trouble about the shroud. You know how finicky he is about his clothes. He'll find fault with the quality of his shroud, and he'll say that it's cut either too short or too long. Then he'll insist, while all the billions wait, on draping the shroud in the finest Greek or Roman toga style, before he marches up to his place on the golden cloud and receives his harp."

Harry laughed.

"That'll be old Arthur, sure," he said. Then his head drooped again. Fatigue was overpowering him. St. Clair and Langdon put a hand on either shoulder and held him erect, but Harry was so far sunk in lethargy that he was not conscious of their grasp. Men looked curiously at the three young officers riding rapidly forward, the one in the center apparently held on his horse by the other two.

St. Clair took prompt measures.

"Harry Kenton!" he called sharply.

"Here!"

"Do you know what they do with a sentinel caught asleep?"

"They shoot him!"

"What of a messenger, bearing great news who has ridden two or three days and nights through a thousand dangers, and then becomes unconscious in his saddle within five hundred yards of his journey's end?"

"The stake wouldn't be too good for him," replied Harry as with a mighty effort he shook himself, both body and mind. Once more his eyes cleared and once more he sat erect in his saddle without help.

"I won't fail, Arthur," he said. "Show the way."

"There's a big tree by the roadside almost straight ahead," said St. Clair. "General Lee is asleep under that, but he'll be as wide awake as any man can be a half-minute after you arrive."

They sprang from their horses, St. Clair spoke quickly with a watching officer who went at once to awaken Lee. Harry dimly saw the form of the general who was sleeping on a blanket, spread over small boughs. Near him a man in brilliant uniform was walking softly back and forth, and now and then impatiently striking the tops of his high yellow-topped boots with a little riding whip. Harry knew at once that it was Stuart, but the cavalry leader had not yet noticed him.

Harry saw the officer bend over the commander-in-chief, who rose in an instant to his feet. He was fully dressed and he showed gray in the dusky light, but he seemed as ever calm and grave. Harry felt instantly the same swell of courage that the presence of Jackson had always brought to him. It was Lee, the indomitable, the man of genius, who could not be beaten. He heard him say to the officer who had awakened him, "Bring him immediately!" and he stepped forward, strengthening himself anew and filled with pride that he should be the first to arrive, as he felt that he certainly now was.

"Lieutenant Kenton!" said Lee.

"Yes, sir," said Harry, lifting his cap.

"You were sent with Colonel Sherburne to see about the fords of the Potomac."

"I was, sir."

"And he has sent you back with the report?"

"He has, sir. He did not give me any written report for fear that I might be captured. He did me the honor to say that my verbal message would be believed."

"It will. I know you, as I do the other members of my staff. Proceed."

"The Potomac is in great flood, sir, and the bridge is destroyed. It can't be crossed until it runs down to its normal depth."

Harry saw other generals of high rank drawing near. One he recognized as Longstreet. They were all silent and eager.

"Colonel Sherburne ordered me to say to you, sir," continued Harry, "that the best fords would be between Williamsport and Hagerstown when the river ran down."

"When did you leave him?"

"Nearly two days ago, sir."

"You have made good speed through a country swarming with our enemy. You are entitled to rest."

"It's not all, sir?"

"What else?"

"On my way I captured a messenger with a letter from General Meade to General Pleasanton. I have the message, sir."

He brought forth the paper from his blouse and extended it to General Lee, who took it eagerly. Some one held up a torch and he read it aloud to his generals.

"And so Meade means to trap me," he said, "by coming down on our flank!"

"Since the river is unfordable he'll have plenty of time to attack us there," said Longstreet.

"But will he dare to attack?" said Stuart defiantly. "He was able to hold his own in defense at Gettysburg, but it's another thing to take the offensive. We hear that General Meade is cautious and that he makes many complaints to his government. A complainer is not the kind of man who can destroy the Army of Northern Virginia."

"Sometimes it's well to be cautious, General," said Lee.

Then he turned to Harry and said:

"Again I commend you."

Harry saluted proudly, and then fell unconscious at the feet of General Lee.

When the young staff officer awoke, he was lying in a wagon which was moving slowly, with many jolts over a very rough road. It was perhaps one of these jolts that awoke him, because his eyes still felt very heavy with sleep. His position was comfortable as he lay on a heap of blankets, and the sides of the wagon looked familiar. Moreover the broad back of the driver was not that of a stranger. Moving his head into a higher place on the blankets he called.

"Hey you, Dick Jones, where are you taking me?"

Jones turned his rubicund and kindly face.

"Don't it beat all how things come about?" he said. "This wagon wasn't built for passengers, but I have you once and then I have you twice, sleepin' like a prince on them blankets. I guess if the road wasn't so rough you'd have slept all the way to Virginia. But I'm proud to have you as a passenger. They say you've been coverin' yourself with glory. I don't know about that, but I never before saw a man who was so all fired tuckered out."

"Where did you find me?"

"I didn't exactly find you myself. They say you saluted General Lee so deep and so strong that you just fell down at his feet an' didn't move, as if you intended to stay there forever. But four of your friends brought you to my wagon feet foremost, with orders from General Lee if I didn't treat you right that I'd get a thousand lashes, be tarred an' feathered, an' hung an' shot an' burned, an' then be buried alive. For all of which there was no need, as I'm your friend and would treat you right anyway."

"I know you would," laughed Harry. "You can't afford to lose your best passenger. How long have I been sleeping in this rough train of yours?"

"Since about three o'clock in the morning."

"And what time might it be now."

"Well it might be ten o'clock in the morning or it might be noon, but it ain't either."

"Well, then, what time is it?"

"It's about six o'clock in the afternoon, Mr. Kenton, and I judge that you've slept nigh on to fifteen hours, which is mighty good for a man who was as tired as you was."

"And what has the army been doing while I slept?"

"Oh, it's been marchin' an' marchin' an' marchin'. Can't you hear the wagons an' the cannons clinkin' an' clankin'? An' the hoofs of the horses beatin' in the road? An the feet of forty or fifty thousand men comin' down kcr-plunk! kcr-plunk! an' all them thousands talkin' off an' on? Yes, we're still marchin', Mr. Kenton, but we're retreatin' with all our teeth showin' an' our claws out, sharpened specially. Most of the boys don't care if Meade would attack us. They'd be glad of the chance to get even for Gettysburg."

There was a beat of hoofs and St. Clair rode up by the side of the wagon.

"All right again, Harry?" he said cheerfully. "I'm mighty glad of it. Other messengers have got through from Sherburne, confirming what you said, but you were the first to arrive and the army already was on the march because of the news you brought. Dalton arrived about noon, dead beat. Happy is coming with a horse for you, and you can rejoin the staff now."

"Before I leave I'll have to thank Mr. Jones once more," said Harry. "He runs the best passenger service that I know."

"Welcome to it any time, either you or your friend," said Jones, saluting with his whip.

CHAPTER VIII
THE CROSSING

Harry left the wagon at midnight and overtook the staff, an orderly providing him with a good horse. Dalton, who had also been sleeping in a wagon, came an hour or two later, and the two, as became modest young officers, rode in the rear of the group that surrounded General Lee.

Although the darkness had come fully, the Army of Northern Virginia had not yet stopped. The infantry flanked by cavalry, and, having no fear of the enemy, marched steadily on. Harry closely observed General Lee, and although he was well into his fifties he could discern no weakness, either physical or mental, in the man who had directed the fortunes of the South in the terrific and unsuccessful three days at Gettysburg and who had now led his army for nearly a week in a retreat, threatened, at any moment, with an attack by a veteran force superior in numbers. All the other generals looked worn and weary, but he alone sat erect, his hair and beard trimmed neatly, his grave eye showing no sign of apprehension.

He seemed once more to Harry—youth is a hero-worshiper—omniscient and omnipotent. The invasion of the North had failed, and there had been a terrible loss of good men, officers and soldiers, but, with Lee standing on the defensive at the head of the Army of Northern Virginia, in Virginia, the South would be invincible. He had always won there, and he always would win there.

Harry sighed, nevertheless. He had two heroes, but one of them was gone. He thought again if only Stonewall Jackson had been at Gettysburg. Lee's terrible striking arm would have smitten with the hammer of Thor. He would have pushed home the attack on the first day, when the Union vanguard was defeated and demoralized. He would have crushed the enemy on the second day, leaving no need for that fatal and terrific charge of Pickett on the third day.

"You reached the general first," said Dalton, "but I tried my best to beat you."

"But I started first, George, old fellow. That gave me the advantage over you."

"It's fine of you to say it. The army has quickened its pace since we came. A part of it, at least, ought to arrive at the river to-morrow, though their cavalry are skirmishing continually on our flanks. Don't you hear the rifles?"

Harry heard them far away to right and left, like the faint buzzing of wasps, but he had heard the same sound so much that it made no impression upon him.

"Let 'em buzz," he said. "They're too distant to reach any of us, and the Army of Northern Virginia is passing on."

Those were precious hours. Harry knew much, but he did not divine the full depths of the suspense, suffered by the people beyond the veil that clothed the two armies. Lincoln had been continually urging Meade to pursue and destroy his opponent, and Meade, knowing how formidable Lee was, and how it had been a matter of touch and go at Gettysburg, pursued, but not with all the ardor of one sure of triumph. Yet the man at the White House hoped continually for victory, and the Southern people feared that his hopes would come true.

It became sure the next day that they would reach the Potomac before Meade could attack them in flank, but the scouts brought word that the Potomac was still a deep and swollen river, impossible to be crossed unless they could rebuild the bridges.

Finally the whole army came against the Potomac and it seemed to Harry that its yellow flood had not diminished one particle since he left. But Lee acted with energy. Men were set to work at once building a new bridge near Falling Waters, parts of the ruined pontoon bridges were recovered, and new boats were built in haste. But while the workmen toiled the army went into strong positions along the river between Williamsport and Hagerstown.

Harry found himself with all of his friends again, and he was proud of the army's defiant attitude. Meade and the Army of the

Potomac were not far away, it was said, but the youthful veterans of the South were entirely willing to fight again. The older men, however, knew their danger. The disproportion of forces would be much greater than at Gettysburg, and even if they fought a successful defensive action with their back to the river the Army of the Potomac could bide its time and await reinforcements. The North would pour forth its numbers without stint.

Harry rode to Sherburne with a message of congratulation from General Lee, who told him that he had selected the possible crossing well, and that he had shown great skill and valor in holding it until the army came up. Sherburne's flush of pride showed under his deep tan.

"I did my best," he said to Harry, who knew the contents of the letter, "and that's all any of us can do."

"But General Lee has a way of inspiring us to do our best."

"It's so, and it's one of the reasons why he's such a great general. Watch those bridge builders work, Harry! They're certainly putting their souls and strength into it."

"And they have need to do so. The scouts say that the Army of the Potomac will be before us to-morrow. Don't you think the river has fallen somewhat, Colonel?"

"A little but look at those clouds over there, Harry. As surely as we sit here it's going to rain. The rivers were low that we might cross them on our march into the North, just smoothing our way to Gettysburg, and now that Gettysburg has happened they're high so we can't get back to the South. It looks as if luck were against us."

"But luck has a habit of changing."

Harry rode back to headquarters, whence he was sent with another dispatch, to Colonel Talbot, whom he found posted well in advance with the Invincibles.

"This note," said the colonel, "bids us to watch thoroughly. General Meade and his army are expected on our front in the morning, and there must be no chance for a surprise in the night, say a dash by their cavalry which would cut up our rear guard or vanguard—upon my soul I don't know which to call it. Harry, as you can see by the note itself, you're to remain with us until about midnight, and then make a full report of all that you and I and the rest of us may have observed upon this portion of the front or rear, whichever it may be. Meanwhile we share with you our humble rations."

Harry was pleased. He was always glad when chance or purpose brought him again into the company of the Invincibles. St. Clair and Langdon were his oldest comrades of the war, and they were like brothers to him. His affection for the two colonels was genuine and deep. If the two lads were like brothers to him, the colonels were like uncles.

"Is the Northern vanguard anywhere near?" asked Harry.

"Skirmishing is going on only four or five miles away," replied Colonel Leonidas Talbot. "It is likely that the sharp shooters will be picking off one another all through the night, but it will not disturb us. That is a great curse of war. It hardens one so for the time being. I'm a soldier, and I've been one all my life, and I suppose soldiers are necessary, but I can't get over this feeling. Isn't it the same way with you, Hector?"

"Exactly the same, Leonidas," replied Lieutenant-Colonel Hector St. Hilaire. "You and I fought together in Mexico, Leonidas, then on the plains, and now in this gigantic struggle, but under whatever guise and, wherever it may be, I find its visage always hideous. I don't think we soldiers are to blame. We don't make the wars although we have to fight 'em."

"Increasing years, Hector, have not dimmed those perceptive faculties of yours, which I may justly call brilliant."

"Thanks, Leonidas, you and I have always had a proper conception of the worth of each other."

"If you will pardon me for speaking, sir," said St. Clair, "there is one man I'd like to find, when this war is over."

"'What is the appearance of this man, Arthur?" asked Colonel Talbot.

"I don't know exactly how he looks, sir, though I've heard of him often, and I shall certainly know him when I meet him. You understand, sir, that, while I've not seen him, he has very remarkable characteristics of manner."

"And what may those be, Arthur? Are they so salient that you would recognize them at once?"

"Certainly, sir. He has an uncommonly loud voice, which he uses nearly all the time and without restraint. Words fairly pour from his tongue. Facts he scorns. He soars aloft on the wings of fancy. Many people who have listened to him have felt persuaded by his talk, but he is perhaps not so popular now."

"An extraordinary person, Arthur. But why are you so anxious to find him?"

"Because I wish, sir, to lay upon him the hands of violence. I would thrash him and beat him until he yelled for mercy, and then I would thrash him and beat him again. I should want the original pair of seven-leagued boots, not that I might make such fast time, but that I might kick him at a single kick from one county to another, and back, and then over and over past counting. I'd duck him in a river until he gasped for breath, I'd drag him naked through a briar patch, and then I'd tar and feather him, and ride him on a rail."

"Heavens, Arthur! I didn't dream that your nature contained so much cruelty! Who is this person over whose torture you would gloat like a red Indian?"

"It is the man who first said that one Southerner could whip five Yankees."

"Arthur," said Colonel Talbot, "your anger is just and becomes you. When the war is over, if we all are spared we'll form a group and hunt this fellow until we find him. And then, please God, if the gallows of Haman is still in existence, we'll hang him on it with promptness and dispatch. I believe in the due and orderly process of the law, but in this case lynching is not only justifiable, but it's an honor to the country."

"Well spoken, Leonidas! Well spoken!" said Lieutenant-Colonel Hector St. Hilaire. "I'm glad that Arthur mentioned the matter, and we'll bear it in mind. You can count upon me."

"And here is coffee," said Happy Tom. "I made this myself, the camp cook liking me and giving me a chance. I'd really be a wonderful cook if I had the proper training, and I may come to it, if we lose the war. Still, the chance even then is slight, because my father, when red war showed its edge over the horizon, put all his money in the best British securities. So we could do no more than lose the plantation."

"Happy," said Colonel Talbot, gravely rebuking, "I am surprised at your father. I thought he was a patriot."

"He is, sir, but he's a financier first, and I may be thankful for it some day. I'll venture the prediction right now that if we lose this war not a single Confederate bill will be in the possession of Thomas Langdon, Sr. Others may have bales of it, worth less per pound than cotton, but not your humble servant's father, who, I sometimes think, has lots more sense than your humble servant's father's son."

Colonel Leonidas Talbot shook his head slowly.

"Finance is a mystery to me," he said. "In the dear old South that I have always known, the law, the army and the church were and are considered the high callings. To speak in fine, rounded periods was considered the great gift. In my young days, Harry, I went with my father by stage coach to your own State, Kentucky, to hear that sublime orator, the great Henry Clay."

"What was he speaking about, sir?" asked Harry.

"I don't remember. That's not important. But surely he was the noblest orator God ever created in His likeness. His words flowing like music and to be heard by everybody, even those farthest from the speaker, made my pulse beat hard, and the blood leap in my veins. I was heart and soul for his cause, whatever it was, and, yet I fear me, though I do not wish to hurt your feelings, Harry, that the state to which he was such ornament, has not gone for the South with the whole spirit that she should have shown. She has not even seceded. I fear sometimes that you Kentuckians are not altogether Southern. You border upon the North, and stretching as you do a long distance from east to west and a comparatively short distance from north to south, you thus face three Northern States across the Ohio—Ohio, Indiana and Illinois, and the pull of three against one is strong. You see your position, don't you? Three Yankee states facing you from the north and only one Southern state, Tennessee, lying across your whole southern border, that is three against one. I fear that these odds have had their effect, because if Kentucky had sent all of her troops to the South, instead of two-thirds of them to the North, the war would have been won by us ere this."

"I admit it," said Harry regretfully. "My own cousin, who was more like a brother to me, is fighting on the other side. Kentucky troops on the Union side have kept us from winning great victories, and many of the Union generals are Kentuckians. I grieve over it, sir, as much as you do."

"But you and your people should not take too much blame to yourselves, Harry," said Lieutenant-Colonel Hector St. Hilaire, who had a very soft heart. "Think of the many influences to which you were exposed daily. Think of those three Yankee states sitting there on the other side of the Ohio—Ohio, Indiana and Illinois—and staring at you so long and so steadily that, in a way, they exerted a certain hypnotic force upon you. No, my boy, don't feel badly about it, because the fault, in a way, is not so much yours as it is that of your neighbors."

"At any rate," said Happy Tom, with his customary boldness and frankness, "we're bound to admit that the Yankees beat us at making money."

"Which may be more to our credit than theirs," said Colonel Talbot, with dignity. "I have found it more conducive to integrity and a lofty mind to serve as an officer at a modest salary in the army rather than to gain riches in trade."

"But somebody has to pay the army, sir."

"Thomas, I regret to tell you that inquiry can be pushed to the point of vulgarity. I have been content with things as they were, and so should you be. Ah, there are our brave boys singing that noble battle song of the South! Listen how it swells! It shows a spirit unconquerable!"

Along the great battle front swelled the mighty chorus:

"Come brothers! Rally for the right!
The bravest of the brave
Sends forth her ringing battle cry
Beside the Atlantic wave!
She leads the way in honor's path;
Come brothers, near and far,
Come rally round the bonnie blue flag
   That bears a single star."

"A fine song! A fine song most truly," said Colonel Talbot. "It heartens one gloriously!"

But Harry, usually so quick to respond, strangely enough felt depression. He felt suddenly in all its truth that they had not only failed in their invasion, but the escape of the army was yet a matter of great doubt. The mood was only momentary, however, and he joined with all his heart as the mighty chorus rolled out another verse:

"Now Georgia marches to the front
And beside her come
Her sisters by the Mexique sea
With pealing trump and drum,
Till answering back from hill and glen
The rallying cry afar,
A Nation hoists the bonnie blue flag
　That bears a single star!"

They sang it all through, and over again, and then, after a little silence, came the notes of a trumpet from a far-distant point. It was played by powerful lungs and the wind was blowing their way but they heard it distinctly. It was a quaint syncopated tune, but not one of the Invincibles had any doubt that it came from some daring detachment of the Union Army. The notes with their odd lilt seemed to swell through the forest, but it was strange to both of the colonels.

"Do any of you know it?" asked Colonel Talbot.

All shook their heads except Harry.

"What is it, Harry?" asked Talbot.

"It's a famous poem, sir, the music of which has not often been heard, but I can translate from music into words the verse that has just been played:

"In their ragged regimentals
Stood the old Continentals
　Yielding not,
When the grenadiers were lunging
And like hail fell the plunging
　Cannon shot;
When the files of the isles
From the smoky night encampment
Bore the banner of the rampant
　Unicorn
And grummer, grummer,
Rolled the roll of the drummer,
　Through the morn!"

The bugler played on. It was the same tune, curious, syncopated and piercing the night shrilly. Whole brigades of the South stood in silence to listen.

"What do you think is its meaning?" asked Lieutenant-Colonel St. Hilaire.

"It's in answer to our song and at the same time a reproach," replied Harry, who had jumped at once to the right conclusion. "The bugler intends to remind us that the old Continentals who stood so well were from both North and South, and perhaps he means, too, that we should stand together again instead of fighting each other."

"Then let the North give up at once," snapped Colonel Talbot.

"But in the trumpeter's opinion that means we should be apart forever."

"Then let him play on to ears that will not heed."

But the bugler was riding away. The music came faintly, and then died in one last sighing note. It left Harry grave and troubled, and he began to ask himself new questions. If the South succeeded in forcing a separation, what then? But the talk of his comrades drove the thought from his mind. Colonel Talbot sent St. Clair, Langdon and a small party of horsemen forward to see what the close approach of the daring bugler meant. Harry went with them.

Scouts in the brushwood quickly told them that a troop of Union cavalry had appeared in a meadow some distance ahead of them, and that it was one of their number who had played the song on the bugle. Should they stalk the detachment and open fire? St. Clair, who was in command, shook his head.

"It would mean nothing now," he said, and rode on with his men, knowing that the watchful Southern sharpshooters were on their flanks. It was night now, and a bright moon was coming out, enabling them to use their glasses with effect.

"There they are!" exclaimed Harry, pointing to the strip of forest on the far side of the opening, "and there is the bugler, too."

He was studying the party intently. The brilliant moonlight, and the strength of his glasses made everything sharp and clear and his gaze concentrated upon the bugler. He knew that man, his powerful chest and shoulders, and the well-shaped head on its strong neck.

Nor did he deny to himself that he had a feeling of gladness when he recognized him.

"It's none other," he said aloud.

"None other what?" asked St. Clair.

"Our warning bugler was Shepard, the Union spy. I can make him out clearly on his horse with his bugle in his hand. You'll remember my telling you how I had that fight with him in the river."

"And perhaps it would have been better for us all if you had finished him off then."

"I couldn't have done it, Arthur, nor could you, if you had been in my place."

"No, I suppose not, but these Yankees are coming up pretty close. It's sure proof that Meade's whole army will be here in the morning, and the bridge won't be built."

"It may be built, but, if Meade chooses a battle, a battle there will be. Heavy forces must be very near. You can see them now signaling to one another from hill to hill."

"So I do, and this is as far as we ought to go. A hundred yards or two farther and we'll be in the territory of the enemy's sharpshooters instead of our own."

They remained for a while among some bushes, and secured positive knowledge that the bulk of the Army of the Potomac was drawing near. Toward midnight Harry returned to his commander-in-chief and found him awake and in consultation with his generals, under some trees near the Potomac. Longstreet, Rhodes, Pickett, Early, Anderson, Pender and a dozen others were there, all of them scarred and tanned by battle, and most of them bearing wounds.

Harry stood back, hesitating to invade this circle, even when he came with dispatches, but the commander-in-chief, catching sight of him, beckoned. Then, taking off his cap, he walked forward and presented a note from Colonel Talbot. It was brief, stating that the enemy was near, and Lee read it aloud to his council.

"And what were your own observations, Lieutenant Kenton?" asked the commander-in-chief.

"As well as I could judge, sir, the enemy will appear on our whole front soon after daybreak."

"And will be in great enough force to defeat us."

"Not while you lead us, sir."

"A courtier! truly a courtier!" exclaimed Stuart, smoothing the great feather of his gorgeous hat, which lay upon his knee.

Harry blushed.

"It may have had that look," he said, "but I meant my words."

"Don't tease the lad," said the crippled Ewell. "I knew him well on Jackson's staff, and he was one of our bravest and best."

"A jest only," said Stuart. "Don't I know him as well as you, Ewell? The first time I saw him he was riding alone among many dangers to bring relief to a beleaguered force of ours."

"And you furnished that relief, sir," said Harry.

"Well, so I did, but it was my luck, not merit."

"Be assured that you have no better friend than General Stuart," said General Lee, smiling. "You have done your duty well, Lieutenant Kenton, and as these have been arduous days for you you may withdraw, and join your young comrades of the staff."

Harry saluted and retired. Before he was out of ear shot the generals resumed their eager talk, but they knew, even as Harry himself, that there was but one thing to do, stand with their backs to the river and fight, if Meade chose to offer battle.

He slept heavily, and when he awoke the next day Dalton, who was up before him, informed him that the Northern army was at hand. Snatching breakfast, he and Dalton, riding close behind the commander-in-chief, advanced a little distance and standing upon a knoll surveyed the thrilling spectacle before them. Far along the front stretched the Army of the Potomac, horse, foot and guns, come up with its enemy again. Harry was sure that Meade was there, and with him Hancock and Buford and Warren and all the other valiant leaders whom they had met at Gettysburg. It was nine days since the close of the great battle, and doubtless the North had poured forward many reinforcements, while the South had none to send.

Harry appreciated the full danger of their situation, with the larger army in front of them, and the deep and swollen torrent of the Potomac behind them. But he did not believe that Meade would attack. Lee had lost at Gettysburg, but in losing he had inflicted such losses upon his opponent, that most generals would hesitate to force another battle. The one who would not have hesitated was consolidating his great triumph at Vicksburg. Harry often thought afterward what would have happened had Grant faced Lee that day on the wrong side of the Potomac.

His opinion that Meade would not attack came from a feeling that might have been called atmospheric, an atmosphere created by the lack of initiative on the Union side, no clouds of skirmishers, no attacks of cavalry, very little rifle firing of any kind, merely generals and soldiers looking at one another. Harry saw, too, that his own opinion was that of his superior officer. Watching the commander-in-chief intently he saw a trace of satisfaction in the blue eyes. Presently all of them rode back.

Thus that day passed and then another wore on. Harry and Dalton had little to do. The whole Army of Northern Virginia was in position, defiant, challenging even, and the Army of the Potomac made no movement forward. Harry watched the strange spectacle with an excitement that he did not allow to appear on his face. It was like many of those periods in the great battles in which he had taken a part, when the combat died, though the lull was merely the omen of a struggle, soon to come more frightful than ever.

But here the struggle did not come. The hours of the afternoon fell peacefully away, and the general and soldiers still looked at one another.

"They're working on the bridge like mad," said Dalton, who had been away with a message, "and it will surely be ready in the morning. Besides, the Potomac is falling fast. You can already see the muddy lines that it's leaving on its banks."

"And Meade's chance is slipping, slipping away!" said Harry exultingly. "In three hours it will be sunset. They can't attack in the night and to-morrow we'll be gone. Meade has delayed like McClellan at Antietam, and, doubtless as McClellan did, he thinks our army much larger than it really is."

"It's so," said Dalton. "We're to be delivered, and we're to be delivered without a battle, a battle that we could ill afford, even if we won it."

Both were in a state of intense anxiety and they looked many times at the sun and their watches. Then they searched the hostile army with their glasses. But nothing of moment was stirring there. Lower and lower sank the sun, and a great thrill ran through the Army of Northern Virginia. In both armies the soldiers were intelligent men—not mere creatures of drill—who thought for themselves, and while those in the Army of Northern Virginia were ready, even eager to fight if it were pushed upon them, they knew the great danger of their position. Now the word ran along the whole line that if they fought at all it would be on their side of the river.

Harry and Dalton did not sleep that night. They could not have done so had the chance been offered. They like others rode all through the darkness carrying messages to the different commands, insuring exact cooperation. As the hours of the night passed the aspect of everything grew better. The river had fallen so fast that it would be fordable before morning.

But after midnight the clouds gathered, thunder crashed, lightning played and the violent rain of a summer storm enveloped them again. Harry viewed it at first with dismay, and then he found consolation. The darkness and the storm would cover their retreat, as it had covered the retreat of their enemy, Hooker, after Chancellorsville.

Harry and Dalton rode close behind Lee, who sat erect on his white horse, supervising the first movement of troops over the new and shaking bridge. Harry noted with amazement that despite his enormous exertions, physical and mental, and an intense anxiety, continuous for many days, he did not yet show signs of fatigue. Word had come that a part of the army was already fording the river, near Williamsport, but this bridge near Falling Waters was the most important point. General Lee and his staff sat there on their horses a long time, while the rain beat unheeded upon them.

Few scenes are engraved more vividly upon the mind of Harry Kenton than those dusky hours before the dawn, the flashes of lightning, the almost incessant rumble of thunder, the turbid and yellow river across which stretched the bridge, a mere black thread in the darkness, swaying and dipping and rising and creaking as horse and foot, and batteries and ammunition wagons passed upon it.

There were torches, but they flared and smoked in the rain and cast a light so weak and fitful that Harry could not see the farther shore. The Army of Northern Virginia marched out upon a shaking bridge and disappeared in the black gulf beyond. Only the lack of an alarm coming back showed that it was reaching the farther shore.

"Dawn will soon be here," said Dalton.

"So it will," said Harry, "and most of the troops are across. Ah, there go the Invincibles! Look how they ride!"

Colonel Leonidas Talbot and Lieutenant-Colonel Hector St. Hilaire at the head of their scanty band were just passing. They took off their hats, and swept a low bow to the great chief who sat silently on his white horse within a few yards of them. Then, side by side, they rode upon the shaking bridge, followed by Langdon, St. Clair and their brave comrades, and disappeared, where the bridge disappeared, in the rain and mist.

"Brave men!" murmured Lee.

Harry, always watching his commander-in-chief, saw now for the first time signs of fatigue and nervousness. The tremendous strain was wearing him down. But while the rain still poured and ran in streams from his gray hair and gray beard, the rear guard of the Army of Northern Virginia passed upon the bridge, and Stuart, all his plumes bedraggled, rode up to his chief, a smoking cup of coffee in his hand.

"Drink this, General, won't you?" he said.

He seized it, drank all of the coffee eagerly, and then handing back the cup, said:

"I never before in my life drank anything that refreshed me so much."

Then he, with his staff, Stuart and some other generals rode over the bridge, disappearing in their turn into the darkness and mist that had swallowed up the others, but emerging, as the others had done, into the safety of the Southern shore.

Meade and his generals had held a council the night before but nearly all the officers advised against attack. This night he made up his mind to move against Lee anyhow, and was ready at dawn, only to find the whole Southern army gone.

CHAPTER IX
IN SOCIETY

Harry, when the dawn had fully come, was sent farther away toward the ford to see if the remainder of the troops had passed, and, when he returned with the welcome news, the rain had ceased to fall. The army was rapidly drying itself in the brilliant sunshine, and marched leisurely on. He felt an immense relief. He knew that a great crisis had been passed, and, if the Northern armies ever reached Richmond, it would be a long and sanguinary road. Meade might get across and attack, but his advantage was gone.

The same spirit of relief pervaded the ranks, and the men sang their battle songs. There had been some fighting at one or two of the fords, but it did not amount to much, and no enemy hung on their rear. But no stop was made by the staff until noon, when a fire was made and food was cooked. Then Harry was notified that he and Dalton were to start that night with dispatches for Richmond. They were to ride through dangerous country, until they reached a point on the railroad, wholly within the Southern lines, when they would take a train for the Confederate capital.

They were glad to go. They felt sure that no great battles would be fought while they were gone. Neither army seemed to be in a mood for further fighting just yet, and they longed for a sight of the little city that was the heart of the Confederacy. They were tired of the rifle and march, of cannon and battles. They wished to be a while where civilized life went on, to hear the bells of churches and to see the faces of women.

It seemed to them both that they had lived almost all their lives in war. Even Jeb Stuart's ball, stopped by the opening guns of a great battle, was far, far away, and to Harry, it was at least a century since he had closed his Tacitus in the Pendleton Academy, and put it away in his desk. That old Roman had written something of battles, but they were no such struggles as Chancellorsville and Gettysburg had been. The legions, he admitted in his youthful pride, could fight well, but they never could have beaten Yank or Reb.

He and Dalton slept through the afternoon and directly after dark, well equipped and well-armed, they made their start into the South. But in going they did not neglect to pass the camp of the Invincibles who were now in the apex of the army farthest south. They had found an unusually comfortable place on a grassy plot beside a fine, cool spring, and most of them were lying down. But Colonel Talbot and Lieutenant-Colonel Hector St. Hilaire sat on empty kegs, with a board on an empty box between them. The great game which ran along with the war had been renewed. St. Clair and Langdon sat on the grass beside them, watching the contest.

The two colonels looked up at the sound of hoofs and paused a moment.

"I'm getting his king into a close corner, Harry," said Colonel Talbot, "and he'll need a lot of time for thinking. Where are you two going, or perhaps I shouldn't ask you such a question?"

"There's no secret about it," replied Harry. "We're going to Richmond with dispatches."

"He was incorrect in saying that he was getting my king into a close corner, as I'll presently show him," said Lieutenant-Colonel St. Hilaire; "but you boys are lucky. I suppose you'll stay a while in the capital. You'll sleep in white beds, you'll eat at tables, with tablecloths on 'em. You'll hear the soft voices of the women and girls of the South, God bless 'em!"

"And if you went on to Charleston you'd find just as fine women there," said Colonel Leonidas Talbot.

He sighed and a shade of sadness crossed his face. Harry heard and saw and understood. He remembered a night long, long ago in that heat of rebellion, when he had looked down from the window of his room, and, in the dark, had seen two figures, a man and a woman, upon a piazza, Colonel Talbot and Madame Delaunay, talking softly together. He had felt then that he was touching almost unconsciously upon the thread of an old romance. A thread slender and delicate, but yet strong enough in its very tenderness and delicacy to hold them both. The perfume of the flowers and of the old romance that night in the town so far away came back. He was moved, and when his eyes met Colonel Talbot's some kind of an understanding passed between them.

"The good are never rewarded," said Happy Tom.

"How so?" asked Harry.

"Because the proof of it sits on his horse here before us. Why should a man like George Dalton be sent to Richmond? A sour Puritan who does not know how to enjoy a dance or anything else, who looks upon the beautiful face of a girl as a sin and an abomination, who thinks to be ugly is to be good, who is by temperament and education unfit to enjoy anything, while Thomas Langdon, who by the same measurements is fit to enjoy everything, is left here to hold back the Army of the Potomac. It's undoubtedly a tribute to my valor, but I don't like it."

"Thomas," said Colonel Leonidas Talbot, gravely, "you're entirely too severe with our worthy young friend, Dalton. The bubbles of pleasure always lie beneath austere and solemn exteriors like his, seeking to break a way to the surface. The longer the process is delayed the more numerous the bubbles are and the greater they expand. If scandalous reports concerning a certain young man in Richmond should reach us here in the North, relating his unparalleled exploits in the giddier circles of our gay capital, I should know without the telling that it was our prim young George Dalton."

"You never spoke truer words, Leonidas," said Lieutenant-Colonel Hector St. Hilaire. "A little judicious gallantry in youth is good for any one. It keeps the temperature from going too high. I recall now the case of Auguste Champigny, who owned an estate in Louisiana, near the Louisiana estate of the St. Hilaires, and the estates of those cousins of mine whom I visited, as I told you once.

"But pardon me. I digress, and to digress is to grow old, so I will not digress, but remain young, in heart at least. I go back now. I was speaking of Auguste Champigny, who in youth thought only of making money and of making his plantation, already great, many times greater. The blood in his veins was old at twenty-two. He did not love the vices that the world calls such. But yet there were times, I knew, when he would have longed to go with the young, because youth cannot be crushed wholly at twenty-two. There was no escape of the spirits, no wholesome blood-letting, so to speak, and that which was within him became corrupt. He acquired riches and more riches, and land and more land, and at fifty he went to New Orleans, and sought the places where pleasures abound. But his true blossoming time had passed. The blood in his veins now became poison. He did the things that twenty should do, and left undone the things that fifty should do. Ah! Harry, one of the saddest things in life is the dissipated boy of fifty! He should have come with us when the first blood of youth was upon him. He could have found time then for play as well as work. He could have rowed with us in the slender boats on the river and bayous with Mimi and Rosalie and Marianne and all those other bright and happy ones. He could have danced, too. It was no strain, we never danced longer than two days and two nights without stopping, and the festivals, the gay fete days, not more than one a week! But it was not Auguste's way. A man when he should have been a boy, and then, alas! a boy when he should have been a man!"

"You speak true words, Hector," said Colonel Leonidas Talbot, "though at times you seem to me to be rather sentimental. Youth is youth and it has the pleasures of youth. It is not fitting that a man should be a boy, but middle-age has pleasures of its own and they are more solid, perhaps more satisfying than those of youth. I can't conceive of twenty getting the pleasure out of the noble game of chess that we do. The most brilliant of your young French Creole dancers never felt the thrill that I feel when the last move is made and I beat you."

"Then if you expect to experience that thrill, Leonidas, continue the pursuit of my king, from which you expect so much, and see what will happen to you."

Colonel Talbot looked keenly at the board, and alarm appeared on his face. He made a rapid retreat with one of his pieces, and Harry and Dalton, knowing that it was time for them to go, reached down from their saddles, shook hands with both, then with St. Clair and Happy Tom, and were soon beyond the bounds of the camp.

They rode on for many hours in silence. They were in a friendly land now, but they knew that it was well to be careful, as Federal scouts and cavalry nevertheless might be encountered at any moment. Two or three times they turned aside from the road to let detachments of horsemen pass. They could not tell in the dark and from their hiding places to which army they belonged, and they were not willing to take the delay necessary to find out. They merely let them ride by and resumed their own place on the road.

Harry told Dalton many more details of his perilous journey from the river to the camp of the commander-in-chief, and he spoke particularly of Shepard.

"Although he's a spy," he said, "I feel that the word scarcely fits him, he's so much greater than the ordinary spy. That man is worth more than a brigade of veterans to the North. He's as brave as a lion, and his craft and cunning are almost superhuman."

He did not tell that he might easily have put Shepard forever out of the way, but that his heart had failed him. Yet he did not feel remorse nor any sense of treachery to his cause. He would do the same were the same chance to come again. But it seemed to him now that a duel had begun between Shepard and himself. They had been drifting into it, either through chance or fate, for a long time. He knew that he had a most formidable antagonist, but he felt a certain elation in matching himself against one so strong.

They rode all night and the next day across the strip of Maryland into Virginia and once more were among their own people, their undoubted own. They were now entering the Valley of Virginia where the great Jackson had leaped into fame, and both Harry and Dalton felt their hearts warm at the greetings they received. Both armies had marched over the valley again and again. It was torn and scarred by battle, and it was destined to be torn and scarred many times more, but its loyalty to the South stood every test. This too was the region in which many of the great Virginia leaders were born, and it rejoiced in the valor of its sons.

Food and refreshment were offered everywhere to the two young horsemen, and the women and the old men—not many young men were left—wanted to hear of Gettysburg. They would not accept it as a defeat. It was merely a delay, they said. General Lee would march North once more next year. Harry knew in his heart that the South would never invade again, that the war would be for her henceforth a purely defensive one, but he said nothing. He could not discourage people who were so sanguine.

Every foot of the way now brought back memories of Jackson. He saw many familiar places, fields of battle, sites of camps, lines of advance or retreat, and his heart grew sad within him, because one whom he admired so much, and for whom he had such a strong affection, was gone forever, gone when he was needed most. He saw again with all the vividness of reality that terrible night at Chancellorsville, when the wounded Jackson lay in the road, his young officers covering his body with their own to protect him from the shells.

When they reached the strip of railroad entering Richmond they left their horses to be sent later, and each took a full seat in the short train, where he could loosen his belt, and stretch his limbs. It was a crude coach, by the standards of to-day, but it was a luxury then. Harry and Dalton enjoyed it, after so much riding horseback, and watched the pleasant landscape, brown now from the July sun, flow past.

Their coach did not contain many passengers, several wounded officers going to Richmond on furlough, some countrymen, carrying provisions to the capital for sale, and a small, thin, elderly woman in a black dress, to whom Harry assigned the part of an old maid. He noticed that her features were fine and she had the appearance of one who had suffered. When they reached Richmond and their passes were examined, he hastened to carry her bag for her and to help her off the train. She thanked him with a smile that made her almost handsome, and quickly disappeared in the streets of the city.

"A nice looking old maid," he said to Dalton.

"How do you know she's an old maid?"

"I don't know. I suppose it's a certain primness of manner."

"You can't judge by appearances. Like as not she's been married thirty years, and it's possible that she may have a family of at least twelve children."

"At any rate, we'll never know. But it's good, George, to be here in Richmond again. It's actually a luxury to see streets and shop windows, and people in civilian clothing, going about their business."

"Looks the same way to me, Harry, but we can't delay. We must be off to the President, with the dispatches from the Army of Northern Virginia."

But they did not hurry greatly. They were young and it had been a long time since they had been in a city of forty thousand inhabitants, where the shop windows were brilliant to them and nobody on the streets was shooting at anybody else. It was late July, the great heats were gone for the time at least, and they were brisk and elated. They paused a little while in Capitol Square, and looked at the Bell Tower, rising like a spire, from the crest of which alarms were rung, then at the fine structure of St. Paul's Church. They intended to go into the State House now used as the Confederate Capitol, but that must wait until they reported to President Davis.

They arrived at the modest building called the White House of the Confederacy, and, after a short wait in the anteroom, they were received by the President. They saw a tall, rather spare man, dressed in a suit of home-knit gray. He received them without either warmth or coldness. Harry, although it was not the first time he had seen him, looked at him with intense curiosity. Davis, like Lincoln, was born in his own State, Kentucky, but like most other Kentuckians, he did not feel any enthusiasm over the President of the Confederacy. There was no magnetism. He felt the presence of intellect, but there was no inspiration in that arid presence.

A man of Oriental features was sitting near with a great bunch of papers in his hand. Mr. Davis did not introduce Harry and Dalton to him, and he remained silent while the President was asking questions of the messengers. But Harry watched him when he had a chance, interested strongly in that shrewd, able, Eastern face, the descendant of an immemorial and intellectual race, the man who while Secretary of State was trying also to help carry the tremendous burden of Confederate finance. What was he thinking, as Harry and Dalton answered the President's questions about the Army of Northern Virginia?

"You say that you left immediately after our army crossed the Potomac?" asked the President.

"Yes, sir," replied Harry. "General Meade could have attacked, but he remained nearly two days on our front without attempting to do so."

A thin gray smile flitted over the face of the President of the Confederacy.

"General Meade was not beaten at Gettysburg, but I fancy he remembered it well enough."

Harry glanced at Benjamin, but his Oriental face was inscrutable. The lad wondered what was lurking at the back of that strong brain. He was shrewd enough himself to know that it was not always the generals on the battlefield who best understood the condition of a state at war, and often the man who held the purse was the one who measured it best of all. But Benjamin never said a word, nor did the expression of his face change a particle.

"The Army of Northern Virginia is safe," said the President, "and it will be able to repel all invasion of Virginia. General Lee gives especial mention of both of you in his letters, and you are not to return to him at once. You are to remain here a while on furlough, and if you will go to General Winder he will assign you to quarters."

Both Harry and Dalton were delighted, and, although thanks were really due to General Lee, they thanked the President, who smiled dryly. Then they saluted and withdrew, the President and the Secretary of State going at once into earnest consultation over the papers Mr. Benjamin had brought.

Harry felt that he had left an atmosphere of depression and said so, when they were outside in the bright sunshine.

"If you were trying to carry as much as Mr. Davis is carrying you'd be depressed too," said Dalton.

"Maybe so, but let's forget it. We've got nothing to do for a few days but enjoy ourselves. General Winder is to give us quarters, but we're not to be under his command. What say you to a little trip through the capitol?"

"Good enough."

Congress had adjourned for the day, but they went through the building, admiring particularly the Houdon Washington, and then strolled again through the streets, which were so interesting and novel to them. Richmond was never gayer and brighter. They were sure that the hated Yankees could never come. For more than two years the Army of Northern Virginia had been an insuperable bar to their advance, and it would continue so.

Harry suddenly lifted his cap as some one passed swiftly, and Dalton glancing backward saw a small vanishing figure.

"Who was it?" he asked.

"The thin little old maid in black whom we saw on the train. She may have nodded to me when I bowed, but it was such a little nod that I'm not certain."

"I rather like your being polite to an insignificant old maid, Harry. I'd expect you, as a matter of course, to be polite to a young and pretty girl, overpolite probably."

"That'll do, George Dalton. I like you best when you're preaching least. Come, let's go into the hotel and hear what they're talking about."

After the custom of the times a large crowd was gathered in the spacious lobby of Richmond's chief hotel. Among them were the local celebrities in other things than war, Daniel, Bagby, Pegram, Randolph, and a half-dozen more, musicians, artists, poets, orators and wits. People were quite democratic, and Harry and Dalton were free to draw their chairs near the edge of the group and listen. Pegram, the humorist, gave them a glance of approval, when he noticed their uniforms, the deep tan of their faces, their honest eyes and their compact, strong figures.

Harry soon learned that a large number of English and French newspapers had been brought by a blockade runner to Wilmington, North Carolina, and had just reached the capital, the news of which these men were discussing with eagerness.

"We learn that the sympathies of both the French and English governments are still with us," said Randolph.

"But these papers were all printed before the news of Vicksburg and Gettysburg had crossed the Atlantic," said Daniel.

"England is for us," said Pegram, "only because she likes us little and the North less. The French Imperialists, too, hate republics, and are in for anything that will damage them. When we beat off the North, until she's had enough, and set up our own free and independent republic, we'll have both England and France annoying us, and demanding favors, because they were for us in the war. Sympathy is something, but it doesn't win any battles."

"A nation has no real friend except itself," said Bagby. "Whatever the South gets she'll have to get with her own good right arm."

"I can predict the first great measure to be put through by the Southern Government after the war."

"What will it be?"

"The abolition of slavery."

"Why, that's one of the things we're fighting to maintain!"

"Exactly so. You're willing to throw away a thing of your own accord, when you're not willing to throw it away because another orders you to do so. Wars are due chiefly to our misunderstanding of human nature."

Then Pegram turned suddenly to Harry. "You're from the field?" he said. "From the Army of Northern Virginia?"

"Yes," replied Harry. "My name is Kenton and I'm a lieutenant on the staff of General Lee. My friend is George Dalton, also of the commander-in-chief's staff."

"Are you from Kentucky?" asked Daniel curiously.

"Yes, from a little town called Pendleton."

"Then I fancy that I've met a relative of yours. I returned recently from a small town in North Georgia, the name of which I may not give, owing to military reasons, necessary at the present time, and I met while I was there a splendid tall man of middle years, Colonel George Kenton of Kentucky."

"That's my father!" said Harry eagerly. "How was he?"

"I thought he must be your father. The resemblance, you know. I should say that if all men were as healthy as he looked there would be no doctors in the world. He has a fine regiment and he'll be in the battle that's breeding down there. Grant has taken Vicksburg, as we all know, but a powerful army of ours is left in that region. It has to be dealt with before we lose the West."

"And it will fight like the Army of Northern Virginia," said Harry. "I know the men of the West. The Yankees win there most of the time, because we have our great generals in the East and they have theirs in the West."

"I've had that thought myself," said Bagby. "We've had men of genius to lead us in the East, but we don't seem to produce them in the West. People are always quoting Napoleon's saying that men are nothing, a man is everything, which I never believed before, but which I'm beginning to believe now."

Then the talk veered away from battle and back to social, literary and artistic affairs, to all of which Harry and Dalton listened eagerly. Both had minds that responded to the more delicate things of life, and they were glad to hear something besides war discussed. It was hard for them to think that everything was going on as usual in Europe, that new books and operas and songs were being written, and that men and women were going about their daily affairs in peace. Yet both were destined to live to see the case reversed, the people of the States setting the world an example in moderation and restraint, while the governments of Europe were deluging that continent with blood.

"If this war should result in our defeat," said Bagby, "we won't get a fair trial before the world for two or three generations, and maybe never."

"Why?" asked Dalton.

"Because we're not a writing people. Oh, yes, there's Poe, I know, the nation's greatest literary genius, but even Europe honored him before the South did. We've devoted our industry and talents to politics, oratory and war. We don't write books, and we don't have any newspapers that amount to much. Why, as sure as I'm sitting here, the moment this war is over New England and New York and Pennsylvania, particularly New England, will begin to pour out books, telling how the wicked Southerners brought on the war, what a cruel and low people we are, the way in which we taught our boys, when they were strong enough, how to beat slaves to death, and the whole world will believe them. Maybe the next generation of Southerners will believe them too."

"Why?" asked Harry.

"Why? Why? Because we don't have any writers, and won't have any for a long time! The writer has not been honored among us. Any fellow with a roaring voice who can get up on the stump and tell his audience that they're the bravest and best and smartest people on earth is the man for them. You know that old story of Andy Jackson. Somebody taunted him with being an uneducated man, so at the close of his next speech he thundered out: _E pluribus unum! Multum in parvo! Sic semper tyrannis!_ So it was all over. Old Andy to that audience, and all the others that heard of it, was the greatest Latin scholar in the world."

"But that may apply to the North, too," objected Harry.

"So it would. Nevertheless they'll write this war, and they'll get their side of it fastened on the world before our people begin to write."

"But if we win we won't care," said Randolph. "Success speaks for itself. You can squirm and twist all you please, and make all the excuses for it that you can think up, but there stands success glaring contemptuously at you. You're like a little boy shooting arrows at the Sphinx."

Thus the conversation ran on. Both Harry and Dalton were glad to be in the company of these men, and to feel that there was something in the world besides war. All the multifarious interests of peace and civilization suddenly came crowding back upon them. Harry remembered Pendleton with its rolling hills, green fields, and clear streams, and Dalton remembered his own home, much like it, in the Valley of Virginia, not so far away.

"Do you remain long in Richmond?" asked Randolph.

"A week at least," replied Harry.

"Then you ought to see a little of social life. Mrs. John Curtis, a leading hostess, gives a reception and a dance to-morrow night. I can easily procure invitations for both of you, and I know that she would be glad to have two young officers freshly arrived from our glorious Army of Northern Virginia."

"But our clothes!" said Dalton. "We have only a change of uniform apiece, and they're not fresh by any means."

All the men laughed.

"You don't think that Richmond is indulging in gorgeous apparel do you?" said Daniel. "We never manufactured much ourselves, and since all the rest of the world is cut off from us where are the clothes to come from even for the women? Brush up your uniforms all you can and you'll be more than welcome. Two gallant young officers from the Army of Northern Virginia! Why, you'll be two Othellos, though white, of course."

Harry glanced at Dalton, and Dalton glanced at Harry. Each saw that the other wanted to go, and Daniel, watching them, smiled.

"I see that you'll come," he said, "and so it's settled. Have you quarters yet?"

"Not yet," replied Harry, "but we'll see about it this afternoon."

"I'll have the invitations sent to you here at this hotel. All of us will be there, and we'll see that you two meet everybody."

Both thanked him profusely. They were about to go, thinking it time to report to General Winder, when Harry noticed a thin woman in a black dress, carrying a large basket, and just leaving the hotel desk. He caught a glimpse of her face and he knew that it was the old maid of the train. Then something else was impressed upon his mind, something which he had not noticed at their first meeting, but which came to him at their second. He had seen a face like hers before, but the resemblance was so faint and fleeting that he could not place it, strive as he would. But he was sure that it was there.

"Who is that woman?" he asked.

Daniel shook his head and so did Randolph, but Bagby spoke up.

"Her name is Henrietta Carden," he said, "and she's a seamstress. I've seen her coming to the hotel often before, bringing new clothes to the women guests, or taking away old ones to be repaired. I believe that the ladies account her most skillful. It's likely that she'll be at the Curtis house, in a surgical capacity, to-morrow night, as a quick repairer of damaged garments, those fine linen and silk and lace affairs that we don't know anything about. Mrs. Curtis relies greatly upon her and I ought to tell you, young gentlemen, that Mr. Curtis is a most successful blockade runner, though he takes no personal risk himself. The Curtis house is perhaps the most sumptuous in Richmond. You'll see no signs of poverty there, though, as I told you, officers in old and faded clothes are welcome."

Harry saw Henrietta Carden carrying the large basket of clothes, go out at a side door, and he felt as if a black shadow like a menace had passed across the floor. But it was only for an instant. He dismissed it promptly, as one of those thoughts that come out of nothing, like idle puffs of summer air. He and Dalton bade a brief farewell to their new friends and left for the headquarters of General Winder. An elderly and childless couple named Lanham had volunteered to take two officers in their house near Capitol Square, and there Harry and Dalton were sent.

They could not have found a better place. Mr. and Mrs. Lanham were quiet people, who gave them an excellent room and a fine supper. Mrs. Lanham showed a motherly solicitude, and when she heard that they were going to the Curtis ball on the following night she demanded that their spare and best uniforms be turned over to her.

"I can make them look fresh," she insisted, "and your appearance must be the finest possible. No, don't refuse again. It's a pleasure to me to do it. When I look at you two, so young and strong and so honest in manner and speech, I wish that I had sons too, and then again I'm glad I have not."

"Why not, Mrs. Lanham?" asked Harry.

"Because I'd be in deadly fear lest I lose them. They'd go to the war—I couldn't help it—and they'd surely be killed."

"We won't grieve over losing what we've never had," smiled Mr. Lanham. "That's morbid."

Harry and Dalton did their best to answer all the questions of their hosts, who they knew would take no pay. The interest of both Mr. and Mrs. Lanham was increased when they found that their young guests were on the staff of General Lee and before that had been on the staff of the great Stonewall Jackson. These two names were mighty in the South, untouched by any kind of malice or envy, and with legends to cluster around them as the years passed.

"And you really saw Stonewall Jackson every day!" said Mrs. Lanham. "You rode with him, talked with him, and went into battle with him?"

"I was in all his campaigns, Mrs. Lanham," replied Harry, modestly, but not without pride. "I was with him in every battle, even to the last, Chancellorsville. I was one of those who sheltered him from the shells, when he was shot by our own men. Alas! what an awful mistake. I—"

He stopped suddenly. He had choked with emotion, and the tears came into his eyes. Mrs. Lanham saw, and, understanding, she quickly changed the subject to Lee. They talked a while after supper, called dinner now, and then they went up to their room on the second floor.

It was a handsome room, containing good furniture, including two single beds. Their baggage had preceded them and everything was in order. Two large windows, open to admit the fresh air, looked out over Richmond. On a table stood a pitcher of ice water and glasses.

"Our lot has certainly been cast in a pleasant place," said Dalton, taking a chair by one of the windows.

"You're right," said Harry, sitting in the chair by the other window. "The Lanhams are fine people, and it's a good house. This is luxury, isn't it, George, old man?"

"The real article. We seem to be having luck all around. And we're going to a big ball to-morrow night, too. Who'd have thought such a thing possible a week ago?"

"And we've made friends who'll see that we're not neglected."

"It's an absolute fact that we've become the favorite children of fortune."

"No earthly doubt of it."

Then ensued a silence, broken at length by a scraping sound as each moved his chair a little nearer to the window.

"Close, George," said Harry at length.

"Yes, a bit hard to breathe."

"When fellows get used to a thing it's hard to change."

"Fine room, though, and those are splendid beds."

"Great on a winter night."

"You've noticed how the commander-in-chief himself seldom sleeps under a tent, but takes his blankets to the open?"

"Wonder how an Indian who has roamed the forest all his life feels when he's shut up between four walls for the first time."

"Fancy it's like a prison cell to him."

"Think so too. But the Lanhams are fine people and they're doing their best for us."

"Do you think they'd be offended if I were to take my blankets, and sleep on the grass in the back yard?"

"Of course they would. You mustn't think of such a thing. After this war is over you've got to emerge slowly from barbarism. Do you remember whether at supper we cut our food with our knives and lifted it to our mouths with forks, or just tore and lifted with our fingers?"

"We used knife and fork, each in its proper place. I happened to think of it and watched myself. You, I suppose, did it through the force of an ancient habit, recalled by civilized surroundings."

"I'm glad you remember about it. Now I'm going to bed, and maybe I'll sleep. I suppose there's no hope of seeing the stars through the roof."

"None on earth! But my bed is fine and soft. We'd be all right if we could only lift the roof off the house. I'd like to hear the wind rubbing the boughs together."

"Stop it! You make me homesick! We've got no right to be pining for blankets and the open, when these good people are doing so much for us!"

Each stretched himself upon his bed, and closed his eyes. They had not been jesting altogether. So long a life in the open made summer skies at night welcome, and roofs and walls almost took from them the power of breathing.

But the feeling wore away after a while and amid pleasurable thoughts of the coming ball both fell asleep.

CHAPTER X
THE MISSING PAPER

Harry and Dalton did not awake until late the next morning and they found they had not suffered at all from sleeping between four walls and under a roof. Their lungs were full of fresh air, and youth with all its joyous irresponsibility had come back. Harry sprang out of bed.

"Up! up! old boy!" Harry cried to Dalton. "Don't you hear the bugles calling? not to battle but to pleasure! There is no enemy in our front! We don't have to cross a river with an overwhelming army pressing down upon us! We don't have to ride before the dawn on a scout which may lead us into a thicket full of hostile riflemen. We're in a city, boy, and our business now is beauty and pleasure!"

"Harry," said Dalton, "you ought to go far."

"Why, George? What induces you to assume the role of a prophet concerning me?"

"Because you're so full of life. You're so keen about everything. You must have a heart and lungs of extra steam power."

"But I notice you don't say anything about brain power. Maybe you think it's the quiet, rather silent fellows like yourself, George, who have an excess of that."

"None of your irony. Am I not looking forward to this ball as much as you are? I was a boy when I entered the war, Harry, but two years of fighting day and night age one terribly. I feel as if I could patronize any woman under twenty-five, and treat her as quite a simple young thing."

"Try it, George, and see what happens to you."

"Oh, no! I merely said I felt that way. I've too much sense to put it into action."

"Do you know, George, that when this war is over it will be really time for us to be thinking about girls. We'll be quite old enough. They say that many of the Yankee maidens in Philadelphia and New York are fine for looks. I wonder if they'll cast a favoring eye on young Southern officers as our conquering armies go marching down their streets!"

"It's too remote. Don't think about it, Harry. Richmond will do us for the present."

"But you can let a fellow project his mind into the future."

"Not so far that we'll be marching as conquerors through Philadelphia and New York. Let's deal with realities."

"I've always thought there was something of the Yankee about you, George, not in political principles—I never question your devotion to the cause—but in calculating, weighing everything and deciding in favor of the one that weighs an ounce the most."

"Are you about through dressing? You've taken a minute longer than the regular time."

There was a knock at the door, and, when Dalton opened it a few inches, a black head announced through the crack that breakfast was ready.

"See what a disgrace you're bringing upon us," said Dalton. "Delaying everything. Mrs. Lanham will say that we're two impostors, that such malingerers cannot possibly belong to the Army of Northern Virginia."

"Lead on," said Harry. "I'm ready, and I'm hungry as every soldier in the Southern army always is."

They had a warm greeting from their hospitable hosts, followed by an abundant breakfast. Then at Mrs. Lanham's earnest solicitation they turned over their dress uniforms to her to be repaired and pressed. Then they went out into the streets again, and spent the whole day rambling about, enjoying everything with the keen and intense delight that can come only to the young, and after long abstinence. Richmond was not depressed. Far from it. There had been a wonderful transformation since those dark days when the army of McClellan was near enough to see the spires of its churches. The flood of battle had rolled far away since then, and it had never come back. It could never come back. It was true that the Army of Northern Virginia had failed at Gettysburg, but it was returning to the South unassailed, and was ready to repeat its former splendid achievements.

Harry went to the post office, and found there, to his great surprise and delight, a letter from his father, written three or four days after Vicksburg.

My dear son: [he wrote]

The news has just come to us that the Army of Northern Virginia, while performing prodigies of valor, has failed to carry all the Northern positions at Gettysburg. Only complete success could warrant a further advance. I assume therefore that General Lee is retreating and I assume also that you, Harry, my beloved son, are alive, that you came unharmed out of that terrible battle. It does not seem possible to me that it could be otherwise. I cannot conceive of you fallen. It may be that it's because you are my son. The sons of others may fall, but not mine, just as we know that all others are doomed to die, but get into the habit of thinking ourselves immortal. So, I address this letter to you in the full belief that it will reach you somewhere, and that you will read it.

You know, of course, of our great loss at Vicksburg. It is disastrous but not irreparable. We still have a powerful army in the West, hardy, indomitable, one with which the enemy will have to reckon. As for myself I have been spared in many battles and I am well. It seems the sport of chance that you and I, while fighting on the same side, should have been separated in this war, you in the East and I in the West. But it has been done by One who knows best, and after all I am glad that you have been in such close contact with two of the greatest and highest-minded soldiers of the ages, Stonewall Jackson and Robert E. Lee. I do not think of them merely as soldiers, but as knights and champions with flaming swords. One of them, alas! is gone, but we have the other, and if man can conquer he will. Here in the West we repose our faith in Lee, as surely as do you in the East, you who see his face and hear his voice every day.

I have had two or three letters from Pendleton. That part of the State is for the present outside the area of conflict, though I hear that the guerilla bands to the east in the mountains still vex and annoy, and that Skelly is growing bolder. I foresee the time when we shall have to reckon with this man, who is a mere brigand.

I hear that the prospects for fruit in our orchards were never finer. You will remember how you prowled in them when you were a little boy, Harry, and what a pirate you were among the apples and peaches and pears and good things that grew on tree and bush and briar in that beautiful old commonwealth of ours. I often upbraided you then, but I should like to see you now, far out on a bough as of old, reaching for a big yellow pear, or a red, red bunch of cherries! Alas! there are many lads who will never return, who will never see the pear trees and the cherry trees again, but I repeat I cannot feel that you will be among them. Who would ever have dreamed when this war began that it could go so far? More than two years of fierce and deadly battles and I can see no end. A deadlock and neither side willing to yield! How glad would be the men who made the war to see both sections back where they were two and a half years ago! and that's no treason.

Water rose in Harry's eyes. He knew how terribly his father's heart had been torn by the quarrel between North and South, and that he had thoughts which he did not tell to his son. Harry was beginning at last to think some of the same thoughts himself. If the South succeeded, then, after the war, what? Another war later on or reunion.

The rest of the letter was wholly personal, and in the end it directed Harry, when writing to him, to address his letters care of the Western Army under General Bragg. Harry was moved and he responded at once. He went to the hotel in which he had met the young men who constituted the leading lights in what was called the Mosaic Club, and, securing writing materials, made a long reply, which he posted with every hope that it would soon reach its destination.

Early in the evening he rejoined Dalton at the house of the Lanhams and they found that Mrs. Lanham had done wonders with their best uniforms. When they were dressed in them they felt that it was no harder to charge the Curtis house than to rush a battery.

"You young men go early," said Mr. Lanham. "Mrs. Lanham and I will appear later."

They departed, daring to practice their dance steps in the street to the delight of small boys who did not hesitate to chaff them. But Harry and Dalton did not care. They answered the chaff in kind, and soon approached the Curtis home, all the windows of which were blazing with light.

The house stood in extensive grounds, and lofty white pillars gave it an imposing appearance. Guests were arriving fast. Most of the men were military, but there was a fair sprinkling of civilians nevertheless. The lads saw their friends of the Mosaic Club pass in just ahead of them, all dressed with extreme care. Generals and colonels and other officers were in most favor now, but these men, with their swift and incisive wit and their ability to talk well about everything, fully made up for the lack of uniform.

Harry and Dalton, before passing through the side gateway that led to the house, paused awhile to look at those who came. Many people, and they ranked among the best in Richmond, walked. They had sent all their horses to the front long ago to be ridden by cavalrymen or to draw cannon. Others, not so self-sacrificing, came in heavy carriages with negroes driving.

Harry noticed that in many cases the clothing of the men showed a little white at the seams, and there were cuffs the ends of which had been trimmed with great care. But it was these whom he respected most. He remembered that Virginia had not really wanted to go into the war, and that she had delayed long, but, being in it, she was making supreme sacrifices.

And there were many young girls who did not need elaborate dress. In their simple white or pink, often but cotton, their cheeks showing the delicate color that is possessed only by the girls in the border states of the South, they seemed very beautiful to Harry and George, who had known nothing but camps and armies so long.

It was the healthy admiration of the brave youth of one sex for the fair youth of the other, but there was in it a deeper note, too. Age can stand misfortune. Youth wonders why it is stricken, and Harry felt as they passed by, bright of face and soft of voice, that the clouds were gathering heavily over them.

But he was too young himself for the feeling to endure long. Dalton was proposing that they go in and they promptly joined the stream of entering guests. Randolph soon found them and presented them to Mrs. Curtis, a large woman of middle years, and dignified manner, related to nearly all the old families of Virginia, and a descendant of a collateral branch of the Washingtons. Her husband, William Curtis, seemed to be of a different type, a man of sixty, tall, thin and more reserved than most Southerners of his time. His thin lips were usually compressed and his pale blue eyes were lacking in warmth. But the long strong line of his jaw showed that he was a man of strength and decision.

"A Northern bough on a Southern tree," whispered Dalton, as they passed on. "He comes from some place up the valley and they say that the North itself has not his superior in financial skill."

"I did not warm to him at first," said Harry, "but I respect him. As you know, George, we've put too little stress upon his kind of ability. We'll need him and more like him when the Confederacy is established. We'll have to build ourselves up as a great power, and that's done by trade and manufactures more than by arms."

"It's so, Harry. But listen to that music!"

A band of four pieces placed behind flowers and shrubbery was playing. Here was no blare of trumpets or call of bugles. It was the music of the dance and the sentimental old songs of the South, nearly all of which had a sad and wailing note. Harry heard the four black men play the songs that he had heard Samuel Jarvis sing, deep in the Kentucky mountains, and his heart beat with an emotion that he could not understand. Was it a cry for peace? Did his soul tell him that an end should come to fighting? Then throbbed the music of the lines:

> Soft o'er the fountain lingering falls the Southern moon
> Far o'er the mountain breaks the day too soon.
> In thy dark eyes' splendor, where the moonlight loves to dwell
> Weary looks, yet tender, speak their fond farewell.
> > Nita, Juanita! Ask thy soul if we should part,
> > Nita, Juanita! Lean thou on my heart!

The music of the sad old song throbbed and throbbed, and sank deep into Harry's heart. At another time he might not have been stirred, but at this moment he was responsive in every fiber. He saw once more the green wilderness, and he heard once more the mellow tones of the singer coming back in far echoes from the gorges.

"Nita, Juanita! Ask thy soul if we should part," hummed Dalton, but Harry was still far away in the green wilderness, listening to the singer of the mountains. Then the singer stopped suddenly, and he was listening once more to the startling prediction of the old, old woman:

"I am proud that our house has sheltered you, but it is not for the last time. You will come again, and you will be thin and pale and in rags, and you will fall at the door. I see you coming with these two eyes of mine."

That prediction had been made a long time ago, years since, it seemed, but whenever it returned to him, and it returned at most unexpected times, it lost nothing of its amazing vividness and power; rather they were increased. Could it be true that the supremely old had a vision or second sight? Then he rebuked himself angrily. There was nothing supernatural in this world.

"Wake up, Harry! What are you thinking about?" whispered Dalton sharply. "You seem to be dreaming, and here's a house full of pretty girls, with more than a half-dozen looking at you, the gallant young officer of the Army of Northern Virginia, the story of whose romantic exploits had already reached Richmond."

"I was dreaming and I apologize," said Harry. That minute in which he had seen so much, so far away, passed utterly, and in another minute both he and Dalton were dancing with Virginia girls, as fair as dreams to these two, who had looked so long only upon the tanned faces of soldiers.

Both he and Dalton were at home in a half-hour. People in the Old South then, as in the New South now, are closely united by ties of kinship which are acknowledged as far as they run. One is usually a member of a huge clan and has all the privileges that clanship can confer. Kentucky was the daughter of Virginia, and mother and daughter were fond of each other, as they are to-day.

After the third dance Harry was sitting with Rosamond Lawrence of Petersburg in a window seat. She was a slender blonde girl, and the dancing had made the pink in her cheeks deepen into a flush.

"You're from Kentucky, I know," said Miss Lawrence, "but you haven't yet told me your town."

"Pendleton. It's small but it's on the map. My father is a colonel in the Western army."

"Aren't you a Virginian by blood? Most all Kentuckians are."

"Partly. My great grandfather, though, was born in Maryland."

"What was his name, Lieutenant Kenton?"

"Henry Ware!"

"Henry Ware! Kentucky's first and greatest governor."

"Yes, he was my great grandfather. I'm proud to be his descendant."

"I should think you would be."

"But his wife, who was Lucy Upton, my great grandmother, was of Virginia blood, and all of the next two generations intermarried with people of Virginia stock."

"Then you are a Kentuckian and a Virginian, too. I knew it! You have a middle name, haven't you?"

"Yes."

"Will you tell me what it is?"

"Cary."

The girl laughed.

"Harry Cary Kenton. Why Cary is one of our best old Virginia names. Will you tell me too what was your mother's name before she was married?"

"Parham."

"Another. Oh, all this unravels finely. And what was your grandmother's name?"

"Brent."

"Nothing could be more Virginian than Brent. Oh, you're one of us, Lieutenant Kenton, a real Virginian of the true blood."

"And heart and soul too!" giving her one of his finest young military glances.

She laughed. It was only quick friendship between them and no more, and a half-hour later he was dancing with another Virginia girl, not so blonde, but just as handsome, and their talk was quite as friendly. Her name was Lockridge, and as they sat down near the musicians to rest, and listen a while, Harry saw a figure, slender and black-robed, pass. He knew at once who she was, and it had been predicted that he might meet her there, but she had stirred his curiosity a little, and thinking he might obtain further information he asked Miss Lockridge:

"Who is the woman who just passed us?"

"That's Miss Carden, Miss Henrietta Carden, a sewing woman, very capable too, who always helps at the big balls. Mrs. Curtis relies greatly upon her. The door through which she went leads to the ladies' dressing-room."

"A native of Richmond?"

"I don't know. But why are you so curious about a sewing woman, Lieutenant Kenton?"

Harry flushed. There was a faint tinge of rebuke in her words, and he knew that he merited it.

"It was just an idle question," he replied quickly, and with an air of indifference. "I noticed her on the train when we came into the capital, and we are so little used to women that we are inquisitive about every one whom we see. Why, Miss Lockridge, I didn't realize until I came to this ball that women could be so extraordinarily beautiful. Every one of you looks like an angel, just lowered gently from Heaven."

"If you're not merely a flatterer then it's long absence that gives charm. I assure you, Lieutenant Kenton, that we're very, very common clay. You should see us eat."

"I'll get you an ice at once."

"Oh, I don't mean that. I mean substantial things!"

"A healthy appetite doesn't keep a girl from being an angel."

"When men marry us they find out that we're not angels."

"The word 'angel' is with me merely a figure of speech. I don't want any real angel. I want my wife, if I ever marry, to be thoroughly human."

Harry's progress was rapid. A handsome figure and face, and an ingenuous manner made him a favorite. After midnight he wandered into a room where older men were smoking and talking. They were mostly officers, some of high rank, one a general, and they talked of that which they could never get wholly from their minds, the war. All knew Harry, and, as he wanted fresh air, they gave him a place by a window which looked upon a small court.

Harry was tired. In dancing he had been compelled to bring into play muscles long unused, and he luxuriated in the cushioned chair, while the pleasant night breeze blew upon him. They were discussing Lee's probable plans to meet Meade, who would certainly follow him in time across the Potomac. They spoke with weight and authority, because they were experienced men who had been in many battles, and they were here on furlough, most of them recovering from wounds.

Harry heard them, but their words were like the flowing of a river. He paid no heed. They did not bring the war back to him. He was thinking of the music and of the brilliant faces of the girls whom he loved collectively. What that Lawrence girl had said was true. He was a Virginian as well as a Kentuckian, and the Kentuckians and Virginians were all one big family. All those pretty Virginia girls were his cousins. It might run to the thirty-second degree, but they were his cousins just the same, and he would claim them with confidence.

He smiled and his eyelids drooped a little. It was rather dark outside, and he was looking directly into the court in which rosebushes and tall flowering plants grew. A shadow passed. He did not see whence it came or went, but he sat up and laughed at himself for dozing and conjuring up phantoms when he was at his first real ball in ages.

All the civilians had gone out and only five or six of the officers, the most important, were left. Their talk had grown more eager, and on the center of the table around which they sat lay a large piece of white canvas upon which they were drawing a map expressing their collective opinion. Every detail was agreed upon, after much discussion, and Harry, as much interested as they, began to watch, while the lines grew upon the canvas. He ventured no opinion, being so much younger than the others.

"We don't know, of course, exactly what General Lee will do," said a colonel, "but we do know that he's always dangerous. He invariably acts on the offensive, even if he's retreating. I should think that he'd strike Meade about here."

"Not there, but not far from it," said the general. "Make a dot at that point, Bathurst, and make another dot here about twenty miles to the east, which represents my opinion."

Bathurst made the dots and the men, wholly absorbed, bent lower over their plans, which were growing almost unconsciously into a map, and a good one too. Harry was as much interested as they, and he still kept himself in the background, owing to his youth and minor rank.

The door to the room was open a little and the music, a waltz, came in a soft ripple from the drawing room. It was rhythmic and languorous, and Harry's feet would have moved to its tune at any other time, but he was too deeply absorbed in the conjectures and certainties that they were drawing with their pencils on the white canvas.

Many of the details, he knew, were absolutely true, and others he was quite sure must be true, because these were men of high rank who carried in their minds the military secrets of the Confederacy.

"I think we're pretty well agreed on the general nature of the plan," said Bathurst. "We differ only in details."

"That's so," said the general, "but we're lingering too long here. God knows that we see little enough of our women folks, and, when we have the chance to see them, and feel the touch of their hands, we waste our time like a lot of fools making military guesses. If I'm not too old to dance to the tune of the shells I'm not too old to dance to the tune of the fiddle and the bow. That's a glorious air floating in from the ballroom. I think I can show some of these youngsters like Kenton here how to shake a foot."

"After you, General," laughed Bathurst. "We know your capacity on both the field and the floor, and how you respond to the shell and the bow. Come on! The ballroom is calling to us, and I doubt whether we'll explain to the satisfaction of everybody why we've been away from it so long. You, too, Harry!"

They rose in a group and went out hastily. Harry was last, and his hand was on the bolt of the door, preparatory to closing it, when the general turned to Bathurst and said:

"You've that diagram of ours, haven't you, Bathurst? It's not a thing to be left lying loose."

"Why, no, sir, I thought you put it in your pocket."

The general laughed.

"You're suffering from astigmatism, Bathurst," he said. "Doubtless it was Colton whom you saw stowing it away. I think we'd better tear it into little bits as we have no further use for it."

"But I haven't it, sir," said Colton, a veteran colonel, just recovering from a wound in the arm. "I supposed of course that one of the others took it."

An uneasy look appeared in the general's eyes, but it passed in an instant.

"You have it, Morton?"

"No, sir. Like Bathurst I thought one of the others took it."

"And you, Kitteridge?"

"I did not take it, sir."

"You surely have it, Johnson?"

"No, sir, I was under the impression that you had taken it away with you."

"And you, McCurdy?"

McCurdy shook his head.

"Then Kenton, as you were the last to rise, you certainly have it."

"I was just a looker-on; I did not touch it," said Harry, whose hand was still on the bolt of the partly opened door.

The general laughed.

"Another case of everybody expecting somebody else to do a thing, and nobody doing it," he said. "Kenton, go back and take it from the table. In our absorption we've been singularly forgetful, and that plan must be destroyed at once."

Harry reentered the room, and in their eagerness all of the officers followed. Then a simultaneous "Ah!" of dismay burst from them all. There was nothing on the table. The plan was gone. They looked at one another, and in the eyes of every one apprehension was growing.

"The window is partly open," said the general, affecting a laugh, although it had an uneasy note, "and of course it has blown off the table. We'll surely find it behind the sofa or a chair."

They searched the room eagerly, going over every inch of space, every possible hiding place, but the plan was not there.

"Perhaps it's in the court," said the general. "It might have fluttered out there. Raise the sash higher, Kenton. Let nobody make any noise. We must be as quiet as possible about this. Luckily there's enough moonlight now for us to find even a small scrap of paper in the court."

They stole through the window silently, one by one, and searched every inch of the court's space. But nothing was in it, save the grass and the flowers and the rosebushes that belonged there. They returned to the room, and once more looked at one another in dismay.

"Shut the window entirely and lock the door, Kenton," said the general.

Harry did so. Then the general looked at them all, and his face was set and very firm.

"We must all be searched," he said. "I know that every one of you is the soul of honor. I know that not one of you has concealed about his person this document which has suddenly become so valuable. I know that not one of you would smuggle through to the enemy such a plan at any price, no matter how large. Nevertheless we must know beyond the shadow of a doubt that none of us has the map. And I insist, too, that I be searched first. Bathurst, Colton, begin!"

They examined one another carefully in turn. Every pocket or possible place of concealment was searched. Harry was the last and when they were done with him the general heaved a huge sigh of relief.

"We know positively that we are not guilty," he said. "We knew it before, but now we've proved it. That is off our minds, but the mystery of the missing map remains. What a strange combination of circumstances. I think, gentlemen, that we had best say nothing about it to outsiders. It's certainly to the interest of every one of us not to do so. It's also to the interest of all of us to watch the best we can for a solution. You're young, Kenton, but from what I hear of you you're able to keep your own counsel."

"You can trust me, sir," said Harry.

"I know it, and now unlock the door. We've held ourselves prisoners long enough, and they'll be wondering about us in the ballroom."

Harry turned the key promptly enough and he was glad to escape from the room. He felt that he had left behind a sinister atmosphere. He had not mentioned to the older men the faint shadow that he thought he had seen crossing the courtyard. But then it was only fancy, nothing more, an idle figment of the brain! There was the music now, softer and more tempting than ever, an irresistible call to flying feet, and another dance with Rosamond Lawrence was due.

"I thought you weren't coming, Lieutenant Kenton," she said. "Some one said that you had gone into the smoking-room and that you were talking war with middle-aged generals and colonels."

"But I escaped as soon as I could, Miss Rosamond," he said—he was thinking of the locked door and the universal search.

"Well, you came just in time. The band is beginning and I was about to give your dance to that good-looking Lieutenant Dalton."

"You wouldn't treat me like that! Throw over your cousin in such a manner! I can't think it!"

"No, I wouldn't!"

Then the full swell of the music caught them both, and they glided away, as light and swift as the melody that bore them on.

CHAPTER XI
A VAIN PURSUIT

Youth was strong in Harry, and, while he danced and the music played, he forgot all about the incident in the smoking-room. With him it was just one pretty girl after another. He had heart enough for them all, and only one who was so young and who had been so long on battlefields could well understand what a keen, even poignant, pleasure it was to be with them.

Those were the days when a ball lasted long. Pleasures did not come often, but when they came they were to be enjoyed to the full. But as the morning hours grew the manner of the older people became slightly feverish and unnatural. They were pursuing pleasure and forgetfulness with so much zeal and energy that it bore the aspect of force rather than spontaneity. Harry noticed it and divined the cause. Beneath his high spirits he now felt it himself. It was that looming shadow in the North and that other in that far Southwest hovering over lost Vicksburg. Serious men and serious women could not keep these shadows from their eyes long.

The incident of the smoking-room and the missing map came back to him with renewed force. It could not have walked away. They had searched the room and the court so thoroughly that they would have found it, had it been there. The disappearance of a document, which men of authority and knowledge had built up almost unconsciously, puzzled and alarmed him.

It was almost day when he and Dalton left. They paid their respects to Mr. and Mrs. Curtis, and said many good-bys to "the girls they left behind them." Then they went out into the street, and inhaled great draughts of the cool night air.

"A splendid night," said Dalton.

"Yes, truly," said Harry.

"I hope you didn't propose to more than six girls."

"To none. But I love them all together."

"I'm glad to hear it, because you're entirely too young to marry, and your occupation is precarious."

"You needn't be so preachy. You're not more'n a hundred years old yourself."

"But I'm two months older than you are and often two months makes a vast difference, particularly in our cases. I notice about you, Harry, at times, a certain juvenility which I feel it my duty to repress."

"Don't do it, George. Let's enjoy it while we can, because as you say my occupation is precarious and yours is the same."

They stopped at the corner of the iron fence enclosing the Curtis home, in which many lights were still shining. It was near a dark alley opening on the street and running by this side of the house.

"I'm going to see what's behind Mr. Curtis's house," said Harry.

Dalton stared at him.

"What's got into your head, Harry!" he exclaimed. "Do you mean to be a burglar prowling about the home of the man who has entertained you?"

Harry hesitated. He was sorry that Dalton was with him. Then he could have gone on without question, but he must make some excuse to Dalton.

"George," he said at last, "will you swear to keep a secret, a most important one which I am pledged to tell to nobody, but which I must confide in you in order to give a good reason for what I am about to do."

"If you are pledged to keep such a secret," replied Dalton, "then don't explain it to me. Your word is good enough, Harry. Go ahead and do what you want to do. I'll ask nothing about any of your actions, no matter how strange it may look."

"You're a man in a million, George. Come on, your confidence is going to be tested. Besides, you'll run the danger of being shot."

But Dalton followed him fearlessly as he led the way down the alley. Richmond was not lighted then, save along the main streets, and a few steps took them into the full dark. The brilliant windows threw bright bands across the lines, but they themselves were in darkness.

The alley ran through the next street and so did the Curtis grounds. They were as extensive in the rear of the house as in front, and contained small pines carefully trimmed, banks of roses and two grape arbors. Harry could hear no sound of any one stirring among them, but people, obviously the cooks and other servants, were talking in the big kitchen at the rear of the house.

The street itself running in the rear of the building was as well lighted as it was in front, but Harry saw no one in it save a member of the city police, who seemed to be keeping a good watch. But as he did not wish to be observed by the man he waited a little while in the mouth of the alley, until he had moved on and was out of sight.

"Now, George," he said, "you and I are going to do a little scouting. You know I'm descended from the greatest natural scout and trailer ever known in the West, one whose senses were preternaturally acute, one who could almost track a bird in the air by its flight."

"Yes, I've heard of the renowned Henry Ware, and I know that you've inherited a lot of his skill and intuition. Go ahead. I promised that I would help you and ask no questions. I keep my word."

Harry climbed silently over the low fence, and Dalton followed in the same manner. The light from the street and house did not penetrate the pines and rosebushes, where Harry quickly found a refuge, Dalton as usual following him.

"What next?" whispered Dalton.

"Now, I do my trailing and scouting, and you help me all you can, George, but be sure you don't make any noise. There's enough moonlight filtering through the pines to show the ground to me, but not enough to disclose us to anybody twenty feet away."

He dropped to his hands and knees, and, crawling back and forth, began to examine every inch of ground with minute care, while Dalton stared at him in amazement.

"I'd help," whispered Dalton, "if I only knew what you were doing."

"Suppose, George, that somebody wanted to see the Curtis house, and yet not be seen, wanted to observe as well as he could, without detection, what was going on there. He'd watch his chance, jump over the fence as we have done and enter this group of pines. He could ask no finer point of observation. We are perfectly hidden and yet we can see the whole rear of the house and one side of it."

"So we can. I infer that you are looking for some one who you think has been acting as a spy."

"Ah! here we are. The earth is a bit soft by this pine, and I see the trace of a footstep! And here is another trace, close by it, undoubtedly the imprint of the other foot. It's as plain as day."

Dalton knelt, looked at the traces, and shook his head. "I can't make out any of them," he said. "I see nothing but a slight displacement of the grass caused by the wind."

"That's because you haven't my keen eye, an inherited and natural ability as a trailer, although you may beat me out of sight in other things. The shape of these traces indicates that they were made by human feet, and their closeness together shows that the man stood looking at the house. If he had been walking along they would be much wider apart."

He examined the traces again with long and minute care.

"The toes point toward the house, consequently he was looking at it," he said. "He was a heavy man, and he stood here a long time, not moving from his tracks. That's why he left these traces, which are so clear and evident to me, George, although they're hidden from a blind man like you."

"Well, what of it?"

"Nothing much to you, but a lot to me."

He rose to his feet and examined the boughs of the pine.

"As I thought," he whispered with great satisfaction. "Despite his courage and power over himself, both of which were very great, he became a little excited. Doubtless he saw something that stirred him deeply."

"What under the stars are you talking about, Harry?"

"See, he broke off three twigs of the pine. Just snapped them in two with nervous fingers. Here are pieces lying on the ground. Now, a man does that sort of thing almost unconsciously. He will not reach up for the twig or down for it, but he breaks it because it presents itself to him at the corner of his eye. This man was six feet in height or more and built very powerfully. I think I know him! Yes, I'm sure I know him! Nor is it at all strange that he should be here."

"Shall we make a thorough search for him among the pines? You say he's tall and built powerfully. But maybe the two of us could master him, and if not we could call for help."

"Too late, George. He left a long time ago, and he took with him what he wanted. We needn't look any farther."

"Lead on, then, King of Trailers and Master of Secrets! If the mighty Caliph, Haroun al Kenton, wishes to prowl in these grounds, seeking the heart of some great conspiracy, it is not for his loyal vizier, the Sheikh Ul Dalton to ask him questions."

"I'm not certain that a vizier is a sheikh."

"Nor am I, but I'm certain that I want to go home and go to bed. Vikings of the land like ourselves can't stand much luxury. It weakens the tissues, made strong on the march and in the fields."

They left the grounds silently and unobserved and soon were in their own quarters, where they slept nearly the whole day. Then they spent three or four days more in the social affairs which were such a keen pleasure to them after such a long deprivation. But wherever they went, and they were in demand everywhere, Harry was always looking for somebody, a man, tall, heavy and broad shouldered, not a man who would come into a room where he was, or who would join a company of people that he had joined, but one who would hang upon the outskirts, and hide behind the corners of buildings or trees. He did not see the shadow, but once or twice he felt that it was there.

The officer, Bathurst, told him one night that some important papers had been stolen from the White House of the Confederacy itself.

"They pertain to our army," said Bathurst, "and they will be of value to the enemy, if they reach him."

"I'm quite certain that the most daring and dangerous of all northern spies is in Richmond," said Harry.

Then he told Bathurst of Shepard and of the trails that he had seen among the pines behind Curtis's house.

"Do you think this man got our map?" asked Bathurst.

"It may have been so. Perhaps he was hidden in the court and when he saw us go out, leaving the map on the table, he slipped in at the window and seized it."

"But the court was enclosed. He would have had to go with the paper through the house itself."

"That's where my theory fails. I can provide for his taking the paper, but I can't provide for his escape."

"I'll tell the General about it. I think you're right, Harry. I've heard of Shepard myself, and he's worth ten thousand men to the Yankees. It's more than that. At such a critical stage of our affairs he might ruin us. We'll make a general search for him. We'll rake the city with a fine tooth comb."

The search was made everywhere. Soldiers pried in every possible place, but they found nobody who could not give an adequate account of his presence in Richmond. Harry felt sure nevertheless that Shepard was somewhere in the capital, protected by his infinite daring and resource, and they received the startling news the next day after the search that a messenger sent northward with dispatches for Lee had been attacked only a short distance from the city. He had been struck from behind, and did not see his assailant, but the wound in the head — the man had been found unconscious — and the missing dispatches were sufficient proof.

A night later precious documents were purloined from the office of the Secretary of War and a list of important earthworks on the North and South Carolina coast disappeared from the office of the Secretary of the Navy. Alarm spread through all the departments of the Confederacy. Some one, spy and burglar too, had come into the very capital, and he was having uncommon success.

Harry had not the least doubt that it was Shepard, and he was filled with an ambition to capture this man, whom he really liked. If Shepard were caught he would certainly be hanged, but then a spy must take his chances.

They heard meanwhile that General Lee had gone to a former camp of his on the Opequan, but that later in response to maneuvers by General Meade, he moved to a position near Front Royal. No orders came for Harry or Dalton to rejoin him, and, as a period of inactivity seemed to be at hand, they were glad to remain a while longer in Richmond. They still stayed with the Lanhams, who refused to take any pay, although the two young officers, chipping together, bought for Mrs. Lanham a little watch which had just come through the blockade from England.

Thus their days lengthened in Richmond, and, despite the shadow of the spy and his doings which was over Harry, they were still very pleasant. The members of the Mosaic Club, although older men, made much of them, and Harry and Dalton, being youths of sprighty wit, were able to hold their own in such company. The time had now passed into August, and they sat one afternoon in the lobby of the big hotel with their new friends. Richmond without was quiet and blazing in the sun. Harry had received a second letter from his father from an unnamed point in Georgia. It did not contain much news, but it was full of cheerfulness, and it intimated in more than one place that Bragg's army was going to strike a great blow.

All eyes were turned toward the West. The opinion had been spreading in the Confederacy that the chief danger was on that line. It seemed that the Army of Northern Virginia could take care of anything to the north and east, but in the south and west affairs did not go well.

"It's a pity that General Bragg is President Davis' brother-in-law," said Randolph.

"Why?" asked Daniel.

"Then he wouldn't be in command of our Western Army."

"Bragg's a fighter, though."

"But not a reaper."

"What do you mean?"

"He wins the victory, but lets the enemy take it."

"It may be so. But to come closer home, what about the Yankee spy in Richmond? It's an established fact that a man of most uncommon daring and skill is here."

"No doubt of it, what's the latest from him?"

"The house of William Curtis was entered last night and robbed."

"Robbed of what?"

"Papers. The man never takes any valuables."

"But Curtis is not in the government!"

"No, but he carries on a lot of blockade running, chiefly through Norfolk and Wilmington. I think the papers related to several blockade running vessels coming out from England, and of course the Yankee blockading ships will be ready for them. There's not a trace of the man who took them."

"Something is deucedly sinister about it," said Bagby. "It seems to be the work of one man, and he must have a hiding place in Richmond, but we can't find it. Kenton, you and Dalton are army officers, supposedly of intelligence. Now, why don't you find this mysterious terror? Ah, will you excuse me for a minute! I see Miss Carden leaving the counter with her basket, and there is no other seamstress in Richmond who can put the ruffles on a man's finest shirt as she can. She's been doing work for me for some time."

He arose, and, leaving them, bowed very politely to the seamstress. Her face, although thin and lined, was that of an educated woman of strong character. Harry thought it probable that she was a lady in the conventional meaning of the word. Many a woman of breeding and culture was now compelled to earn her own living in the South. She and Bagby exchanged only a few words, he returning to his chair, and she leaving the hotel at a side door, walking with dignity.

"I've seen Miss Carden three times before, once on the train, once at this hotel and once at Mr. Curtis's house; can you tell me anything about her?" said Harry.

"It's an ordinary tale," replied Bagby. "I think she lived well up the valley and her house being destroyed in some raid of the Federal troops she came down to the capital to earn a living. She's been doing work for me and others I know for a year past, and I know she's not been out of Richmond in that time."

The talk changed now to the books that had come through from Europe in the blockade runners. There was a new novel by Dickens and another by Thackeray, new at least to the South, and the members of the Mosaic Club were soon deep in criticism and defense.

Harry strolled away after a while. He did not tell his friends — nothing was to be gained by telling them — that he was absolutely sure of the identity of the spy, that it was Shepard. The question of identity did not matter if they caught him, and his old feeling that it was a duel between Shepard and himself returned. He believed that the duty to catch the man had been laid upon him.

He began to haunt Richmond at all hours of the night. More than once he had to give explanations to watchmen about public buildings, but he clung to the task that he had imposed upon himself. He explained to Dalton and the Virginian found no fault except for Harry's loss of time that might be devoted to amusement. Harry sometimes rebuked himself for his own persistency, but Bagby's taunt had stung a little, and he felt that it applied more to himself than to Dalton. He knew Shepard and he knew something of his ways. Moreover, his was the blood of the greatest of all trailers, and it was incumbent upon him to find the spy. Yet he was trailing in a city and not in a forest. In spite of everything he clung to his work.

On a later night about one o'clock in the morning he was near the building that housed army headquarters, and he noticed a figure come from some bushes near it. He instantly stepped back into the shadow and saw a man glance up and down the street, probably to see if it was clear. It was a night to favor the spy, dark, with heavy clouds and gusts of rain.

The figure, evidently satisfied that no one was watching, walked briskly down the street, and Harry's heart beat hard against his side. He knew that it was Shepard, the king of spies, against whom he had matched himself. He could not mistake, despite the darkness, his figure, his walk and the swing of his powerful shoulders.

His impulse was to cry for help, to shout that the spy was here, but at the first sound of his voice Shepard would at once dart into the shrubbery, and escape through the alleys of Richmond. No, his old feeling that it was a duel between Shepard and himself was right, and so they must fight it out.

Shepard walked swiftly toward the narrower and more obscure streets, and Harry followed at equal speed. The night grew darker and the rain, instead of coming in gusts, now fell steadily. Twice Shepard stopped and looked back. But on each occasion Harry flattened himself against a plank fence and he did not believe the spy had seen him.

Then Shepard went faster and his pursuer had difficulty in keeping him in view. He went through an alley, turned into a street, and Harry ran in order not to lose sight of him.

The alley came into the street at a right angle, and, when Harry turned the corner, a heavy, dark figure thrust itself into his path.

"Shepard!" he cried.

"Yes!" said the man, "and I hate to do this, but I must."

His heavy fist shot out and caught his pursuer on the jaw. Harry saw stars in constellations, then floated away into blackness, and, when he came out of it, found himself lying on a bed in a small room. His jaw was bandaged and very sore, but otherwise he felt all right. A candle was burning on a table near him and an unshuttered window on the other side of the room told him that it was still night and raining.

Harry looked leisurely about the room, into which he had been wafted on the magic carpet of the Arabian genii, so far as he knew. It was small and without splendor and he knew at once from the character of its belongings that it was a woman's room.

He sat up. His head throbbed, but touching it cautiously he knew that he had sustained no serious injury. But he felt chagrin, and a lot of it. Shepard had known that he was following him and had laid a trap, into which he had walked without hesitation. The man, however, had spared his life, although he could have killed him as easily as he had stunned him. Then he laughed bitterly at himself. A duel between them, he had called it! Shepard wouldn't regard it as much of a duel.

His head became so dizzy that he lay down again rather abruptly and began to wonder. What was he doing in a woman's room, and who was the woman and how had he got there? This would be a great joke for Dalton and St. Clair and Happy Tom.

He was fully dressed, except for his boots, and he saw them standing on the floor against the wall. He surveyed once more the immaculate neatness of the room. It was certainly a woman's, and most likely that of an old maid. He sat up again, but his head throbbed so fearfully that he was compelled to lie down quickly. Shepard had certainly put a lot in that right hand punch of his and he had obtained a considerable percentage of revenge for his defeat in the river.

Then Harry forgot his pain in the intensity of his curiosity. He had sustained a certain temporary numbing of the faculties from the blow and his fancy, though vivid now, was vague. He was not at all sure that he was still in Richmond. The window still showed that it was night, and the rain was pouring so hard that he could hear it beating against the walls. At all events, he thought whimsically, he had secured shelter, though at an uncommon high price.

He heard a creak, and a door at the end of the room opened, revealing the figure and the strong, haggard features of Henrietta Carden. Evidently she had taken off a hood and cloak in an outer room, as there were rain drops on her hair and her shoes were wet.

"How are you feeling, Mr. Kenton?" she asked.

"Full of aches and wonder."

"Both will pass."

She smiled, and, although she was not young, Harry thought her distinctly handsome, when she smiled.

"I seem to have driven you out of your room and to have taken your bed from you, Miss Carden," he said, "but I assure you it was unintentional. I ran against something pretty hard, and since then I haven't been exactly responsible for what I was doing."

She smiled again, and this time Harry found the smile positively winning.

"I'm responsible for your being here," she said.

Then she went back to the door and said to some one waiting in the outer room:

"You can come in, Lieutenant Dalton. He's all right except for his headache, and an extraordinary spell of curiosity."

Dalton stalked solemnly in, and regarded Harry with a stern and reproving eye.

"You're a fine fellow," he said. "A lady finds you dripping blood from the chin, and out of your head, wandering about the street in the darkness and rain. Fortunately she knows who you are, takes you into her own house, gives you an opiate or some kind of a drug, binds up your jaw where some man good and true has hit you with all his goodness and truth, and then goes for me, your guardian, who should never have let you out of his sight. I was awakened out of a sound sleep in our very comfortable room at the Lanham house, and I've come here through a pouring rain with Miss Carden to see you."

"I do seem to be the original trouble maker," said Harry. "How did you happen to find me, Miss Carden?"

"I was sitting at my window, working very late on a dress that Mrs. Curtis wants to-morrow. It was not raining hard then, and I could see very well outside. I saw a dark shadow in the street at the mouth of the alley. I saw that it was the figure of a man staggering very much. I ran out and found that it was you, Lieutenant Kenton. You were bleeding at the chin, where apparently some one had struck you very hard, and you were so thoroughly dazed that you did not know where you were or who you were."

"Yes, he hit me very hard, just as you supposed, Miss Carden," said Harry, feeling gently his sore and swollen chin.

"I half led and half dragged you into my house—there was nowhere else I could take you—and, as you were sinking into a stupor, I managed to make you lie down on my bed. I bound up your wound, while you were unconscious, and then I went for Lieutenant Dalton."

"And she saved your life, too, you young wanderer. No doubt of that," said Dalton reprovingly. "This is what you get for roaming away from my care. Lucky you were that an angel like Miss Carden saved you from dying of exposure. If I didn't know you so well, Harry, I should say that you had been in some drunken row."

"Oh, no! not that!" exclaimed Miss Carden. "There was no odor of liquor on his breath."

"I was merely joking, Miss Carden," said Dalton. "Old Harry here is one of the best of boys, and I'm grateful to you for saving him and coming to me. If there is any way we can repay you we'll do it."

"I don't want any repayment. We must all help in these times."

"But we won't forget it. We can't. How are you feeling, Harry?"

"My head doesn't throb so hard. The jarred works inside are gradually getting into place, and I think that in a half-hour I can walk again, that is, resting upon that stout right arm of yours, George."

"Then we'll go. I've brought an extra coat that will protect you from the rain."

"You are welcome to stay here!" exclaimed Miss Carden. "Perhaps you'd be wiser to do so."

"We thank you for such generous hospitality," said Dalton gallantly, "but it will be best for many reasons that we go back to Mrs. Lanham's as soon as we can. But first can we ask one favor of you, Miss Carden?"

"Of course."

"That you say nothing of Mr. Kenton's accident. Remember that he was on military duty and that in the darkness and rain he fell, striking upon his jaw."

"I'll remember it. Our first impression that he had been struck by somebody was a mistake, of course. You can depend upon me, both of you. Neither of you was ever in my house. The incident never occurred."

"But we're just as grateful to you as if it had happened."

A half-hour later they left the cottage, Miss Carden holding open the door a little to watch them until they were out of sight. But Harry had recovered his strength and he was able to walk without Dalton's assistance, although the Virginian kept close by his side in case of necessity.

"Harry," said Dalton, when they were nearly to the Lanham house, "are you willing to tell what happened?"

"As nearly as I know. I got upon the trail of that spy who has been infesting Richmond. I knew at the time that it couldn't have been any one else. I followed him up an alley, but he waited for me at the turn, and before I could defend myself he let loose with his right. When I came drifting back into the world I was lying upon the bed in Miss Carden's cottage."

"He showed you some consideration. He might have quietly put you out of the way with a knife."

"Shepard and I don't care to kill each other. Each wants to defeat the other's plans. It's got to be a sort of duel between us."

"So I see, and he has scored latest."

"But not last."

"We'd better stick to the tale about the fall. Such a thing could happen to anybody in these dark streets. But that Miss Carden is a fine woman. She showed true human sympathy, and what's more, she gave help."

"She's all that," agreed Harry heartily.

They had their own keys to the Lanham house and slipped in without awakening anybody. Their explanations the next day were received without question and in another day Harry's jaw was no longer sore, though his spirit was. Yet the taking of important documents ceased suddenly, and Harry was quite sure that his encounter with Shepard had at least caused him to leave the city.

CHAPTER XII
IN WINTER QUARTERS

Harry was sent a few days later with dispatches from the president to General Lee, who was still in his camp beside the Opequan. Dalton was held in the capital for further messages, but Harry was not sorry to make the journey alone. The stay in Richmond had been very pleasant. The spirits of youth, confined, had overflowed, but he was beginning to feel a reaction. One must return soon to the battlefield. This was merely a lull in the storm which would sweep with greater fury than ever. The North, encouraged by Gettysburg and Vicksburg, was gathering vast masses which would soon be hurled upon the South, and Harry knew how thin the lines there were becoming.

He thought, too, of Shepard, who was the latest to score in their duel, and he believed that this man had already sent to the Northern leaders information beyond value. Harry felt that he must strive in some manner to make the score even.

It was late in the summer when he rejoined the Army of Northern Virginia and delivered the letters to the commander-in-chief, who sat in the shade of a large tree. Harry observed him closely. He seemed a little grayer than before the Battle of Gettysburg, but his manner was as confident as ever. He filled to both eye and mind the measure of a great general. After asking Harry many questions he dismissed him for a while, to play, so he said.

The young Kentuckian at once, and, as a matter of course, sought the Invincibles. St. Clair and Langdon hailed him with shouts of joy, but to his great surprise, Colonel Leonidas Talbot and Lieutenant-Colonel Hector St. Hilaire were not playing chess.

"We were getting on with the game last night, Harry," explained Colonel Talbot, "but we came to a point where we were about to develop heat over a projected move. Then, in order to avoid such a lamentable occurrence, we decided to postpone further play until tonight. But we find you looking uncommonly well, Harry. The flesh pots of Egypt have agreed with you."

"I had a good time in Richmond, sir, a fine one," replied Harry. "The people there have certainly been kind to me, as they are to all the officers of the Army of Northern Virginia."

"What have you done with the grave Dalton, who was your comrade on your journey to the capital?"

"They've kept him there for the present. They think he's stronger proof against the luxuries and temptations of a city than I am."

"Youth is youth, and I'm glad that you've had this little fling, Harry. Perhaps you'll have another, as I think you'll be sent back to Richmond very soon."

"What has been going on here, Colonel?"

"Very little. Nothing, in fact, of any importance. When we crossed the swollen Potomac, although threatened by an enemy superior to us in numbers, I felt that we would not be pushed. General Meade has been deliberate, extremely deliberate in his offensive movements. Up North they call Gettysburg a great victory, but we're resting here calmly and peacefully. Hector and I and our young friends have found rural peace and ease among these Virginia hills and valleys. You, of course, found Richmond very gay and bright?"

"Very gay and bright, Colonel, and full of handsome ladies."

Colonel Talbot sighed and Lieutenant-Colonel Hector St. Hilaire sighed also.

"Hector and I should have been there," said Colonel Talbot. "Although we've never married, we have a tremendous admiration for the ladies, and in our best uniforms we're not wholly unpopular among them, eh, Hector?"

"Not by any means, Leonidas. We're not as young as Harry here, but I know that you're a fine figure of a man, and you know that I am. Moreover, our experience of the dangerous sex is so much greater than that of mere boys like Harry and Arthur and Tom here, that we know how to make ourselves much more welcome. You talk to them about frivolous things, mere chit chat, while we explain grave and important matters to them."

"Are you sure, sir," asked St. Clair, "that the ladies don't really prefer chit chat?"

"I was not speaking of little girls. I was alluding to those ornaments of their sex who have arrived at years of discretion. Ah, if Leonidas and I were only a while in Richmond! It would be the next best thing to being in Charleston."

"Maybe the Invincibles will be sent there for a while."

"Perhaps. I don't foresee any great activity here in the autumn. How do they regard the Army of Northern Virginia in Richmond now, Harry?"

"With supreme confidence."

The talk soon drifted to the people whom Harry had met at the capital, and then he told of his adventure with Shepard, the spy.

"He seems to be a most daring man," said Talbot; "not a mere ordinary spy, but a man of a higher type. I think he's likely to do us great harm. But the woman, Miss Carden, was surely kind to you. If she hadn't found you wandering around in the rain you'd have doubtless dropped down and died. God bless the ladies."

"And so say we all of us," said Harry.

He returned to Richmond in a few days, bearing more dispatches, and to his great delight all that was left of the Invincibles arrived a week later to recuperate and see a little of the world. St. Clair and Happy Tom plunged at once and with all the ardor of youth into the gayeties of social life, and the two colonels followed them at a more dignified but none the less earnest pace. All four appeared in fine new uniforms, for which they had saved their money, and they were conspicuous upon every occasion.

Harry was again at the Curtis house, and although it was not a great ball this time the assemblage was numerous, including all his friends. The two colonels had become especial favorites everywhere, and they were telling stories of the old South, which Harry had divined was passing; passing whether the South won or not.

Although there had been much light talk through the evening and an abundance of real gayety, nearly every member of the company, nevertheless, had serious moments. The news from Tennessee and Georgia was heavy with import. It was vague in some particulars, but it was definite enough in others to tell that the armies of Rosecrans and Bragg were approaching each other. All eyes turned to the West. A great battle could not be long delayed, and a powerful division of the Army of Northern Virginia under Longstreet had been sent to help Bragg.

Harry found himself late at night once more in that very room in which the map had disappeared so mysteriously. The two colonels, St. Clair and Langdon, and one or two others had drifted in, and the older men were smoking. Inevitably they talked of the battle which they foresaw with such certainty, and Harry's anxiety about it was increased, because he knew his father would be there on one side, and the cousin, for whom he cared so much, would be on the other.

"If only General Lee were in command there," said Colonel Talbot, "we might reckon upon a great and decisive victory."

"But Bragg is a good general," said Lieutenant-Colonel St. Hilaire.

"It's not enough to be merely a good general. He must have the soul of fire that Lee has, and that Jackson had. Bragg is the Southern McClellan. He is brave enough personally, but he always overrates the strength of the enemy, and, if he is victorious on the field, he does not reap the fruits of victory."

"Where were the armies when we last heard from them?" asked a captain.

"Bragg was turning north to attack Rosecrans, who stood somewhere between him and Chattanooga."

"I'm glad that it's Rosecrans and not Grant who commands the Northern army there," said Harry.

"Why?" asked Colonel Talbot.

"I've studied the manner in which he took Vicksburg, and I've heard about him from my father, and others. He won't be whipped. He isn't like the other Northern generals. He hangs on, whatever happens. I heard some one quoting him as saying that no matter how badly his army was suffering in battle, the army of the other fellow might be suffering worse. It seems to me that a general who is able to think that way is very dangerous."

"And so he is, Harry," said Colonel Talbot. "I, too, am glad that it's Rosecrans and not Grant. If there's any news of a battle, we're not in a bad place to hear it. It's said that Mr. Curtis always knows as soon as our government what's happened."

The talk drifted on to another subject and then a hum came from the larger room. A murmur only, but it struck such an intense and earnest note that Harry was convinced.

"It's news of battle! I know it!" he exclaimed.

They sprang to their feet and hurried into the ballroom. William Curtis, his habitual calm broken, was standing upon a chair and all the people had gathered in front of him. A piece of paper, evidently a telegram, was clutched in his hand.

"Friends," he said in a strained, but exultant voice, "a great battle has been fought near Chattanooga on a little river called the Chickamauga, and we have won a magnificent victory."

A mighty cheer came from the crowd.

"The army of Rosecrans, attacked with sudden and invincible force by Bragg, has been shattered and driven into Chattanooga."

Another cheer burst forth.

"No part of the Union army was able to hold fast, save one wing under Thomas."

A third mighty cheer arose, but this time Harry did not join in it. He felt a sudden sinking of the heart at the words, "save one wing under Thomas." Then the victory was not complete. It could be complete only when the whole Union army was driven from the field. As long as Thomas stood, there was a flaw in the triumph. He had heard many times of this man, Thomas. He had Grant's qualities. He was at his best in apparent defeat.

"Is there anything else, Mr. Curtis?" asked Colonel Talbot.

"That is all my agent sends me concerning its results, but he says that it lasted two days, and that it was fierce and bloody beyond all comparison with anything that has happened in the West. He estimated that the combined losses are between thirty and forty thousand men."

A heavy silence fell upon them all. The victory was great, but the price for it was great, too. Yet exultation could not be subdued long. They were soon smiling over it, and congratulating one another. But Harry was still unable to share wholly in the joy of victory.

"Why this gloom in your face, when all the rest of us are so happy?" asked St. Clair.

"My father was there. He may have fallen. How do I know?"

"That's not it. He always comes through. What's the real cause? Out with it!"

"You know that part of the dispatch saying, 'No part of the Union army was able to hold fast save one wing under Thomas.' How about that wing! You heard, too, what the colonel said about General Bragg. He always overestimates the strength of the enemy, and while he may win a victory he will not reap the fruits of it. That wing under Thomas still may be standing there, protecting all the rest of the Union army."

"Come now, old Sober Face! This isn't like you. We've won a grand victory! We've more than paid them back for their Gettysburg."

Harry rejoiced then with the others, but at times the thought came to him that Thomas with one wing might yet be standing between Bragg and complete victory. When he and Dalton went back home—they were again with the Lanhams—they found the whole population of Richmond ablaze with triumph. The Yankee army in the West had been routed. Not only was Chickamauga an offset for Gettysburg, but for Vicksburg as well, and once more the fortunes of the South were rising toward the zenith.

Dalton had returned from the army a little later this time than Harry, but he had joined him at the Lanhams', and he too showed gravity amid the almost universal rejoicing.

"I see that you're afraid the next news won't be so complete, Harry," he said.

"That's it, George. We don't really know much, except that Thomas was holding his ground. Oh, if only Stonewall Jackson were there! Remember how he came down on them at the Second Manassas and at Chancellorsville! Thomas would be swept off his feet and as Rosecrans retreated into Chattanooga our army would pour right on his heels!"

They waited eagerly the next day and the next for news, and while Richmond was still filled with rejoicings over Chickamauga, Harry saw that his fears were justified. Thomas stood till the end. Bragg had not followed Rosecrans into Chattanooga. The South had won a great battle, but not a decisive victory. The commanding general had not reaped all the rewards that were his for the taking. Bragg had justified in every way Colonel Talbot's estimate of him.

And yet Richmond, like the rest of the South, felt the great uplift of Chickamauga, the most gigantic battle of the West. It told South as well as North that the war was far from over. The South could no longer invade the North, nor could the North invade the South at will. Even on the northernmost border of the rebelling section the Army of Northern Virginia under its matchless leader, rested in its camp, challenging and defiant.

Harry was glad to return with his friends to the army. His brief period of festival was over, and his fears for his father had been relieved by a letter, stating that he had received no serious harm in the great and terrible battle of Chickamauga.

After the failure of the armies of Lee and Meade to bring about a decisive battle at Mine Run, the Army of Northern Virginia established its autumn and winter headquarters on a jutting spur of the great range called Clarke's Mountain, Orange Court House lying only a few miles to the west. The huge camp was made in a wide-open space, surrounded by dense masses of pines and cedars. Tents were pitched securely, and, feeling that they were to stay here a long time many of the soldiers built rude log cabins.

General Lee himself continued to use his tent, which stood in the center of the camp, the streets of tents and cabins radiating from it like the spokes of a wheel. Close about Lee's own tent were others occupied by Colonel Taylor, his adjutant general, Colonel Peyton, Colonel Marshall, and other and younger officers, including Harry and Dalton. A little distance down one of the main avenues, which they were pleased to call Victory Street, the Invincibles were encamped, and Harry saw them almost every day.

The troops were well fed now, and the brooks provided an abundance of clear water. The days were still warm, but the evenings were cold, and, inhaling the healing odors of the pines and cedars, wounded soldiers returned rapidly to health.

It was a wonderful interval for Harry and his friends associated with him so closely. Save for the presence of armies, it seemed at times that there was no war. Deep peace prevailed along the Rapidan and the slopes of the mountain. It was the longest period of rest that he and his comrades were to know in the course of the mighty struggle. The action of the war was now chiefly in the Southwest, where Grant, taking the place of Rosecrans, was seeking to recover all that was lost at Chickamauga.

Harry had another letter from his father, telling him that his own had been received, and giving personal details of the titanic struggle on the Chickamauga. He did not speak out directly, but Harry saw in his words the vain regret that the great opportunity won at Chickamauga at such a terrible price had not been used. In his belief the whole Federal army might have been destroyed, and the star of the South would have risen again to the zenith.

Here Harry sighed and remembered his own forebodings. Oh, if only a Stonewall Jackson had been there! His mighty sweep would have driven Thomas and the rest in a wild rout. A tear rose in his eye as he remembered his lost hero. He sincerely believed then and always that the Confederacy would have won had he not fallen on that fatal evening at Chancellorsville. It was an emotion with him, a permanent emotion with which logic could not interfere.

Harry was conscious, too, that the long quiet on the Eastern front was but a lull. There was nothing to signify peace in it. If the North had ever felt despair about the war Gettysburg and Vicksburg had removed every trace of it. He knew that beyond the blue ranges of mountains, both to east and west, vast preparations were going forward. The North, the region of great population, of illimitable resources, of free access to the sea, and of mechanical genius that had counted for so much in arming her soldiers, was gathering herself for a supreme effort. The great defeats of the war's first period were to be ignored, and her armies were to come again, more numerous, better equipped and perhaps better commanded than ever.

Nevertheless, his mind was still the mind of youth, and he could not dwell continuously upon this prospect. The camp in the hills was pleasant. The heats had passed, and autumn in the full richness of its coloring had come. The forests blazed in all the brilliancy of red and yellow and brown. The whole landscape had the color and intensity that only a North American autumn can know, and the October air had the freshness and vitality sufficient to make an old man young.

The great army of youth—it was composed chiefly of boys, like the one opposing it—enjoyed itself during these comparatively idle months. The soldiers played rural games, marbles even, pitching the horseshoe, wrestling, jumping and running. It was to Harry like Hannibal in winter quarters at Capua, without the Capua. There was certainly no luxury here. While food was more abundant than for a long time, it was of the simplest. Instead of dissipation there was a great religious revival. Ministers of different creeds, but united in a common object, appeared in the camp, and preached with power and energy. The South was emotional then and perhaps the war had made it more so. The ministers secured thousands of converts. All day long the preaching and singing could be heard through the groves of pine and cedar, and Harry knew that when the time for battle came they would fight all the better because of it. Yielding to the enemy was no part of the Christianity that these ministers preached.

Harry also saw the growth of the hero-worship accorded to his great commander. He did not believe that any other general, except perhaps Napoleon in his earlier career, had ever received such trust and admiration. Many soldiers who had felt his guiding hand in battle now saw him for the first time. He had an appearance and manner to inspire respect, and, back of that, was something much greater, a firm conviction in the minds of all that he had illimitable patience, a willingness to accept responsibility, and a military genius that had never been surpassed. Such was the attitude of the Southern people toward their great leader then, and, to an even greater degree now, when his figure, like that of Lincoln, instead of becoming smaller grows larger as it recedes into the past.

Harry often rode with him. He seemed to have an especial liking for the very young members of his staff, or for old private soldiers, bearded and gray like himself, whom he knew by name. Far in October he rode down toward the Rapidan where Stuart was encamped, taking with him only Harry and Dalton. He was mounted on his great white war horse, Traveller, which the soldiers knew from afar. Cheering arose, but when he raised his hand in a deprecating way the soldiers, obedient to his wish, ceased, and they heard only the murmur of many voices, as they went on. The general made the lads ride, one on his right and the other on his left hand, and brilliant

October coloring and crisp air seemed to put him in a mood that was far from war.

"I pine for Arlington," he said at length to Harry, "that ancestral home of mine that is held by the enemy. I should like to see the ripening of the crops there. We Virginians of the old stock hold to the land, and you Kentuckians, who are really of the same race, hold to it, too."

"It is true, sir," said Harry. "My father loves the land. After his retirement from the army, following the Mexican war, he worked harder upon our place in Kentucky than any slave or hired man. He was going to free his slaves, but I suppose, sir, that the war has made him feel different about it."

"Yes, we're often willing to do things by our own free will, but not under compulsion. The great Washington himself wrote of the evils of slave labor. The 'old fields' scattered all over Virginia show what it has done for this noble commonwealth."

Harry remembered quite well similar "old fields" in Kentucky. Slaves were far less numerous there than in Virginia, and he was old enough to have observed that, in addition to the wrong of slavery, they were a liability rather than an asset. But he too felt anew the instinctive rebellion against being compelled to do what he would perhaps do anyhow.

General Lee talked more of the land and Harry and Dalton listened respectfully. Harry saw that his commander's heart turned strongly toward it. He knew that Jefferson had dreamed of the United States as an agricultural community, having no part in the quarrels of other nations, but he knew that it was only a dream. The South, the section that had followed Jefferson's dream, was now at a great disadvantage. It had no ships, and it did not have the mills to equip it for the great war it was waging. He realized more keenly than ever the one-sided nature of the South's development.

The general turned his horse toward the banks of the Rapidan, and a resplendent figure came forward to meet him. It was that incarnation of youth and fantastic knighthood, Jeb Stuart, who had just returned from a ride toward the north. He wore a new and brilliant uniform and the usual broad yellow sash about his waist. His tunic was embroidered, too, and his epaulets were heavy with gold.

The thick gold braid about his hat was tied in a gorgeous loop in front. His hands were encased in long gloves of the finest buckskin, and he tapped the high yellow tops of his riding boots with a little whip.

Harry always felt that Stuart did not really belong to the present. His place was with the medieval knights who loved gorgeous armor, who fought by day for the love of it and who sat in the evening on the castle steps with fair ladies for the love of it, and who in the dark listened to the troubadours below, also for the love of it. A great cavalry leader, he shone at his brightest in the chase, and, when there was no fighting to be done, his were the spirits of a boy, and he was as quick for a prank as any lad under his own command.

But Stuart, although he had joked with Jackson, never took any liberties with Lee. He instantly swept the ground with his plumed hat and said in his most respectful manner:

"General, will you honor us by dining with us? We've just returned from a long ride northward and we've made some captures."

Lee caught a twinkle in his eye, and he smiled.

"I see no prisoners, General Stuart," he replied, "and I take it that your captures do not mean human beings."

"No, sir, there are other things just now more valuable to us than prisoners. We raided a little Yankee outpost. Nobody was hurt, but, sir, we've captured some provisions, the like of which the Army of Northern Virginia has not tasted in a long time. Would you mind coming with me and taking a look? And bring Kenton and Dalton with you, if you don't mind, sir."

"This indeed sounds tempting," said the commander-in-chief of the Army of Northern Virginia. "I accept your invitation, General Stuart, in behalf of myself and my two young aides."

He dismounted, giving the reins of Traveller to an orderly, and walked toward Stuart's tent, which was pitched near the river. The "captures" were heaped in a grassy place.

"Here, sir," said General Stuart, "are twenty dozen boxes of the finest French sardines. I haven't tasted sardines in a year and I love them."

"I've always liked them," said General Lee.

"And here, sir, are several cases of Yorkshire ham, brought all the way across the sea—and for us. It isn't as good as our Virginia ham, which is growing scarce, but we'll like it. And cove oysters, cases and cases of 'em. I like 'em almost as well as sardines."

"Most excellent."

"And real old New England pies, baked, I suppose, in Washington. We can warm 'em over."

"I see that you have the fire ready."

"And jars of preserves, a half-dozen kinds at least, and all of 'em look as if two likely youngsters like Kenton and Dalton would be anxious to get at 'em."

"You judge us rightly, General," said Harry. "We'll show no mercy to such prisoners as we have here."

"You wouldn't be boys and you wouldn't be human if you did," rejoined Stuart, "would they, General?"

"They would not," replied Lee. "One of the principal recollections of my boyhood is that I was always hungry. Our regular three meals a day were not enough for us, however much we ate at one time. Virginia, like your own Kentucky, Harry, is full of forage, and we moved in groups. Now, didn't you find a lot of food in the woods and fields?"

"Oh, yes, sir," rejoined Harry with animation. "I was hungry all the time, too. An hour after breakfast I was hungry again, and an hour after dinner, which we had in the middle of the day, I was hungry once more."

"But you knew where to go for supplies."

"Yes, sir; we had berries, strawberries, blackberries, raspberries, gooseberries, dewberries, cherries, all of them growing wild although some of them started tame. And then we could forage for pears, peaches, plums, damsons, all kinds of apples, paw paws, and then later for the nuts, hickory nuts, walnuts, chestnuts, hazel nuts, chinquapins, and a lot more. We could have almost lived in the woods and fields from early spring until late fall."

"We did the same in Virginia," said the commander-in-chief. "I've often thought that our forest Indians did not develop a higher civilization, because it was so easy for them to live, save in the depths of a hard winter. They had most of the berries and fruits and nuts that we white boys had. The woods were full of game, and the lakes and rivers full of fish. They were not driven by the hard necessity that creates civilization."

"Dinner is ready, sir," announced General Stuart, who had been directing the orderlies. "I can offer you and the others nothing but boxes and kegs to sit on, but I can assure you that this Northern food, some of which comes in cans, is excellent."

The two lads and General Stuart fell to work with energy. General Lee ate more sparingly. Stuart was a boy himself, talking much and running over with fun.

"Have you heard what happened to General Early, sir?" he asked the commander-in-chief.

"Not yet."

"But you will, sir, to-morrow. Early will be slow in sending you that dispatch. He hasn't had time to write it yet. He's not through swearing."

"General Early is a valiant and able man, but I disapprove of his swearing."

"Why, sir, 'Old Jube' can't help it. It's a part of his breathing, and man cannot live without breath. He sent one of his best aides with a dispatch to General Hill, who is posted some distance away. Passing through a thick cedar wood the aide was suddenly set upon by a genuine stage villain, large, dark and powerful, who clubbed him over the head with the butt of a pistol, and then departed with his dispatch."

"And what happened then?"

"The aide returned to General Early with his story, but without his dispatch. The general believed his account, of course, but he called him names for allowing himself to be surprised and overcome by a single Yankee. He cursed until the air for fifty yards about him smelled strongly of sulphur and brimstone."

"Did he do anything more?"

"Yes, General. He sent a duplicate of the dispatch by an aide whom he said he could trust. In an hour the second man came back with the same big lump on his head and with the same story. He had been ambushed at the crossing of a ravine full of small cedars, and the highwayman was undoubtedly the same, too, a big, powerful fellow, as bold as you please."

Harry's pulse throbbed hard for a few moments, when he first heard mention of the man. The description, not only physical, but of manner and action as well, answered perfectly. He had not the slightest doubt that it was Shepard.

"A daring deed," said General Lee. "We must see that it is not repeated."

"But that wasn't all of the tale, sir. While the second man was sitting on the bank, nursing his broken head, the Yankee Dick Turpin read the dispatch and saw that it was a duplicate of the first. He became red-hot with wrath, and talked furiously about the extra and unnecessary work that General Early was forcing upon him. He ended by cramming the dispatch into the man's hands, directing him to take it back, and to tell General Early to stop his foolishness. The aide was a bit dazed from the blow he received and he delivered that message word for word. Why, sir, General Early exploded. People who have heard him swear for years and who know what an artist he is in swearing, heard him then utter swear words that they had never heard before, words invented on the spur of the moment, and in the heat of passion, words full of pith and meaning."

"And that was all, I suppose?"

"Not by any means, sir. General Early picked two sharpshooters and sent them with another copy of the dispatch. They passed the place of the first hold-up, and next the ravine without seeing anybody. But as they were riding some distance further on both of their horses were killed by shots from a small clump of pines. Before they could regain their feet Dick Turpin came out and covered them with his rifle—it seems that he had one of those new repeating weapons.

"The men saw that his eye was so keen and his hand so steady that they did not dare to move a hand to a pistol. Then as he looked down the sights of his rifle he lectured them. He told them they were foolish to come that way, when the two who came before them had found out that it was a closed road. He said that real soldiers learned by experience, and would not try again to do what they had learned to be impossible.

"Then he said that after all they were not to blame, as they had been sent by General Early, and he made one of them who had the stub of a pencil write on the back of the dispatch these words: 'General Jubal Early, C. S. A.: This has ceased to be a joke. After your first man was stopped, it was not necessary to do anything more. I have the dispatch. Why insist on sending duplicate after duplicate?' And the two had to walk all the way back to General Early with that note, because they didn't dare make away with the dispatch.

"I have a certain respect for that man's skill and daring, but General Early had a series of spells. He retired to his tent and if the reports are not exaggerated, a continuous muttering like low thunder came from the tent, and all the cloth of it turned blue from the lightnings imprisoned inside."

General Lee himself smiled.

"It was certainly annoying," he said. "I hope the dispatch was not of importance."

"It contained nothing that will help the Yankees, but it shows that the enemy has some spies — or at least one spy — who are Napoleons at their trade."

CHAPTER XIII
THE COMING OF GRANT

The little dinner ended. Despite his disapproval of General Early's swearing, General Lee laughed heartily at further details of the strange Yankee spy's exploits. But it was well known that in this particular General Early was the champion of the East. Harry did not know that in the person of Colonel Charles Woodville, his cousin, Dick Mason, had encountered one of equal ability in the Southwest.

Presently General Lee and his two young aides mounted their horses for the return. The commander-in-chief seemed gayer than usual. He was always very fond of Stuart, whose high spirits pleased him, and before his departure he thanked him for his thoughtfulness.

"Whenever we get any particularly choice shipments from the North I shall always be pleased to notify you, General, and send you your share," said Stuart, sweeping the air in front of him again with his great plumed hat. With his fine, heroic face and his gorgeous uniform he had never looked more a knight of the Middle Ages.

General Lee smiled and thanked him again, and then rode soberly back, followed at a short distance by his two young aides. Although the view of hills and mountains and valleys and river and brooks was now magnificent, the sumach burning in red and the leaves vivid in many colors, Lee, deeply sensitive, like all his rural forbears, to rural beauty, nevertheless seemed not to notice it, and soon sank into deep thought.

It is believed by many that Lee knew then that the Confederacy had already received a mortal blow. It was not alone sufficient for the South to win victories. She must keep on winning them, and the failure at Gettysburg and the defeat at Vicksburg had put her on the defensive everywhere. Fewer blockade runners were getting through.

Above all, there was less human material upon which to draw. But he roused himself presently and said to Harry:

"There was something humorous in the exploits of the man who held up General Early's messengers, but the fellow is dangerous, exceedingly dangerous at such a time."

"I've an idea who he is, sir," said Harry.

"Indeed! What do you know?"

Then Harry told nearly all that he knew about Shepard, but not all—that struggle in the river, and his sparing of the spy and the filching of the map at the Curtis house, for instance—and the commander-in-chief listened with great attention.

"A bold man, uncommonly bold, and it appears uncommonly skilled, too. We must send out a general alarm, that is, we must have all our own scouts and spies watching for him."

Harry said nothing, but he did not believe that anybody would catch Shepard. The man's achievements had been so startling that they had created the spell of invincibility. His old belief that he was worth ten thousand men on the Northern battle line returned. No movement of the Army of Northern Virginia could escape him, and no lone messenger could ever be safe from him.

Lee returned to his camp on Clarke's Mountain, and, a great revival meeting being in progress, he joined it, sitting with a group of officers. Fitzhugh Lee, W. H. F. Lee, Jones, Rosser, Wickham, Munford, Young, Wade Hampton and a dozen others were there. Taylor and Marshall and Peyton of his staff were also in the company.

The preacher was a man of singular power and earnestness, and after the sermon he led the singing himself, in which often thirty or forty thousand voices joined. It was a moving sight to Harry, all these men, lads, mostly, but veterans of many fields, united in a chorus mightier than any other that he had ever heard. It would have pleased Stonewall Jackson to his inmost soul, and once more, as always, a tear rose to his eye as he thought of his lost hero.

Harry and Dalton left their horses with an orderly and came back to the edge of the great grove, in which the meeting was being held. They had expected to find St. Clair and Happy Tom there, but not seeing them, wandered on and finally drifted apart. Harry stood alone for a while on the outskirts of the throng. They were all singing again, and the mighty volume of sound rolled through the wood. It was not only a singular, it was a majestic scene also to Harry. How like unto little children young soldiers were! and how varied and perplexing were the problems of human nature! They were singing with the utmost fervor of Him who had preached continuously of peace, who was willing to turn one cheek when the other was smitten, and because of their religious zeal they would rush the very next day into battle, if need be, with increased fire and zeal.

He saw a heavily built, powerful man on the outskirts, but some distance away, singing in a deep rolling voice, but something vaguely familiar in the figure drew his glance again. He looked long and well and then began to edge quietly toward the singer, who was clothed in the faded butternut uniform that so many of the Confederate soldiers wore.

The fervor of the singer did not decrease, but Harry noticed that he too was moving, moving slowly toward the eastern end of the grove, the same direction that Harry was pursuing. Now he was sure. He would have called out, but his voice would not have been heard above the vast volume of sound. He might have pointed out the singer to others, but, although he felt sure, he did not wish to be laughed at in case of mistake. But strongest of all was the feeling that it had become a duel between Shepard and himself.

He walked slowly on, keeping the man in view, but Shepard, although he never ceased singing, moved away at about the same pace. Harry inferred at once that Shepard had seen him and was taking precautions. The temptation to cry out at the top of his voice that the most dangerous of all spies was among them was almost irresistible, but it would only create an uproar in which Shepard could escape easily, leaving to him a load of ridicule.

He continued his singular pursuit. Shepard was about a hundred yards away, and they had made half the circuit of this huge congregation. Then the spy passed into a narrow belt of pines, and when Harry moved forward to see him emerge on the other side he failed to reappear. He hastened to the pines, which led some distance down a little gully, and he was sure that Shepard had gone that way. He followed fast, but he could discover no sign. He had vanished utterly, like thin smoke swept away by a breeze.

He returned deeply stirred by the appearance and disappearance—easy, alike—of Shepard. His sense of the man's uncanny powers and of his danger to the Confederacy was increased. He seemed to come and go absolutely as he pleased. It was true that in the American Civil War the opportunities for spies were great. All men spoke the same language, and all looked very much alike. It was not such a hard task to enter the opposing lines, but Shepard had shown a daring and success beyond all comparison. He seemed to have both the seven league boots and the invisible cloak of very young childhood. He came as he pleased, and when pursuit came he vanished in thin air.

Harry bit his lips in chagrin. He felt that Shepard had scored on him again. It was true that he had been victorious in that fight in the river, when victory meant so much, but since then Shepard had triumphed, and it was bitter. He hardened his determination, and resolved that he would always be on the watch for him. He even felt a certain glow, because he was one of two in such a conflict of skill and courage.

The meeting having been finished, he went down one of the streets of tents to the camp of the Invincibles. Colonel Leonidas Talbot and Lieutenant-Colonel Hector St. Hilaire were not playing chess. Instead they were sitting on a pine log with Happy Tom and St. Clair and other officers, listening to young Julien de Langeais, who sat on another log, playing a violin with surpassing skill. Lieutenant-Colonel St. Hilaire, knowing his prowess as a violinist, had asked him to come and play for the Invincibles. Now he was playing for them and for several thousand more who were gathered in the pine woods.

Young de Langeais sat on a low stump, and the great crowd made a solid mass around him. But he did not see them, nor the pine woods nor the heavy cannon sitting on the ridges. He looked instead into a region of fancy, where the colors were brilliant or gay or tender as he imagined them. Harry, with no technical knowledge of music but with a great love of it, recognized at once the touch of a master, and what was more, the soul of one.

To him the violin was not great, unless the player was great, but when the player was great it was the greatest musical instrument of all. He watched de Langeais' wrapt face, and for him too the thousands of soldiers, the pines and the cannon on the ridges melted away. He did not know what the young musician was playing, probably some old French air or a great lyric outburst of the fiery Verdi, whose music had already spread through America.

"A great artist," whispered Lieutenant-Colonel St. Hilaire in his ear. "He studied at the schools in New Orleans and then for two years in Paris. But he came back to fight. Nothing could keep Julien from the army, but he brought his violin with him. We Latins, or at least we who are called Latins, steep our souls in music. It's not merely intellectual with us. It's passion, fire, abandonment, triumph and all the great primitive emotions of the human race."

Harry's feelings differed somewhat from those of Lieutenant-Colonel St. Hilaire—in character but not in power—and as young de Langeais played on he began to think what a loss a stray bullet could make. Why should a great artist be allowed to come on the battle line? There were hundreds of thousands of common men. One could replace another, but nobody could replace the genius, a genius in which the whole world shared. It was not possible for either drill or training to do it, and yet a little bullet might take away his life as easily as it would that of a plowboy. They were all alike to the bullets and the shells.

De Langeais finished, and a great shout of applause arose. The cheering became so insistent that he was compelled to play again.

"His family is well-to-do," said Lieutenant-Colonel St. Hilaire just before he began playing once more, "and they'll see that he goes back to Paris for study as soon as the war is over. If they didn't I would."

It did not seem to occur to Lieutenant-Colonel St. Hilaire that young de Langeais could be killed, and Harry began to share his confidence. De Langeais now played the simple songs of the old South, and there was many a tear in the eyes of war-hardened youth. The sun was setting in a sea of fire, and the pine forests turned red in its blaze. In the distance the waters of the Rapidan were crimson, too, and a light wind out of the west sighed among the pines, forming a subdued chorus to the violin.

De Langeais began to play a famous old song of home, and Harry's mind traveled back on its lingering note to his father's beautiful house and grounds, close by Pendleton, and all the fine country about it, in which he and Dick Mason and the boys of their age had roamed. He remembered all the brooks and ponds and the groves that produced the best hickory nuts. When should he see them again and would his father be there, and Dick, and all the other boys of their age! Not all! Certainly not all, because some were gone already. And yet this plaintive note of the homes they had left behind, while it brought a tear to many an eye, made no decrease in martial determination. It merely hardened their resolution to win the victory all the sooner, and bring the homecoming march nearer.

De Langeais ended on a wailing note that died like a faint sigh in the pine forest. Then he came back to earth, sprang up, and put his violin in its case. Applause spread out and swelled in a low, thunderous note, but de Langeais, who was as modest as he was talented, quickly hid himself among his friends.

The sun sank behind the blue mountains, and twilight came readily over the pine and cedar forests. Colonel Talbot and Lieutenant-Colonel St. Hilaire, who had a large tent together, invited the youths to stay awhile with them as their guests and talk. All the soldiers dispersed to their own portions of the great camp, and there would be an hour of quiet and rest, until the camp cooks served supper.

It had been a lively day for Harry, his emotions had been much stirred, and now he was glad to sit in the peace of the evening on a stone near the entrance of the tent, and listen to his friends. War drew comrades together in closer bonds than those of peace. He was quite sure that St. Clair, Dalton and Happy Tom were his friends for life, as he was theirs, and the two colonels seemed to have the same quality of youth. Simple men, of high faith and honor, they were often childlike in the ways of the world, their horizons sometimes not so wide as those of the lads who now sat with them.

"As I told Harry," said Lieutenant-Colonel St. Hilaire to Julien, "you shall have that talent of yours cultivated further after the war. Two years more of study and you will be among the greatest. You must know, lads, that for us who are of French descent, Paris is the world's capital in the arts."

"And for many of English blood, too," said Colonel Talbot.

Then they talked of more immediate things, of the war, the armies and the prospect of the campaigns. Harry, after an hour or so, returned to headquarters and he found soldiers making a bed for the commander-in-chief under the largest of the pines. Lee in his campaigns always preferred to sleep in the open air, when he could, and it required severe weather to drive him to a tent. Meanwhile he sat by a small fire—the October nights were growing cold—and talked with Peyton and other members of his staff.

Harry and Dalton decided to imitate his example and sleep between the blankets under the pines. Harry found a soft place, spread his blankets and in a few minutes slept soundly. In fact, the whole Army of Northern Virginia was a great family that retired early, slept well and rose early.

The next morning there was frost on the grass, but the lads were so hardy that they took no harm. The autumn deepened. The leaves blazed for a while in their most vivid colors and then began to fall under the strong west winds. Brown and wrinkled, they often whirled past in clouds. The air had a bite in it, and the soldiers built more and larger fires.

The Army of Northern Virginia never before had been quiescent so long. The Army of the Potomac was not such a tremendous distance away, but it seemed that neither side was willing to attack, and as the autumn advanced and began to merge into winter the minds of all turned toward the Southwest.

For the valiant soldiers encamped on the Virginia hills the news was not good. Grant, grim and inflexible, was deserving the great name that was gradually coming to him. He had gathered together all the broken parts of the army defeated at Chickamauga and was turning Union defeat into Union victory.

Winter closed in with the knowledge that Grant had defeated the South disastrously on Lookout Mountain and all around Chattanooga. Chickamauga had gone for nothing, the whole flank of the Confederacy was turned and the Army of Northern Virginia remained the one great barrier against the invading legions of the North. Yet the confidence of the men in that army remained undimmed. They felt that on their own ground, and under such a man as Lee, they were invincible.

In the course of these months Harry, as a messenger and often as a secretary, was very close to Lee. He wrote a swift and clear hand, and took many dispatches. Almost daily messages were sent in one direction or another and Harry read from them the thoughts of his leader, which he kept locked in his breast. He knew perhaps better than many an older officer the precarious condition of the Confederacy. These letters, which he took from dictation, and the letters from Richmond that he read to his chief, told him too plainly that the limits of the Confederacy were shrinking. Its money declined steadily. Happy Tom said that he had to "swap it pound for pound now to the sutlers for groceries." Yet it is the historical truth that the heart of the Army of Northern Virginia never beat with more fearless pride, as the famous and "bloody" year of '63 was drawing to its close.

The news arrived that Grant, the Sledge Hammer of the West, had been put by Lincoln in command of all the armies of the Union, and would come east to lead the Army of the Potomac in person, with Meade still as its nominal chief, but subject, like all the others, to his command.

Harry heard the report with a thrill. He knew now that decisive action would come soon enough. He had always felt that Meade in front of them was a wavering foe, and perhaps too cautious. But Grant was of another kind. He was a pounder. Defeats did not daunt him. He would attack and then attack again and again, and the diminishing forces of the Confederacy were ill fitted to stand up against the continued blows of the hammer. Harry's thrill was partly of apprehension, but whenever he looked at the steadfast face of his chief his confidence returned.

Winter passed without much activity and spring began to show its first buds. The earth was drying, after melting snows and icy rains, and Harry knew that action would not be delayed much longer. Grant was in the East now. He had gone in January to St. Louis to visit his daughter, who lay there very ill, and then, after military delays, he had reached Washington.

Harry afterward heard the circumstances of his arrival, so characteristic of plain and republican America. He came into Washington by train as a simple passenger, accompanied only by his son, who was but fourteen years of age. They were not recognized, and arriving at a hotel, valise in hand, with a crowd of passengers, he registered in his turn: "U. S. Grant and son, Galena, Ill." The clerk, not noticing the name, assigned the modest arrival and his boy to a small room on the fifth floor. Then they moved away, a porter carrying the valise. But the clerk happened to look again at the register, and when he saw more clearly he rushed after them with a thousand apologies. He did not expect the victor of great battles, the lieutenant-general commanding all the armies of the Union, a battle front of more than a million men, to come so modestly.

When Harry heard the story he liked it. It seemed to him to be the same simple and manly quality that he found in Lee, both worthy of republican institutions. But he did not have time to think about it long. The signs were multiplying that the advance would soon come. The North had never ceased to resound with preparations, and Grant would march with veterans. All the spies and scouts brought in the same report. Butler would move up from Fortress Monroe toward Richmond with thirty thousand men and Grant with a hundred and fifty thousand would cross the Rapidan, moving by the right flank of Lee until they could unite and destroy the Confederacy. Such was the plan, said the scouts and spies in gray.

Longstreet with his corps had returned from the West and Lee gathered his force of about sixty thousand men to meet the mighty onslaught—he alone perhaps divined how mighty it would be—and when he was faced by the greatest of his adversaries his genius perhaps never shone more brightly.

May and the full spring came. It was the third day of the month, and the camp of the Army of Northern Virginia was as usual. Many of the young soldiers played games among the trees. Here and there they lay in groups on the new grass, singing their favorite songs. The cooks were preparing their suppers over the big fires. Several bands were playing. Had it not been for the presence of so many weapons the whole might have been taken for one vast picnic, but Harry, who sat in the tent of the commander-in-chief, was writing as fast as he could dispatch after dispatch that the Southern leader was dictating to him. He knew perfectly well, of course, that the commander-in-chief was gathering his forces and that they would move quickly for battle. He knew, too, how inadequate was the equipment of the army. Only a short time before he had taken from the dictation of his chief a letter to the President of the Confederacy a part of which ran:

My anxiety on the subject of provisions for the army is so great that I cannot refrain from expressing it to your Excellency. I cannot see how we can operate with our present supplies. Any derangement in their arrival or disaster to the railroad would render it impossible for me to keep the army together and might force a retreat into North Carolina. There is nothing to be had in this section for men or animals. We have rations for the troops to-day and to-morrow. I hope a new supply arrived last night, but I have not yet had a report.

Harry had thought long over this letter and he knew from his own observation its absolute truth. The depleted South was no longer able to feed its troops well. The abundance of the preceding autumn had quickly passed, and in winter they were mostly on half rations.

Lee, better than any other man in the whole South, had understood what lay before them, and his foes both of the battlefield and of the spirit have long since done him justice. Less than a week before this eve of mighty events he had written to a young woman in Virginia, a relative:

I dislike to send letters within reach of the enemy, as they might serve, if captured, to bring distress on others. But you must sometimes cast your thoughts on the Army of Northern Virginia, and never forget it in your prayers. It is preparing for a great struggle, but I pray and trust that the great God, mighty to deliver, will spread over it His Almighty arms and drive its enemies before it.

Harry had seen this letter before its sending, and he was not surprised now when Lee was sending messengers to all parts of his army. With all the hero-worshiping quality of youth he was once more deeply grateful that he should have served on the staffs and been brought into close personal relations with two men, Stonewall Jackson and Lee, who seemed to him so great. As he saw it, it was not alone military greatness but greatness of the soul, which was greater. Both were deeply religious—Lee, the Episcopalian, and Jackson, the Presbyterian, and it was a piety that contained no trace of cant.

Harry felt that the crisis of the great Civil War was at hand. It had been in the air all that day, and news had come that Grant had broken up his camps and was crossing the Rapidan with a huge force. He knew how small in comparison was the army that Lee could bring against him, and yet he had supreme confidence in the military genius of his chief.

He had written a letter with which an aide had galloped away, and then he sat at the little table in the great tent, pen in hand and ink and paper before him, but Lee was silent. He was dressed as usual with great neatness and care, though without ostentation. His face had its usual serious cast, but tinged now with melancholy. Harry knew that he no longer saw the tent and those around him. His mind dwelled for a few moments upon his own family and the ancient home that he had loved so well.

The interval was very brief. He was back in the present, and the principal generals for whom he had sent were entering the tent. Hill, Longstreet, Ewell, Stuart and others came, but they did not stay long. They talked earnestly with their leader for a little while, and then every one departed to lead his brigades.

The secretaries put away pen, ink and paper. Twilight was advancing in the east and night suddenly fell outside. The songs ceased, the bands played no more, and there was only the deep rumble of marching men and moving cannon.

"We'll ride now, gentlemen," said Lee to his staff.

Traveller, saddled and bridled, was waiting and the commander-in-chief sprang into the saddle with all the agility of a young man. The others mounted, too, Harry and Dalton as usual taking their places modestly in the rear.

A regiment, small in numbers but famous throughout the army for valor, was just passing, and its colonel and its lieutenant-colonel, erect men, riding splendidly, but gray like Lee, drew their swords and gave the proud and flashing salute of the saber as they went by. Lee and his staff almost with involuntary impulse returned the salute in like fashion. Then the Invincibles passed on, and were lost from view in the depths of the forest.

Harry felt a sudden constriction of the heart. He knew that he might never see Colonel Leonidas Talbot nor Lieutenant-Colonel Hector St. Hilaire again, nor St. Clair, nor Happy Tom either.

But his friends could not remain long in his mind at such a time. They were marching, marching swiftly, the presence of the man on the great white horse seeming to urge them on to greater speed. As the stars came out Lee's brow, which had been seamed by thought, cleared. His plan which he had formed in the day was moving well. His three corps were bearing away toward the old battlefield of Chancellorsville. Grant would be drawn into the thickets of the

Wilderness as Hooker had been the year before, although a greater than Hooker was now leading the Army of the Potomac.

Harry, who foresaw it all, thrilled and shuddered at the remembrance. It was in there that the great Jackson had fallen in the hour of supreme triumph. Not far away were the heights of Fredericksburg, where Burnside had led the bravest of the brave to unavailing slaughter. As Belgium had been for centuries the cockpit of Europe, so the wild and sterile region in Virginia that men call the Wilderness became the cockpit of North America.

While Lee and his army were turning into the Wilderness Grant and the greatest force that the Union had yet assembled were seeking him. It was composed of men who had tasted alike of victory and defeat, veterans skilled in all the wiles and stratagems of war, and with hearts to endure anything. In this host was a veteran regiment that had come East to serve under Grant as it had served under him so valiantly in the West. Colonel Winchester rode at its head and beside him rode his favorite aide, young Richard Mason. Not far away was Colonel Hertford, with a numerous troop of splendid cavalry.

Grant, alert and resolved to win, carried in his pocket a letter which he had received from Lincoln, saying:

Not expecting to see you before the spring campaign opens, I wish to express in this way my entire satisfaction with what you have done up to this time, so far as I understand it. The particulars of your plans I neither know nor seek to know. You are vigilant and self-reliant, and, pleased with this, I wish not to obtrude any constraints or restraints upon you. While I am very anxious that any great disaster or the capture of our men in great numbers should be avoided, I know these points are less likely to escape your attention than they would mine. If there is anything wanting which is within my power to give, do not fail to let me know it. And now, with a brave army and a just cause, may God sustain you.

A noble letter, breathing the loftiest spirit, and showing that moral grandeur which has been so characteristic of America's greatest men. He had put all in Grant's hands and he had given to him an army, the like of which had never been seen until now on the American continent. Never before had the North poured forth its wealth and energy in such abundance.

Four thousand wagons loaded with food and ammunition followed the army, and there was a perfect system by which a wagon emptied of its contents was sent back to a depot to be refilled, while a loaded wagon took its place at the front. Complete telegram equipments, poles, wires, instruments and all were carried with every division. The wires could be strung easily and the lieutenant-general could talk to every part of his army. There were, also, staffs of signalmen, in case the wires should fail at any time. Grant held in his hand all the resources of the North, and if he could not win no one could.

All through the night the hostile armies marched, and before them went the spies and scouts.

CHAPTER XIV
THE GHOSTLY RIDE

Harry and Dalton kept close together during the long hours of the ghostly ride. Just ahead of them were Taylor and Marshall and Peyton, and in front Lee rode in silence. Now and then they passed regiments, and at other times they would halt and let regiments pass them. Then the troops, seeing the man sitting on the white horse, would start to cheer, but always their officers promptly subdued it, and they marched on feeling more confident than ever that their general was leading them to victory.

Many hours passed and still the army marched through the forests. The trees, however, were dwindling in size and even in the night they saw that the earth was growing red and sterile. Dense thickets grew everywhere, and the marching became more difficult. Harry felt a sudden thrill of awe.

"George," he whispered, "do you know the country into which we're riding?"

"I think I do, Harry. It's the Wilderness."

"It can't be anything else, George, because I see the ghosts."

"What are you talking about, Harry? What ghosts?"

"The thousands and thousands who have fallen in that waste. Why the Wilderness is so full of dead men that they must walk at night to give one another room. I only hope that the ghost of Old Jack will ride before us and show us the way."

"I almost feel like that, too," admitted Dalton, who, however, was of a less imaginative mind than Harry. "As sure as I'm sitting in the saddle we're bound for the Wilderness. Now, what is the day going to give us?"

"Marching mostly, I think, and with the next noon will come battle. Grant doesn't hesitate and hold back. We know that, George."

"No, it's not his character."

Morning came and found them still in the forests, seeking the deep thickets of the Wilderness, and Grant, warned by his scouts and spies, and most earnestly by one whose skill, daring and judgment were unequaled, turned from his chosen line of march to meet his enemy. Once more Lee had selected the field of battle, where his inferiority in numbers would not count so much against him.

It was nearly morning when the march ceased, and officers and troops, save those on guard, lay down in the forest for rest. Harry, a seasoned veteran, could sleep under any conditions and with a blanket over him and a saddle for a pillow closed his eyes almost immediately. Lee and his older aides, Taylor and Peyton and Marshall, slept also. Around them the brigades, too, lay sleeping.

A while before dawn a large man in Confederate uniform, using the soft, lingering speech of the South, appeared almost in the center of the army of Northern Virginia. He knew all the pass words and told the officers commanding the watch that the wing under Ewell was advancing more rapidly than any of the others. Inside the line he could go about almost as he chose, and one could see little of him, save that he was large of figure and deeply tanned, like all the rest.

He approached the little opening in which Lee and his staff lay, although he kept back from the sentinels who watched over the sleeping leader. But Shepard knew that it was the great Confederate chieftain who lay in the shadow of the oak and he could identify him by the glances of the sentinels so often directed toward the figure.

There were wild thoughts for a moment or two in the mind of Shepard. A single bullet fired by an unerring hand would take from the Confederacy its arm and brain, and then what happened to himself afterward would not matter at all. And the war would be over in a month or two. But he put the thought fiercely from him. A spy he was and in his heart proud of his calling, but no such secret bullet could be fired by him.

He turned away from the little opening, wandered an hour through the camp and then, diving into the deep bushes, vanished like a shadow through the Confederate lines, and was gone to Grant to report that Lee's army was advancing swiftly to attack, and that the command of Ewell would come in touch with him first.

Not long after dawn Harry was again on the march, riding behind his general. From time to time Lee sent messengers to the various divisions of his army, four in number, commanded by Longstreet, Early, Hill and Stuart, the front or Stuart's composed of cavalry. Harry's own time came, when he received a dispatch of the utmost importance to take to Ewell. He memorized it first, and, if capture seemed probable, he was to tear it into bits and throw it away. Harry was glad he was to go to Ewell. In the great campaign in the valley he had been second to Jackson, his right arm, as Jackson had been Lee's right arm. Ewell had lost a leg since then, and his soldiers had to strap him in the saddle when he led them into battle, but he was as daring and cheerful as ever, trusted implicitly by Lee.

Harry with a salute to his chief rode away. Part of the country was familiar to him and in addition his directions were so explicit that he could not miss the way.

The four divisions of the army were in fairly close touch, but in a country of forests and many waters Northern scouts might come between, and he rode with caution, his hand ever near the pistol in his belt. The midday sun however clouded as the afternoon passed on. The thickets and forests grew more dense. From the distance came now and then the faint, sweet call of a trumpet, but everything was hidden from sight by the dense tangle of the Wilderness, a wilderness as wild and dangerous as any in which Henry Ware had ever fought. How it all came back to him! Almost exactly a year ago he had ridden into it with Jackson and here the armies were gathering again.

Imagination, fancy, always so strong in him, leaped into vivid life. The year had not passed and he was riding to meet Stonewall Jackson, who was somewhere ahead, preparing for his great curve about Hooker and the lightning stroke at Chancellorsville. Rabbits sprang out of the undergrowth and fled away before his horse's hoofs. In the lonely wilderness, which nevertheless had little to offer to the hunter, birds chattered from every tree. Small streams flowed slowly between dense walls of bushes. Here and there in the protection of the thickets wild flowers were in early bloom.

It was spring, fresh spring everywhere, but the bushes and the grass alike were tinged with red for Harry. The strange mental illusion that he was riding to Chancellorsville remained with him and he did not seek to shake it off. He almost expected to see Old Jack ahead on a hill, bent over a little, and sitting on Little Sorrel, with the old slouch hat drawn over his eyes. They had talked of the ghost of Jackson leading them in the Wilderness. He shivered. Could it be so? All the time he knew it was an illusion, but he permitted it to cast its spell over him, as one who dreams knowingly.

And Harry was dreaming back. Old Jack, the earlier of his two heroes, was leading them. He foresaw the long march through the thickets of the Wilderness, Stonewall forming the line of battle in the deep roads late in the evening, almost in sight of Hooker's camp, the sudden rush of his brigades and then the terrible battle far into the night.

He shook himself. It was uncanny. The past was the past. Dreams were thin and vanished stuff. Once more he was in the present and saw clearly. Old Jack was gone to take his place with the great heroes of the past, but the Army of Northern Virginia was there, with Lee leading them, and the most formidable of all the Northern chiefs with the most formidable of all the Northern armies was before them.

He heard the distant thud of hoofs and with instinctive caution drew back into a dense clump of bushes. A half-dozen horsemen were near and their eager looks in every direction told Harry that they were scouts. There was little difference then between a well worn uniform of blue or gray, and they were very close before Harry was able to tell that they belonged to Grant's army.

He was devoutly glad that his horse was trained thoroughly and stood quite still while the Northern scouts passed. A movement of the bushes would have attracted their attention, and he did not wish to be captured at any time, least of all on the certain eve of a great battle. After a battle he always felt an extra regret for those who had fallen, because they would never know whether they had won or lost.

They were alert, keen and vigorous men, or lads rather, as young as himself, and they rode as if they had been Southern youths almost born in the saddle. Harry was not the only one to notice how the Northern cavalry under the whip hand of defeat had improved so fast that it was now a match, man for man, for that of the South.

The young riders rode on and the tread of their hoofs died in the undergrowth. Then Harry emerged from his own kindly clump of bushes and increased his speed, anxious to reach Ewell, without any more of those encounters. He made good progress through the thickets, and soon after sundown saw a glow which he took to be that of campfires. He advanced cautiously, met the Southern sentinels and knew that he was right.

The very first of these sentinels was an old soldier of Jackson, who knew him well.

"Mr. Kenton!" he exclaimed.

"Yes, Thorn! It's you!" said Harry without hesitation.

The soldier was pleased that he should be recognized thus in the dusk, and he was still more pleased when the young aide leaned down and shook his hand.

"I might have known, Thorn, that I'd find you here, rifle on your arm, watching," he said.

"Thank you, Mr. Kenton. You'll find the general over there on a log by the fire."

Harry dismounted, gave his horse to a soldier and walked into the glade. Ewell sat alone, his crutch under his arms, his one foot kicking back the coals, his bald head a white disc in the glow.

"General Ewell, sir," said Harry.

General Ewell turned about and when he saw Harry his face clearly showed gladness. He could not rise easily, but he stretched out a welcoming hand.

"Ah! Kenton," he said, "you're a pleasant sight to tired eyes like mine. You bring back the glorious old days in the valley. So it's a message from the commander-in-chief?"

"Yes, sir. Here it is."

Ewell read it rapidly by the firelight and smiled.

"He tells us we're nearest to the enemy," he said, "and to hold fast, if we're attacked. You're to remain with us and report what happens, but doubtless you knew all this."

"Yes, I had to commit it to memory before I started."

"Then stay here with me. I may want to report to General Lee at any time. The enemy is in our front only three or four miles away. He knows we're here and it was a villainous surprise to him to find us in his way. They say this man Grant is a pounder. So is Lee, when the time comes to pound, but he's that and far more. I tell you, young man, that General Lee has had to trim a lot of Northern generals. McClellan and Pope and Burnside and Hooker and Meade have been going to school to him, and now Grant is qualifying for his class."

"But Grant is a great general. So our men in the West themselves say."

"He may be, but Lee is greater, greatest. And, Harry, you and I, who knew him and loved him, wish that another who alone was fit to ride by his side was here with him."

"I wish it from the bottom of my heart," said Harry.

"Well, well, regrets are useless. Help me up, Harry. I'm only part of a man, but I can still fight."

"We saw you do that at Gettysburg," said Harry, as he put his arm under Ewell's shoulder. Then Ewell took his crutch and they walked to the far side of the glade, where several officers of his staff gathered around him.

"Lieutenant Kenton, whom you all know," said General Ewell, "has brought a message from the commander-in-chief that we will be attacked first, and to be on guard. We consider it an honor, do we not, my lads?"

"Yes, let them come," they said.

"Harry, you may want to see the enemy. Clayton, you and Campbell take him forward through the pickets. But don't go too far. We don't want to lose three perfectly good young officers before the battle begins. After that it may be your business to get yourselves shot."

The two rode nearly two miles to the crest of a hill and then, using their strong glasses in the moonlight, they were able to see the lights of a vast camp.

"We hear that it is Warren's corps," said Clayton. "As General Ewell doubtless has told you, the enemy know that we're in front, but I don't believe they know our exact location. I believe we'll be in battle with those men in the morning."

Harry thought so too. In truth, it was inevitable. Warren would advance and Ewell would stand in his way. Yet he slept soundly when he went back to camp, although he was awakened long before dawn the next day. Then he ate breakfast, mounted and sat his horse not far away from Ewell, whom two soldiers had strapped into his saddle, and who was watching with eager eyes for the sunrise.

Harry, listening intently, heard no sound in front of them, save the wind rippling through the dwarfed forests of the Wilderness, and he knew that no battle had yet begun elsewhere. Sound would come far on that placid May morning, and it was a certainty that Ewell was nearest to contact with the enemy.

But Ewell did not yet move. All his men had been served with early breakfast, such as it was, and remained in silent masses, partly hidden by the forest and thickets. The dawn was cold, and Harry felt a little chill, but it soon passed, as the red edge of the sun showed over the eastern border of the Wilderness. Then the light spread toward the zenith, but the golden glow failed to penetrate the somber thickets.

"It's going to be a good day," said Harry to an aide.

"A good day for a battle."

"We'll hear from the Yankees soon. They can't fail to discover our exact location by sunrise, and they'll fight. Be sure of that."

It was now nearly six o'clock, and General Ewell, growing impatient, rode forward a little. Harry followed with his staff. A half-dozen Southern sharpshooters rose suddenly out of the thickets, and one of them dared to lay his hands on the reins of the general's horse. But Ewell was not offended. He looked down at the man and said:

"What is it, Strother?"

"Riflemen of the enemy are not more than three or four hundred yards away. If you go much farther, General, they will certainly see you and fire upon you."

"Thanks, Strother. So they've located us?"

"They're about to do it. They're feeling around. We've seen 'em in the bushes. We ask you not to go on, General. We wouldn't know what to do without you. There, sir! They're firing on our pickets!"

A half-dozen shots came from the front, and then a half-dozen or so in reply. Harry saw pink flashes, and then spirals of smoke rising.

More shots were fired presently on their right, and then others on their left. The Northern riflemen were evidently on a long line, and intended to make a thorough test of their enemy's strength. Harry had no doubt that Shepard was there. He would surely come to the point where his enemy was nearest, and his eyes and ears would be the keenest of all.

The little skirmish continued for a few minutes, extending along a winding line of nearly a mile through the thickets. Only two or three were wounded and nobody killed on the Southern side. Harry understood thoroughly, as Ewell had said, that the sharpshooters of the enemy were merely feeling for them. They wanted to know if a strong force was there, and now they knew.

The firing ceased, not in dying shots, but abruptly. The Wilderness in front of them returned to silence, broken only by the rippling leaves. Harry knew that the Northern sharpshooters had discovered all they wanted, and were now returning to their leaders.

Ewell turned his horse and rode back toward the main camp, his staff following. The cooking fires had been put out, the lines were formed and every gun was in position. As little noise as possible was allowed, while they waited for Grant; not for Grant himself, but for one of his lieutenants, pushed forward by his master hand.

Harry and most of the staff officers dismounted, holding their horses by the bridle. The young lieutenant often searched the thickets with his glasses, but he saw nothing. Nevertheless he knew that the enemy would come. Grant having set out to find his foe, would never draw back when he found him.

A much longer period of silence than he had expected passed. The sun, flaming red, was moving on toward the zenith, and no sounds of battle came from either right or left. The suspense became acute, almost unbearable, and it was made all the more trying by the blindness of that terrible forest. Harry felt at times as if he would rather fight in the open fields; but he knew that his commander-in-chief was right when he drew Grant into the shades of the Wilderness.

When the suspense became so great that heavy weights seemed to be pressing upon his nerves, rifle shots were fired in front, and skirmishers uttered the long, shrill rebel yell. Then above both shots and shouts rose the far, clear call of a bugle.

"Here they come!" Harry heard Ewell say to himself, and the next moment the sound of human voices was drowned in the thunder of great guns and the crash of fifty thousand rifles. The battle was so sudden and the charge so swift that it seemed to leap into full volume in an instant. Warren, a resolute and daring general, led the Northern column and it struck with such weight and force that the Southern division was driven back. Harry felt it yielding, as if the ground were sliding under his feet.

There was so much flame and smoke that he could not see well, but the sensation of slipping was distinct. General Ewell was near him, shouting orders. His hat had fallen off, and his round, bald head had turned red, either from the rush of blood or the cannon's glare. It shone like a red dome, but Harry knew that there was no better man in such a crisis than this veteran lieutenant of Stonewall Jackson.

The Wilderness, usually so silent, was an inferno now. The battle, despite its tremendous beginning, increased in violence and fury. Although Grant himself was not there, the spirit that had animated him at Shiloh and Vicksburg was. He had communicated it to his generals, and Warren brought every ounce of his strength into action. The long line of his bayonets gleamed through the thickets and the Northern artillery, superb as usual, rained shells upon the Southern army.

Ewell's men, fighting with all the courage and desperation that they had shown on so many a field, were driven back further and further. Ewell, strapped in his saddle, flourishing his sword, his round, bald head glowing, rode among them, bidding them to stand, that help would soon come. They continued to go backward, but those veterans of so many campaigns never lost cohesion nor showed sign of panic. Their own artillery and rifles replied in full volume. The heads of the charging columns were blown away, but other men took their places, and Warren's force came on with undiminished fire and strength.

Harry wondered if the attack at other points had been made with such impetuosity, but there was such a roar and crash about him that it was impossible to hear sounds of battle elsewhere. Men were falling very fast, but the general was unharmed, and neither the young lieutenant nor his horse was touched.

A sudden shout arose, and it was immediately followed by the piercing rebel yell, swelling wild and fierce above the tumult of the battle. Help was coming. Regiments in gray were charging down the paths and on the left flank rose the thunder of hoofs as a formidable body of cavalry under Sherburne, sabers aloft, swept down on the Northern flank.

Ewell's entire division stopped its retreat and, reinforced by the new men, charged directly upon the Northern bayonets. Men met almost face to face. The saplings and bushes were mown down by cannon and rifles and the air was full of bursting shells. From time to time Ewell's men uttered their fierce, defiant yell, and with a great bound of the heart Harry saw that they were gaining. Warren was being driven back. Two of his cannon were captured already, and the Southern men, feeling the glow of the advance after retreat, charged again and again, reckless of death. But Harry soon saw that ultimate victory here would rest with the South. The troops of Warren, exhausted by their early rush, were driven from one position to another by the seasoned veterans who faced them. The Confederates retained the captured cannon and thrust harder and harder. It became obvious that Warren must soon fall back to the main Northern line, and though the battle was still raging with great fury Ewell beckoned Harry to him.

"Don't stay here any longer," he shouted in his ear. "Ride to General Lee and tell him we're victorious at this point for the day at least!"

Harry saluted and galloped away through the thickets. Behind him the battle still roared and thundered. A stray shell burst just in front of him, and another just behind him, but he and his horse were untouched. Once or twice he glanced back and it looked as if the Wilderness were on fire, but he knew that it was instead the blaze of battle. He saw also that Ewell was still moving forward, winning more ground, and his heart swelled with gladness.

How proud Jackson would have been had he been able to see the valor and skill of his old lieutenant! Perhaps his ghost did really hover over the Wilderness, where a year before he had fallen in the moment of his greatest triumph! Harry urged his horse into a gallop. All his faculties now became acute. He was beyond the zone of fire, but the roar of the battle behind him seemed as loud as ever. Yet it was steadily moving back on the main Union lines, and there could be no doubt of Ewell's continued success.

The curves of the low hills and the thick bushes hid everything from Harry's sight, as he rode swiftly through the winding paths of the Wilderness. When the tumult sank at last he heard a new thunder in front of him, and now he knew that the Southern center under Hill had been attacked also, and with the greatest fierceness.

As Harry approached, the roar of the second battle became terrific. Uncertain where General Lee would now be, he rode through the sleet of steel, and found Hill engaged with the very flower of the Northern army. Hancock, the hero of Gettysburg, was making desperate exertions to crush him, pouring in brigade after brigade, while Sheridan, regardless of thickets, made charge after charge with his numerous cavalry.

Harry remained in the rear on his horse, watching this furious struggle. The day had become much darker, either from clouds or the vast volume of smoke, and the thickets were so dense that the officers often could not see their enemy at all, only their own men who stood close to them. The struggle was vast, confused, carried on under appalling conditions. The charging horsemen were sometimes swept from the saddle by bushes and not by bullets. Infantrymen stepped into a dark ooze left by spring rains, and pulling themselves out, charged, black to the waist with mud. Sometimes the field pieces became mired, and men and horses together dragged them to firmer ground.

Grant here, as before Ewell, continually reinforced his veterans, but Hill, although he was not able to advance, held fast. The difficult nature of the ground that Lee had chosen helped him. In marsh and thickets it was impossible for the more numerous enemy to outflank him. Harry saw Hill twice, a slender man, who had suffered severe wounds but one of the greatest fighters in the Southern army. He had been ordered to hold the center, and Harry knew now that he would do it, for the day at least. Night was not very far away, and Grant was making no progress.

He rode on in search of Lee and before he was yet beyond the range of fire he met Dalton, mounted and emerging from the smoke.

"The commander-in-chief, where is he?" asked Harry.

"On a little hill not far from here, watching the battle. I'm just returning with a dispatch from Hill."

"I saw that Hill was holding his ground."

"So my dispatch says, and it says also that he will continue to hold it. You come from Ewell?"

"Yes, and he has done more than stand fast. He was driven back at first, but when reinforcements came he drove Warren back in his turn, and took guns and prisoners."

"The chief will be glad to hear it. We'll ride together. Look out for your horse! He may go knee deep into mire at any time. Harry, the Wilderness looks even more somber to me than it did a year ago when we fought Chancellorsville."

"I feel the same way about it. But see, George, how they're fighting! General Hill is making a great resistance!"

"Never better. But if you look over those low bushes you can see General Lee on the hill."

Harry made out the figure of Lee on Traveller, outlined against the sky, with about a dozen men sitting on their horses behind him. He hurried forward as fast as he could. The commander-in-chief was reading a dispatch, while the fierce struggle in the thickets was going on, but when Harry saluted and Marshall told him that he had come to report the general put away the dispatch and said:

"What news from General Ewell?"

"General Ewell was at first borne back by the enemy's numbers, but when help came he returned to the charge, and has been victorious. He has gained much ground."

A gleam of triumph shot from Lee's eyes, usually so calm.

"Well done, Ewell!" he said. "The loss of a leg has not dimmed his ardor or judgment. I truly believe that if he were to lose the other one also he would still have himself strapped into the saddle and lead his men to victory. We thank you for the news you have brought, Lieutenant Kenton."

He put his glasses to his eyes and Harry and Dalton as usual withdrew to the rear of the staff. But they used their glasses also, bringing nearer to them the different phases of the battle, which now raged through the Wilderness. They saw at some points the continuous blaze of guns, and the acrid powder smoke, lying low, was floating through all the thickets.

But Harry now knew that the combat, however violent and fierce, was only a prelude. The sun was already setting, and they could not fight at night in those wild thickets, where men and guns would become mired and tangled beyond extrication. The great struggle, with both leaders hurling in their full forces, would come on the morrow.

The sun already hung very low, and in the twilight and smoke the savagery of the Wilderness became fiercer than ever. The dusk gathered around Lee, but his erect figure and white horse still showed distinctly through it. Harry, his spirit touched by the tremendous scenes in the very center of which he stood, regarded him with a fresh measure of respect and admiration. He was the bulwark of the Confederacy, and he did not doubt that on the morrow he would stop Grant as he had stopped the others.

The darkness increased, sweeping down like a great black pall over the Wilderness. The battle in the center and on the left died. Lee and his staff dismounting, prepared for the labors of the night.

CHAPTER XV
THE WILDERNESS

When night settled down over the Wilderness the two armies lay almost face to face on a long line. The preliminary battle, on the whole, had favored the Confederacy. Hill had held his ground and Ewell had gained, but Grant had immense forces, and, though naturally kind of heart, he had made up his mind to strike and keep on striking, no matter what the loss. He could afford to lose two men where the Confederacy lost one.

Harry, like many others, felt that this would be the great Northern general's plan. To-morrow's battle might end in Southern success, but Grant would be there to fight the following day with undiminished resolution. He was as sure of this as he was sure that the day would come.

The night itself was somber and sinister, the heavens dusky and a raw chill in the air. Heavy vapors rose from the marshes, and clouds of smoke from the afternoon's battle floated about over the thickets, poisoning the air as if with gas, and making the men cough as they breathed it. It made Harry's heart beat harder than usual, and his head felt as if it were swollen. Everything seemed clothed in a black mist with a slightly reddish tint.

A small fire had been built in a sheltered place for the commander-in-chief and his staff, and the cooks were preparing the supper, which was of the simplest kind. While they ate the food and drank their coffee, the darkness increased, with the faint lights of other fires showing here and there through it. Around the muddy places frogs croaked in defiance of armies, and, from distant points, came the crackling fire of skirmishers prowling in the dusk.

Harry's horse, saddled and bridled, was tied to a bush not far away. He knew that it was to be no night of rest for him, or any other member of the staff. Lee would be sending messages continually. Longstreet, although he had been marching hard, was not yet up on the right, and he and his veterans must be present when the shock of Grant's mighty attack came in the morning.

Hill, thin and pale, yet suffering from the effects of his wounds, but burning as usual with the fire of battle, rode up and consulted long and earnestly with Lee. Presently he went back to his own place nearer the center, and then Lee began to send away his staff one by one with messages. Harry was among the last to go, but he bore a dispatch to Longstreet.

He had heard that Longstreet had criticized Lee for ordering Pickett's famous charge at Gettysburg, but if so, Lee had taken no notice of it, and Longstreet had proved himself the same stalwart fighter as of old. He and the prompt arrival of his veterans had enabled Bragg to win Chickamauga, and it was not Longstreet's fault that the advantage gained there was lost afterward. Now Harry knew that he would be up in time with his seasoned veterans.

As the young lieutenant rode away he saw General Lee walking back and forth before the low fire, his hands clasped behind him, and his eyes as serious as those of any human being could be. Harry appreciated the immensity of his task, and in his heart was a sincere pity for the man who bore so great a burden. He was familiar with the statement that to Lee had been offered the command of the Northern armies at the beginning of the war, but believing his first duty was to his State he had gone with Virginia when Virginia reluctantly went out of the Union. Truly no one could regret the war more than he, and yet he had struck giant blows for its success.

A moment more and the tall figure standing beside the low fire was lost to sight. Then Harry rode among the thickets in the rear of the Confederate line and it was a weird and ghastly ride. Now and then his horse's feet sank in mud, and the frogs still dared to croak around the pools, making on such a night the most ominous of all sounds. It seemed a sort of funeral dirge for both North and South, a croak telling of the ruin and death that were to come on the morrow.

Damp boughs swept across his face, and the vapors, rising from the earth and mingled with the battle smoke, were still bitter to the tongue and poisonous to the breath. Rotten logs crushed beneath his horse's feet and Harry felt a shiver as if the hoofs had cut through a body of the dead. Riflemen rose out of the thickets, but he always gave them the password, and rode on without stopping.

Then came a space where he met no human being, the gap between Hill and Longstreet, and now the Wilderness became incredibly lonely and dreary. Harry felt that if ever a region was haunted by ghosts it was this. The dead of last year's battle might be lying everywhere, and as the breeze sprang up the melancholy thickets waved over them.

He was two-thirds of the way toward the point where he expected to find Longstreet when he heard the sough of a hoof in the mud behind him.

Harry listened and hearing the hoof again he was instantly on his guard. He did not know it, but the character of the night and the wild aspect of the Wilderness were bringing out all the primeval and elemental qualities in his nature. He was the great borderer, Henry Ware, in the Indian-haunted forest, feeling with a sixth sense, even a seventh sense, the presence of danger.

He was following a path, scarcely traceable, used by charcoal burners and wood-cutters, but when he heard the hoof a second time he turned aside into the deepest of the thickets and halted there. The hoofbeat came a third time, a little nearer, and then no more. Evidently the horseman behind him knew that he had turned aside, and was waiting and watching. He was surely an enemy of great skill and boldness, and it was equally sure that he was Shepard. Harry never felt a doubt that he was pursued by the formidable Union spy, and he felt too that he had never been in greater danger, as Shepard at such a moment would not spare his best friend.

But he was not afraid. Danger had become so common that one looked upon it merely as a risk. Moreover, he was never cooler or more ample of resource. He dismounted softly, standing beside his horse's head, holding the reins with one hand and a heavy pistol with the other. He suspected that Shepard would do the same, but he believed that his eyes and ears were the keener. The man must have been inside the Confederate lines all the afternoon. Probably he had seen Harry riding away, and, deftly appropriating a horse, had followed him. There was no end to Shepard's ingenuity and daring.

Harry's horse was trained to stand still indefinitely, and the young man, with the heavy pistol, who held the reins was also immovable.

The silence about him was so deep that Harry could hear the frogs croaking at a distant pool.

He waited a full five minutes, and now, like the wild animals, he relied more upon ear than eye. He had learned the faculty of concentration and he bent all his powers upon his hearing. Not the slightest sound could escape the tightly drawn drums of his ears.

He was motionless a full ten minutes. Nor did the horse beside him stir. It was a test of human endurance, the capacity to keep himself absolutely silent, but with every nerve attuned, while he waited for an invisible danger. And those minutes were precious, too. The value of not a single one of them could have been measured or weighed. It was his duty to reach Longstreet at speed, because the general and his veterans must be in line in the morning, when the battle was joined. Yet the incessant duel between Shepard and himself was at its height again, and he did not yet see how he could end it.

Harry felt that it must be essentially a struggle of patience, but when he waited a few minutes longer, the idea to wait with ears close to the earth, one of the oldest devices of primitive man, occurred to him. It was fairly dry in the bushes, and he lay down, pressing his ear to the soil. Then he heard a faint sound, as if some one crawling through the grass, like a wild animal stalking its prey. It was Shepard, of course, and then Harry planned his campaign. Shepard had left his horse, and was endeavoring to reach him by stealth.

Leaving his own horse, he crept a little to the right, and then rising carefully in another thicket he picked out every dark spot in the gloom. He made out presently the figure of a riderless horse, standing partly behind the trunk of an oak, larger than most of those that grew in the Wilderness.

Harry knew that it was Shepard's mount and that Shepard himself was some distance in front of it creeping toward the thicket which he supposed sheltered his foe. There was barely enough light for Harry to see the horse's head and regretfully he raised his heavy pistol. But it had to be done, and when his aim was true he pulled the trigger.

The report of the pistol was almost like the roar of a cannon in the desolate Wilderness and made Harry himself jump. Then he promptly threw himself flat upon his face. Shepard's answering fire came from a point about thirty yards in front of the horse, and the bullet passed very close over Harry's head. It was a marvelous shot to be made merely at the place from which a sound had come. It all passed in a flash, and the next moment Harry heard the sound of a horse falling and kicking a little. Then it too was still.

He remained only a half minute in the grass. Then he began to creep back, curving a little in his course, toward his own horse. He did not believe that Shepard's faculty of hearing was as keen as his own, and he moved with the greatest deftness. He relied upon the fact that Shepard had not yet located the horse, and if Harry could reach it quickly it would not be hard for him, a mounted man, to leave behind Shepard, dismounted. It might be possible, too, that Shepard had gone back to see about his own horse, not knowing that it was slain.

He saw the dusky outline of his horse, and, rising, made two or three jumps. Then he snatched the rein loose, sprang upon his back, and lying down upon his neck to avoid bullets, crashed away, reckless of bushes and briars. He heard one bullet flying near him, but he laughed in delight and relief as his horse sped on toward Longstreet.

He did not diminish his speed until he had gone two or three miles, and then, knowing that Shepard had been left hopelessly behind, even if he had attempted pursuit, he brought his horse down to a walk, and laughed. There was a bit of nervous excitement in the laugh. He had outwitted Shepard again. He had never seen the man, but it did not enter his mind that it was not he. Each had scored largely over the other from time to time, but Harry believed that he was at least even.

He steadied his nerves now and rode calmly toward Longstreet, coming soon upon his scouts, who informed him that the heavy columns were not far behind, marching with stalwart step to their appointed place in the line. But it was Harry's business to see Longstreet himself, and he continued his way toward the center of the division, where they told him the general could be found.

He rode forward and in the moonlight recognized Longstreet at once, a heavy-set, bearded man, mounted on a strong bay horse. He had a very small staff, and he was first to notice the young lieutenant advancing. He knew Harry well, having seen him with Lee at Gettysburg and with Jackson before. He stopped and said abruptly:

"You come from the commander-in-chief, do you not?"

"Yes, sir," replied Harry, "and I've been coming as fast as I could."

He did not deem it necessary to say anything about his encounter with Shepard.

"There has been heavy fighting. What are his orders?"

Harry told him, also giving him a written message, which the general read by the light of a torch an aide held.

"You can tell General Lee that all my men will be in position for battle before dawn," said the Georgian crisply.

Even as he spoke, Harry heard the heavy, regular tread of the brigades marching forward through the Wilderness. He saluted General Longstreet.

"I shall return at once with your message," he said.

But Harry, having had one such experience, was resolved not to risk another. He would make a wider circuit in the rear of the army. Shepard, on foot, and anxious to avenge his defeat, might be waiting for him, but he would go around him. So when he started back he made a wide curve, and soon was in the darkness and silence again.

He had a good horse and his idea of direction being very clear he rode swiftly in the direction he had chosen. But his curve was so great that when he reached the center of it he was so far in the rear of the army that no sound came from it. If the skirmishers were still firing the reports of their rifles were lost in the distance. Where he rode the only noises were those made by the wild animals that inhabited the Wilderness, creatures that had settled back into their usual haunts after the armies had passed beyond.

Once a startled deer sprang from a clump of bushes and crashed away through the thickets. Rabbits darted from his path, and an owl, wondering what all the disturbance was about, hooted mournfully from a bough.

Long before dawn Harry reached the Southern sentinels in the center and was then passed to General Lee, who remained at the same camp, sitting on a log by some smothered coals. Several other members of his staff had returned already, and the general, looking up when Harry came forward, merely said:

"Well!"

"I have seen General Longstreet, sir," said Harry, "and he bids me tell you that he and his men will be in position before dawn. He was nearly up when I left, and he has also sent you this note."

He handed the note to General Lee, who, bending low over the coals, read it.

"Everything goes well," he said with satisfaction. "We shall be ready for them. What time is it, Peyton?"

"Five minutes past four o'clock, sir."

"Then I think the attack should come within an hour."

"Perhaps before daybreak, sir."

"Perhaps. And even after the sun begins to rise it will be like twilight in this gloomy place."

Grant, in truth, prompt and ready as always, had ordered the advance to be begun at half-past four, but Meade, asking more time for arrangements and requesting that it be delayed until six, he had consented to a postponement until five o'clock and no more.

Harry had one more message to carry, a short distance only, and on his return he found the Invincibles posted on the commander-in-chief's right, and not more than two hundred yards away.

"You must be a body guard for the general," he said to Colonel Leonidas Talbot.

"There could be no greater honor for the Invincibles, nor could General Lee have a better guard."

"I'm sure of that, sir."

"What's happening, Harry? Tell us what's been going on in the night!"

"Our line of battle has been formed. General Longstreet and his men on the right are soon to be in touch with General Hill. I returned from him a little while ago. I can't yet smell the dawn, but I think the battle will come before then."

Harry rode back and resumed his place beside Dalton. The troops everywhere were on their feet, cannon and rifles ready, because it was a certainty that the two armies would meet very early.

In fact, the Army of Northern Virginia began to slide slowly forward. It was not the habit of these troops to await attack. Lee nearly always had taken the offensive, and the motion of his men was involuntary. They felt that the enemy was there and they must go to meet him.

"What time is it now?" whispered Dalton.

Harry was barely able to discern the face of his watch.

"Ten minutes to five," he replied.

"And the dawn comes early. It won't be long before Grant comes poking his nose through the Wilderness."

Harry was silent. A few minutes more, and there was a sudden crackle of rifles in front of them.

"The dawn isn't here, but Grant is," said Harry.

The crackling fire doubled and tripled, and then the fire of the Southern rifles replied in heavy volume. The lighter field guns opened with a crash, and the heavier batteries followed with rolling thunder. Leaves and twigs fell in showers, and men fell with them. The deep Northern cheer swelled through the Wilderness and the fierce rebel yell replied.

Gray dawn, rising as if with effort, over the sodden Wilderness found two hundred thousand men locked fast in battle. It might have been a bright sun elsewhere, but not here among the gloomy shades and the pine barrens. The firing was already so tremendous that the smoke hung low and thick, directly over the tops of the bushes, and the men, as they fought, breathed mixed and frightful vapors.

Both sides fought for a long time in a heavy, smoky dusk, that was practically night. Officers coming from far points, led, compass in hand, having no other guide save the roar of battle. As the Southern leaders had foreseen, Grant was throwing in the full strength of his powerful army, hoping with superior numbers and better equipment to crush Lee utterly that day.

The great Northern artillery was raking the whole Southern front. Hancock, the superb, was hurling the heavy Northern masses directly upon the main position of the South. He had half the Army of the Potomac, and at other points Warren, Wadsworth, Sedgwick and Burnside were advancing with equal energy and contempt of death. Fiercer and fiercer grew the conflict. Hancock, remembering how he had held the fatal hill at Gettysburg, and resolved to win a complete victory now, poured in regiment after regiment. But in all the fire and smoke and excitement and danger he did not neglect to keep a cool head. Hearing that a portion of Longstreet's corps was near, he sent a division and numerous heavy artillery to attack it, driving it back after a sanguinary struggle of more than an hour.

Then he redoubled his attack upon the Southern center, compelling it to give ground, though slowly. Harry felt that gliding movement backward and a chill ran through his blood. The heavy masses of Grant and his powerful artillery were prevailing. The strongest portion of the Southern army was being forced back, and a gap was cut between Hill and Longstreet. Had Hancock perceived the gap that he had made he might have severed the Southern army, inflicting irretrievable retreat, but the smoke and the dusk of the Wilderness hid it, and the moment passed into one of the great "Ifs" of history.

Harry, on horseback, witnessed this conflict, all the more terrible because of the theater in which it was fought. The batteries and the riflemen alike were frequently hidden by the thickets. The great banks of smoke hung low, only to be split apart incessantly by the flashes of fire from the big guns. But the bullets were more dangerous than the cannon balls and shells. They whistled and shrieked in thousands and countless thousands.

Lee sat on his horse impassive, watching as well as he could the tide of battle. Messengers covered with smoke and sweat had informed him of the gap between Hill and Longstreet, and he was dispatching fresh troops to close it up. Harry saw the Invincibles march by. The two colonels at their head beheld Lee on his white horse, and their swords flew from their scabbards as they made a salute in perfect unison. Close behind them rode St. Clair and Happy Tom, and they too saluted in like manner. Lee took off his hat in reply and Harry choked. "About to die, we salute thee," he murmured under his breath.

Then with a shout the Invincibles, their officers at their head, plunged into the fire and smoke, and were lost from Harry's view. But he could not stay there long and wonder at their fate. In a few minutes he was riding to Longstreet with a message for him to bear steadily toward Hill, that the gap might be closed entirely, and as soon as possible.

He galloped behind the lines, but bullets fell all around him, and often a shell tore the earth. The air had become more bitter and poisonous. Fumes from swamps seemed to mingle with the smoke and odors of burned gunpowder. His lips and his tongue were scorched. But he kept on, without exhaustion or mishap, and reached Longstreet, who had divined his message.

"The line will be solid in a few minutes," he said, and while the battle was still at its height on the long front he touched hands with Hill. Then both drove forward with all their might against Hancock, rushing to the charge, with the Southern fire and recklessness of death that had proved irresistible on so many fields. The advance, despite the most desperate efforts of Hancock and his generals, was stopped. Then he was driven back. All the ground gained at so much cost was lost and the Southern troops, shouting in exultation, pushed on, pouring in a terrible rifle fire. Longstreet, in his eagerness, rode a little ahead of his troops to see the result. Turning back, he was mistaken in the smoke by his own men for a Northern cavalryman, and they fired upon him, just as Jackson had been shot down by his own troops in the dusk at Chancellorsville.

The leader fell from his horse, wounded severely, and the troops advancing to victory became confused. The rumor spread that Longstreet had been killed. There was no one to give orders, and the charge stopped. Harry and a half-dozen others who had seen the accident or heard of it, galloped to Lee, who at once rode into the very thick of the command, giving personal orders and sending his aides right and left with others. The whole division was reformed under his eye, and he sent it anew to the attack.

The battle now closed in with the full strength of both armies. Hancock strove to keep his place. The valiant Wadsworth had been killed already. The dense thickets largely nullified Grant's superior numbers. Lee poured everything on Hancock, who was driven from every position. Fighting furiously behind a breastwork built the night before, he was driven from that too.

Often in the dense shades the soldiers met one another face to face and furious struggles hand-to-hand ensued. Bushes and trees, set on fire by the shells, burned slowly like torches put there to light up the ghastly scene of man's bravery and folly. Jenkins, a Confederate general, was killed and colonels and majors fell by the dozen. But neither side would yield, and Grant hurried help to his hard-pressed troops.

Harry had been grazed on the shoulder by a bullet, but his horse was unharmed, and he kept close to Lee, who continued to direct the battle personally. He knew that they were advancing. Once more the genius of the great Confederate leader was triumphing. Grant, the redoubtable and tenacious, despite his numbers, could set no trap for him! Instead he had been drawn into battle on a field of Lee's own choosing.

The conflict had now continued for a long time, and was terrible in all its aspects. It was far past noon, and for miles a dense cloud of smoke hung over the Wilderness, which was filled with the roar of cannon, the crash of rifles and the shouts of two hundred thousand men in deadly conflict. The first meeting of the two great protagonists of the war, Lee and Grant, was sanguinary and terrible, beyond all expectation.

Hundreds fell dead, their bodies lying hidden under the thickets. The forest burned fiercely here and there, casting circles of lurid light over the combatants, while the wind rained down charred leaves and twigs. The fires spread and joined, and at points swept wide areas of the forest, yet the fury of the battle was not diminished, the two armies forgetting everything else in their desire to crush each other.

Harry's horse was killed, as he sat near Lee, but he quickly obtained another, and not long afterward he was sent with a second message to Ewell. He rode on a long battle front, not far behind the lines, and he shuddered with awe as he looked upon the titanic struggle. The smoke was often so heavy and the bushes so thick that he could not see the combatants, except when the flame of the firing or the burning trees lighted up a segment of the circle.

Halfway to Ewell and he stopped when he saw two familiar figures, sitting on a log. They were elderly men in uniforms riddled by bullets. The right arm of one and the left leg of the other were tightly bandaged. Their faces were very white and it was obvious that they were sitting there, because they were not strong enough to stand.

Harry stopped. No message, no matter how important, could have kept him from stopping.

"Colonel Talbot! Colonel St. Hilaire!" he cried.

"Yes, here we are, Harry," replied Colonel Leonidas Talbot in a voice, thin but full of courage. "Hector has been shot through the leg and has lost much blood, but I have bound up his wound, and he has done as much for my arm, which has been bored through from side to side by a bullet, which must have been as large as my fist."

"And so for a few minutes," said Lieutenant-Colonel St. Hilaire, valiantly, "we must let General Lee conduct the victory alone."

"And the Invincibles!" exclaimed Harry, horrified. "Are they all gone but you?"

"Not at all," replied Colonel Talbot. "There is so much smoke about that you can't see much, but if it clears a little you will behold Lieutenant St. Clair and the youth rightly called Happy Tom and some three score others, lying among the bushes, not far ahead of you, giving thorough attention to the enemy."

"And is that all that's left of the Invincibles?"

"It's a wonder that they're so many. You were right about this man, Grant, Harry. He's a fighter, and their artillery is numerous and wonderful. John Carrington himself must be in front of us. We have not seen him, but the circumstantial evidence is conclusive. Nobody else in the world could have swept this portion of the Wilderness with shell and shrapnel in such a manner. Why, he has mowed down the bushes in long swathes as the scythe takes the grass and he has cut down our men with them. How does the battle go elsewhere?"

"We're succeeding. We're driving 'em back. I can stop only a moment now. I'm on my way to General Ewell."

"Then hurry. Don't be worried about us. I'll help Hector and Hector will help me. And do you curve further to the rear, Harry. The worst thing that a dispatch bearer can do is to get himself shot."

Waving his hand in farewell Harry galloped away. He knew that Colonel Talbot had given him sound advice, and he bore back from the front, coming once more into lonely thickets, although the flash of the battle was plainly visible in front of him, and its roar filled his ears. Yet when he rode alone he almost expected to see Shepard rise up before him, and bid him halt. His encounters with this man had been under such startling circumstances that it now seemed the rule, and not the exception, for him to appear at any moment.

But Shepard did not come. Instead Harry began to see the badly wounded of his own side drifting to the rear, helping one another as hurt soldiers learn to do. Two of them he allowed to hang on his stirrups a little while.

"They're fighting hard," said one, a long, gaunt Texan, "an' they're so many they might lap roun' us. This man of theirs, Grant, ain't much of a fellow to get scared, but I guess Marse Bob will take care of him just ez he has took care of the others who came into Virginia."

"They're led in the main attack by Hancock," said the other, a Virginian. "I caught a glimpse of him through the smoke, just as I had a view of him for a minute back there by the clump of trees on the ridge at Gettysburg."

"Are you one of Pickett's men?" asked Harry.

"I am, sir, one of the few that's left. I went clear to the clump of trees and how I got back I've never known. It was a sort of red dream, in which I couldn't pick out anything in particular, but I was back with the army, carrying three bullets that the doctors took away from me, and here I've gathered up two more they'll rob me of in just the same way."

He spoke quite cheerfully, and when Harry, curving again, was compelled to release them, both, although badly wounded, wished him good luck.

He found General Ewell in front, stamping back and forth on his crutches, watching the battle with excitement.

"And so you're here again, Harry. Well it's good news at present!" he cried. "It seems that their man, Grant, is going to school to Lee just like the others."

"But some pupils learn too fast, sir!"

"That's so, but, Harry, I wish I could see more of the field. An invisible battle like this shakes my nerves. Batteries that we can't see send tornadoes of shot and shell among us. Riflemen, by the thousands, hidden in the thickets rain bullets into our ranks. It's inhuman, wicked, and our only salvation lies in the fact that it's as bad for them as it is for us. If we can't see them they can't see us."

"You can hold your ground here?"

"Against anything and everything. Tell General Lee that we intend to eat our suppers on the enemy's ground."

"That's all he wants to know."

As Harry rode back he saw that the first fires were spreading, passing over new portions of the battlefield. Sparks flew in myriads and fine, thin ashes were mingled with the powder smoke. The small trees, burnt through, fell with a crash, and the flames ran as if they were alive up boughs. Other trees fell too, cut through by cannon balls, and some were actually mown down by sheets of bullets, as if they had been grass.

His way now led through human wreckage, made all the more appalling by an approaching twilight, heavy with fumes and smoke, and reddened with the cannon and rifle blaze. His frightened horse pulled wildly at the bit, and tried to run away, but Harry held him to the path, although he stepped more than once in hot ashes and sprang wildly. The dead were thick too and Harry was in horror lest the hoof of his horse be planted upon some unheeding face.

He knew that the day was waning fast and that the dark was due in some degree to the setting sun, and not wholly to the smoke and ashes. Yet the fury of the battle was sustained. The southern left maintained the ground that it had gained, and in the center and right it could not be driven back. It became obvious to Grant that Lee was not to be beaten in the Wilderness. His advance suffered from all kinds of disadvantages. In the swamps and thickets he could mass neither his guns nor his cannon. Communications were broken, the telegraph wires could be used but little and as the twilight darkened to night he let the attack die.

Harry was back with the commander-in-chief, when the great battle of the Wilderness, one of the fiercest ever fought, sank under cover of the night. It was not open and spectacular like Gettysburg, but it had a gloomy and savage grandeur all its own. Grant had learned, like the others before him, that he could not drive headlong over Lee, but sitting in silence by his campfire, chewing his cigar, he had no thought, unlike the others, of turning back. Nearly twenty thousand of his men had fallen, but huge resources and a President who supported him absolutely were behind him and he was merely planning a new method of attack.

In the Southern camp there was exultation, but it was qualified and rather grim. These men, veterans of many battles and able to judge for themselves, believed that they had won the victory, but they knew that it was by no means decisive. The numerous foe with his powerful artillery was still before them. They could see his campfires shining through the thickets, and their spies told them that, despite his great losses, there was no sign of retreat in Grant's camp.

An appalling night settled down on the Wilderness. The North American Continent never saw one more savage and terrible. Twenty thousand wounded were scattered through the thickets and dense shades, and spreading fires soon brought death to many whom the bullets had not killed at once. The smoke, the mists and vapors gathered into one dense cloud, that hung low and made everything clammy to the touch.

Lee stood under the boughs of an oak, and ate food that had been prepared for him hastily. But, as Harry saw, the act was purely mechanical. He was watching as well as he could what was going on in front, and he was giving orders in turns to his aides. Harry's time had not yet come, and he kept his eyes on his chief.

There was no exultation in the face of Lee. He had drawn Grant into the Wilderness and then he had held him fast in a battle of uncommon size and fierceness. But nothing was decided. He had studied the career of Grant, and he knew that he had a foe of great qualities with whom to deal. He would have to fight him again, and fight very soon. He heard too with a sorrow, hard to conceal, the reports of his own losses. They were heavy enough and the gaps now made could never be refilled. The Army of Northern Virginia, which had been such a powerful instrument in his hands, must fight with ever diminishing numbers.

Harry was sent to inquire into the condition of Longstreet, whom he found weak physically and suffering much pain. But the veteran was upborne by the success of the day and his belief in ultimate victory. He bade Harry tell the commander-in-chief that his men were fit to fight again and better than ever, at the first shoot of dawn.

Harry rode back in the night, the burning trees serving him for torches. Nearly all the soldiers were busy. Some were gathering up the wounded and others were building breastworks. His eyes were reddened by the powder-smoke, and often the heavy black masses of vapor were impenetrable, save where the forest burned. Now he came to a region where the dead and wounded were so thick that he dismounted and led his horse, lest a hoof be planted upon any one of them. But he noticed that here as in other battles the wounded made but little complaint. They suffered in silence, waiting for their comrades to take them away.

Then he passed around a section of forest that was burning fiercely. Here Southern and Union soldiers had met on terms of peace and were making desperate efforts to save their helpless comrades. Harry would have been glad to give aid himself, but he was too well trained now to turn aside when he rode for Lee.

He saw many dark figures passing before the flaming background, and as he walked more slowly than he thought, he saw one that looked remarkably familiar to him. It was impossible to see the face, but he knew the walk and the lift of the shoulders. Discipline gave way to impulse now, and he ran forward crying:

"Dick! Dick!"

Dick Mason, who had just dragged a wounded man beyond the range of the flames, turned at the sound of the voice. Even had Harry seen his face at first he would not have known him nor would Dick have known Harry. Both were black with ashes, smoke and burned gunpowder. But Dick knew the voice in an instant. Once more were the two cousins to meet in peace on an unfinished battlefield.

Each driven by the same impulse stepped forward, and their hands met in the strong grasp of blood kindred and friendship, which war itself could not sever.

"You're alive, Harry!" said Dick. "It seems almost impossible after what has happened to-day."

"And you too are all right. Not harmed, I see, though your face is an African black."

"I should call your own color dark and smoky."

"I wasn't sure that you were in the East. When did you come?"

"With General Grant, and I knew that you were on General Lee's staff. I've a message to give him by you. Oh! you needn't laugh. It's a good straight talk."

"Go ahead then and say it to me."

"You say to General Lee that it's all over. Tell him to quit and send his soldiers home. If he doesn't he'll be crushed."

Harry laughed again and waved his finger at the somber battlefield, upon which he stood.

"Does this look like it?" he asked. "We're farther forward to-night than we were this morning. Wouldn't General Grant be glad if he could say as much?"

"It makes no difference. I know you don't believe me, but it's so. The North is prepared as it never was before. And Grant will hammer and hammer forever. We know what a man Lee is. The whole North admits it, but I tell you the sun of the South is setting."

"You're growing poetical and poetry is no argument."

"But unlimited men, unlimited cannon and rifles, unlimited ammunition and supplies and a general who is willing to use them, are. Of course I know that you can't carry any such message to General Lee, but I feel it to be the truth."

"We've a great general and a great army that say, no."

Nobody paid any attention to the two. It was merely another one of those occasions when men of the opposing sides stood together amid the dead and wounded, and talked in friendly fashion. But Harry knew that he could not delay long.

"I've got to go, Dick," he said. "And I've a message too, one that I want you to deliver to General Grant."

"What is it?"

"Tell him that we've more than held our own to-day, and that we'll thrash him like thunder to-morrow, and whenever and wherever he may choose, no matter what the odds are against us."

Dick laughed.

"I see that you won't believe even a little bit of what I tell you," he said "and maybe if I were in your place I wouldn't either. But it's true all the same. Good-by, Harry."

The two hands, covered with battle grime, met again in the strong grasp of blood kindred and friendship.

"Take care of yourself, old man!"

The words, exactly alike, were uttered by the two simultaneously.

Both were stirred deeply. Harry sprang on his horse, looked back once, waving his hand, and rode rapidly to General Lee. Later in the night, he received permission to hunt up the Invincibles, his heart full of fear that they had perished utterly in the gloomy pit called the Wilderness, lit now only by the fire of death.

He left his horse with an orderly and walked toward the point where he had last seen them. He passed thousands of soldiers, many wounded, but silent as usual, while the unhurt were sleeping where they had dropped. The Invincibles were not at the point where he had seen them last, and the colonels of several scattered regiments could not tell him what had become of them. But he continued to seek them although the fear was growing in his heart that the last man of the Invincibles had died under the Northern cannon.

His search led toward the enemy's lines. Almost unconsciously he went in that direction, however, his knowledge of the two colonels telling him that they would take the same course. He turned into a little cove, partly sheltered by the dwarfed trees and he heard a thin voice saying:

"Nonsense, Leonidas. I scarcely felt it, but yours, old friend, is pretty bad. You must let me attend to it. Keep still! I'll adjust the bandage."

"Hector, why do you make a fuss over me, when I'm only slightly hurt, and sacrifice yourself, a severely injured man!"

"With all due respect you'd better let me attend to you both," said a voice that Harry recognized as St. Clair's.

"And maybe I could help a little," said another that he knew to be Happy Tom's. But their voices, like those of the colonels, were weak. Still he had positive proof that they were alive, and, as his heart gave a joyful throb or two, he stepped into the glade. There was enough light for him to see Colonel Leonidas Talbot, and Lieutenant-Colonel Hector St. Hilaire, sitting side by side on the grass with their backs against the earthly wall, very pale from loss of blood, but with heads erect and eyes shining with a certain pride. St. Clair and Langdon lay on the grass, one with an old handkerchief, blood-soaked, bound about his head and the other with a bandage tightly fastened over his left shoulder. Beyond them lay a group of soldiers.

"Good evening, heroes!" said Harry lightly as he stepped forward.

He was welcomed with an exclamation of joy from them all.

"We meet again, Harry," said Colonel Talbot, "and it is the second time since morning. I fancy that second meetings to-day have not been common. We have the taste of success in our mouths, but you'll excuse us for not rising to greet you. We are all more or less affected by the missiles of the enemy and for some hours at least neither walking nor standing will be good for us."

"Mohammed must come to all the mountains," said St. Clair, weakly holding out a hand.

Harry greeted them all in turn, and sat down with them. He was overflowing with sympathy, but it was not needed.

"A glorious day," said Colonel Leonidas Talbot.

"Truly," said Harry.

"A most glorious day," said Lieutenant-Colonel Hector St. Hilaire.

"Most truly," said Harry.

"An especially glorious day for the Invincibles," said Colonel Talbot.

"The most glorious of all possible days for the Invincibles," said Lieutenant-Colonel Hector St. Hilaire.

There was an especial emphasis to their words that aroused Harry's attention.

"The Invincibles have had many glorious days," he said. "Why should this be the most glorious of them all?"

"We went into battle one hundred and forty-seven strong," replied Colonel Talbot quietly, "and we came out with one hundred and forty-seven casualties, thirty-nine killed and one hundred and eight wounded. We lay no claim to valor, exceeding that of many other regiments in General Lee's glorious army, but we do think we've made a fairly excellent record. Do you see those men?"

He pointed to a silent group stretched upon the turf, and Harry nodded.

"Not one of them has escaped unhurt, but most of us will muster up strength enough to meet the enemy again to-morrow, when our great general calls."

Harry's throat contracted for a moment.

"I know it, Colonel Talbot," he said. "The Invincibles have proved themselves truly worthy of their name. General Lee shall hear of this."

"But in no boastful vein, Harry," said Colonel Talbot. "We would not have you to speak thus of your friends."

"I do not have to boast for you. The simple truth is enough. I shall see that a surgeon comes here at once to attend to your wounded. Good night, gentlemen."

"Good night," said the four together. Harry walked back toward General Lee's headquarters, full of pride in his old comrades.

CHAPTER XVI
SPOTTSYLVANIA

Harry secured a little sleep toward morning, and, although his nervous tension had been very great, when he lay down, he felt greatly strengthened in body and mind. He awakened Dalton in turn, and the two, securing a hasty breakfast, sat near the older members of the staff, awaiting orders. The commander-in-chief was at the edge of the little glade, talking earnestly with Hill, and several other important generals.

Harry often saw through the medium of his own feelings, and the rim of the sun, beginning to show over the eastern edge of the Wilderness, was blood red. The same crimson and sinister tinge showed through the west which was yet in the dusk. But in east and west there were certain areas of light, where the forest fires yet smoldered.

Both sides had thrown up hasty breastworks of earth or timber, but the two armies were unusually silent. A space of perhaps a mile and a half lay between them, but as the light increased neither moved. There was no crackle of rifle fire along their fronts. The skirmishers, usually so active, seemed to be exhausted, and the big guns were at rest. The fierce and tremendous fighting of the two days before seemed to have taken all the life out of both North and South.

Harry, inured to war, understood the reasons for silence and lack of movement. Grant had been drawn into a region that he did not like, where he could not use his superior numbers to advantage, and he must be shuddering at the huge losses he had suffered already. He would seek better ground. Lee too, was in no condition to take advantage of his successful defense. The old days when he could send Jackson on a great turning movement, to fall with all the crushing impact of a surprise upon the Northern flank, were gone forever.

Stuart, the brilliant cavalryman, was there, but his men were not numerous enough, and, however brilliant, he was not Jackson.

The sun rose higher. Midmorning came, and the two armies still lay close. Harry grew stronger in his opinion that they would not fight again that day, although he watched, like the others, for any sign of movement in the Northern camp.

Noon came, and the same dead silence. The fires had burned themselves out now and the dusk that had reigned over the Wilderness, before the battle, recovered its ground, thickened still further by the vast quantities of smoke still hanging low under a cloudy sky. But the aspect of the Wilderness itself was more mournful than ever. Coals smoldered in the burned areas, and now and then puffs of wind picked up the hot ashes and sent them in the faces of the soldiers. Thickets and bushes had been cut down by bullets and cannon balls, and lay heaped together in tangled confusion. Back of the lines, the surgeons, with aching backs, toiled over the wounded, as they had toiled through the night.

Harry saw nearly the whole Southern front. The members of Lee's staff were busy that day, carrying orders to all his generals to rectify their lines, and to be prepared, to the last detail, for another tremendous assault. It was not until the afternoon that he was able to look up the Invincibles again. The two colonels and the two lieutenants were doing well, and the colonels were happy.

"We've already been notified," said Colonel Talbot, "that we're to retain our organization as a regiment. We're to have about a hundred new men now, the fragments of destroyed regiments. Of course, they won't be like the veterans of the Invincibles, but a half-dozen battles like that of yesterday should lick them into shape."

"I should think so," said Harry.

"Do you believe that Grant is retreating?" asked Lieutenant-Colonel St. Hilaire.

"Our scouts don't say so."

"Then he is merely putting off the evil day. The sooner he withdraws the more men he will save. No Yankee general can ever get by General Lee. Keep that in your mind, Harry Kenton."

Harry was silent, but rejoicing to find that his friends would soon recover from their wounds, he went back to his place, and saw all the afternoon pass, without any movement indicating battle.

Night came again and the scouts reported to Lee that the Union army was breaking camp, evidently with the intention of getting out of the Wilderness and marching to Fredericksburg. Harry was with the general when he received the news, and he saw him think over it long. Other scouts brought in the same evidence.

Harry did not know what the general thought, but as for himself, although he was too young to say anything, it was incredible that Grant should retreat. It was not at all in accordance with his character, now tested on many fields, and his resources also were too great for withdrawal.

But the night was very dark and no definite knowledge yet came out of it. Lee stayed by his little campfire and received reports. Far after dusk Harry saw the look of doubt disappear from his eyes, and then he began to send out messengers. It was evident that he had formed his opinion, and intended to act upon it at once.

He beckoned to Harry and Dalton, and bade them go together with written instructions to General Anderson, who had taken the place of General Longstreet.

"You will stay with General Anderson subject to his orders," he said, as Harry and Dalton, saluting, rode toward Anderson's command.

Their way led through torn, tangled and burned thickets. Sometimes a horse sprang violently to one side and neighed in pain. His hoof had come down on earth, yet so hot that it scorched like fire. Now and then sparks fell upon them, but they pursued their way, disregarding all obstacles, and delivered their sealed orders to General Anderson, who at once gathered up his full force, and marched away from the heart of the Wilderness toward Spottsylvania Court House.

Harry surmised that Grant was attempting some great turning movement, and Lee, divining it, was sending Anderson to meet his advance. He never knew whether it was positive knowledge or a happy guess.

But he was quite sure that the night's ride was one of the most singular and sinister ever made by an army. If any troops ever marched through the infernal regions it was they. In this part of the Wilderness the fires had been of the worst. Trees still smoldered. In the hollows, where the bushes had grown thickest, were great beds of coals. The smoke which the low heavy skies kept close to the earth was thick and hot. Gusts of wind sent showers of sparks flying, and, despite the greatest care to protect the ammunition, they marched in constant danger of explosion.

Harry thought at one time that General Anderson intended to camp in the Wilderness for the night, but he soon saw that it was impossible. One could not camp on hot ground in a smoldering forest.

"I believe it's a march till day," he said to Dalton. "It's bound to be. If a man were to lie down here, he'd find himself a mass of cinders in the morning, and it will take us till daylight and maybe past to get out of the Wilderness."

"If he didn't burn to death he'd choke to death. I never breathed such smoke before."

"That's because it's mixed with ashes and the fumes of burned gunpowder. A villainous compound like this can't be called air. How long is it until dawn?"

"About three hours, I think."

"You remember those old Greek stories about somebody or other going down to Hades, and then having a hard climb out again. We're the modern imitators. If this isn't Hades then I don't know what it is."

"It surely is. Phew, but that hurt!"

"What happened?"

"I brushed my hand against a burning bush. The result was not happy. Don't imitate me."

Dalton's horse leaped to one side, and he had difficulty in keeping the saddle. His hoof had been planted squarely in the midst of a mass of hot twigs.

"The sooner I get out of this Inferno or Hades of a place the happier I'll be!" said Dalton.

"I've never seen the like," said Harry, "but there's one thing about it that makes me glad."

"And what's the saving grace?"

"That it's in Virginia and not in Kentucky, though for the matter of that it couldn't be in Kentucky."

"And why couldn't it be in Kentucky?"

"Because there's no such God-forsaken region in all that state of mine."

"It certainly gets upon one's soul," said Dalton, looking at the gloomy region, so terribly torn by battle.

"But if we keep going we're bound to come out of it some time or other."

"And we're not stopping. A man can't make his bed on a mass of coals, and there'll be no rest for us until we're clear out of the Wilderness."

They marched on a long time, and, as day dawned, hundreds of voices united in a shout of gladness. Behind them were the shades of the Wilderness, that dismal region reeking with slaughter and ruin, and before them lay firm soil, and green fields, in all the flush of a brilliant May morning.

"Well, we did come out of Hades, Harry," said Dalton.

"And it does look like Heaven, but the trouble with our Hades, George, is that the inmates will follow us. Put your glasses to your eyes and look off there."

"Horsemen as sure as we're sitting in our own saddles."

"And Northern horsemen, too. Their uniforms are new enough for me to tell their color. I take it that Grant's vanguard has moved by our right flank and has come out of the Wilderness."

"And our surmises that we were to meet it are right. Spottsylvania Court House is not far away, and maybe we are bound for it."

"And maybe the Yankees are too."

Harry's words were caused by the sound of a distant and scattering fire. In obedience to an order from Anderson, he and Dalton galloped forward, and, from a ridge, saw through their glasses a formidable Union column advancing toward Spottsylvania. As they looked they saw many men fall and they also saw flashes of flame from bushes and fences not far from its flank.

"Our sharpshooters are there," said Harry. And he was right. While the Union force was advancing in the night Stuart had dismounted many of his men and using them as skirmishers had incessantly harassed the march of Grant's vanguard led by Warren.

"Each army has been trying to catch the other napping," said Dalton.

"And neither has succeeded," said Harry.

"Now we make a race for the Spottsylvania ridge," said Dalton. "You see if we don't! I know this country. It's a strong position there, and both generals want it."

Dalton was right. A small Union force had already occupied Spottsylvania, but the heavy Southern division crossing the narrow, but deep, river Po, drove it out and seized the defensive position.

Here they rested, while the masses of the two armies swung toward them, as if preparing for a new battlefield, one that Harry surveyed with great interest. They were in a land of numerous and deep rivers. Here were four spreading out, like the fingers of a human hand, without the thumb, and uniting at the wrist. The fingers were the Mat, the Ta, the Po, and the Nye, and the unit when they united was called the Mattopony.

Lee's army was gathering behind the Po. A large Union force crossed it on his flank, but, recognizing the danger of such a position, withdrew. Lee himself came in time. Hill, overcome by illness and old wounds, was compelled to give up the command of his division, and Early took his place. Longstreet also was still suffering severely from his injuries. Lee had but few of the able and daring generals who had served him in so many fields. But Stuart, the gay and brilliant, the medieval knight who had such a strong place in the commander-in-chief's affections, was there. Nor was his plumage one bit less splendid. The yellow feather stood in his hat. There was no speck or stain on the broad yellow sash and his undimmed courage was contagious.

But Harry with his sensitive and imaginative mind, that leaped ahead, knew their situation to be desperate. His opinion of Grant had proved to be correct. Although he had found in Lee an opponent far superior to any other that he had ever faced, the Union general, undaunted by his repulse and tremendous losses in the Wilderness, was preparing for a new battle, before the fire from the other had grown cold.

He knew too that another strong Union army was operating far to the south of them, in order to cut them off from Richmond, and scouts had brought word that a powerful force of cavalry was about to circle upon their flank. The Confederacy was propped up alone by the Army of Northern Virginia, which having just fought one great battle was about to begin another, and by its dauntless commander.

The Southern admiration for Lee, both as the general and as the man, can never be shaken. How much greater then was the effect that he created in the mind of impressionable youth, looking upon him with youth's own eyes in his moments of supreme danger! He was in very truth to Harry another Hannibal as great, and better. The long list of his triumphs, as youth counted them, was indeed superior to those of the great Carthaginian, and he believed that Lee would repel this new danger.

Nearly all that day the two armies constructed breastworks which stood for many years afterward, but neither made any attempt at serious work, although there was incessant firing by the skirmishers and an occasional cannon shot. Harry, whether carrying an order or not, had ample chance to see, and he noted with increasing alarm the growing masses of the Union army, as they gathered along the Spottsylvania front.

"Can we beat them?" "Can we beat them?" was the question that he continually asked himself. He wondered too where the Winchester regiment and Dick Mason lay, and where the spy, Shepard, was. But Shepard was not likely to remain long in one place. Skill and courage such as his would be used to the utmost in a time like this. Doubtless he was somewhere in the Confederate lines, discovering for Grant the relatively small size of the army that opposed him.

Near dusk and having the time he followed his custom and sought the Invincibles. Both colonels had recovered considerable strength, and, although one of them could not walk, he would be helped upon his horse whenever the battle began, and would ride into the thick of it. But the faces of St. Clair and Happy Tom glowed and their wounds apparently were forgotten.

"Lieutenant Arthur St. Clair and Lieutenant Thomas Langdon are gone forever," said Colonel Talbot. "In their places we have Major Arthur St. Clair and Captain Thomas Langdon. All our majors and captains have been killed, and with our reduced numbers these two will fill their places, as best they can; and that they can do so most worthily we all know. They received their promotions this afternoon."

Harry congratulated them both with the greatest warmth. They were very young for such rank, but in this war the toll of officers was so great that men sometimes became generals when they were but little older.

"Is it to be to-morrow?" asked Colonel Talbot.

"I think it likely that we'll fight again then," said Harry.

"And Grant has not yet had enough. He wants a little more of the same, does he!"

"It would appear so, sir."

"Then I take it without consulting General Lee that he is ready to deal with the Yankees as he dealt with them in the Wilderness."

"I hope so. Good night."

"Good night!" they called to him, and Harry returned to the staff. Taylor, the adjutant general, told him and Dalton to lie down and seek a little sleep. Harry was not at all averse, as he was completely exhausted again after the tremendous excitement of the battle, and the long hours of strain and danger. But his nerves were so much on edge that he could not yet sleep. His eyes were red and smarting from the smoke and burned powder, and he felt as if accumulated smoke and dust encased him like a suit of armor.

"I'd give a hundred dollars for a good long drink, just as long as I liked to make it," he groaned, "and I mean a drink of pure cold water, too."

"Confederate paper or money?" said Dalton.

"I mean real money, but at the same time you oughtn't to make invidious comparisons."

"Then the money's mine, but you can pay me whenever you feel like it, which I suppose will be never. There's a spring in the thick woods just back of your quarters. It flows out from under rocks, at the distance of several yards makes a deep pool, and then the overflow of the pool goes on through the forest to the Po. Come on, Harry! We'll luxuriate and then tell the others."

Harry found that it was a most glorious spring, indeed; clear and cold. He and Dalton drank slowly at first, and then deeply.

"I didn't know I could hold so much," said Dalton.

"Nor I," said Harry.

"Let's take another."

"I'm with you."

"Let's make it two more."

"I still follow you."

"Horace wrote about his old Falernian, and the other wines which he enjoyed, as he and the leading Roman sports sat around the fountain, flirting with the girls," said Dalton, "but I don't believe any wine ever brewed in Latium was the equal of this water."

"I've always had an idea that Horace wasn't as gay as he pretended to be, else he wouldn't have written so much about Chloe and her comrades. I imagine that an old Roman boy would keep pretty quiet about his dancing and singing, and not publish it to the public."

"Well, let him be. He's dead and the Romans are dead, and the Americans are doing their best to kill off one another, but let's forget it for a few minutes. That pool there is about four feet deep, the water is clear and the bottom is firm ground; now do you know what I'm going to do?"

"Yes, and I'm going to do the same. Bet you even that I beat you into the water."

"Taken."

They threw off their clothes rapidly, but the splashes were simultaneous as their bodies struck the water. Although the limits of the pool were narrow they splashed and paddled there for a while, and it was a long time since they had known such a luxury. Then they walked out, dried themselves and spread the good news. All night long the pool was filled with the bathers, following one another in turn.

The water taken internally and externally soothed Harry's nerves. His excitement was gone. A great army with which they were sure to fight on the morrow was not far away, but for the time he was indifferent. The morrow could take care of itself. It was night, and he had permission to go to sleep. Hence he slumbered fifteen minutes later.

He slept almost through the night, and, when he was awakened shortly before dawn, he found that his strength and elasticity had returned. He and Dalton went down to the spring again, drank many times, and then ate breakfast with the older members of the staff, a breakfast that differed very little from that of the common soldiers.

Then a day or two of waiting, and watching, and of confused but terrible fighting ensued. The forests were again set on fire by the bursting shells and they were not able to rescue many of the wounded from the flames. Vast clouds again floated over the whole region, drawing a veil of dusk between the soldiers and the sun. But neither army was willing to attack the other in full force.

Grant commanding all the armies of the East was moving meanwhile. A powerful cavalry division, he heard, had got behind Beauregard, who was to protect Richmond, and was tearing up an important railway line used by the Confederacy. The daring Sheridan with another great division of cavalry had gone around Lee's left and was wrecking another railway, and with it the rations and medical supplies so necessary to the Confederates. Grant, recognizing his antagonist's skill and courage and knowing that to succeed he must destroy the main Southern army, resolved to attack again with his whole force.

The day had been comparatively quiet and the Army of Northern Virginia had devoted nearly the whole time to fortifying with earthworks and breastworks of logs. The young aides, as they rode on their missions, could easily see the Northern lines through their glasses. Harry's heart sank as he observed their extent. The Southern army was sadly reduced in numbers, and Grant could get reinforcement continually.

But such is the saving grace of human nature that even in these moments of suspense, with one terrible battle just over and another about to begin, soldiers of the Blue and Gray would speak to one another in friendly fashion in the bushes or across the Po. It was on the banks of this narrow river that Harry at last saw Shepard once more. He happened to be on foot that time, the slope being too densely wooded for his horse, and Shepard hailed him from the other side.

"Good day, Mr. Kenton. Don't fire! I want to talk," he said, holding up both hands as a sign of peace.

"A curious place for talking," Harry could not keep from saying.

"So it is, but we're not observed here. It was almost inevitable while the armies remained face to face that we should meet in time. I want to tell you that I've met your cousin, Richard Mason, here, and his commanding officer, Colonel Winchester. Oh, I know much more about you and your relationships than you think."

"How is Dick?"

"He has not been hurt, nor has Colonel Winchester. Mr. Mason has received a letter from his home and your home in Pendleton in Kentucky. The outlaws to the eastward are troublesome, but the town is occupied by an efficient Union garrison and is in no danger. His mother and all of his and your old friends, who did not go to the war, are in good health. He thought that in my various capacities as ranger, scout and spy I might meet you, and he asked me, if it so happened, to tell these things to you."

"I thank you," said Harry very earnestly, "and I'm truly sorry, Mr. Shepard, that you and I are on different sides."

"I suppose it's too late for you to come over to the Union and the true cause."

Harry laughed.

"You know, Mr. Shepard, there are no traitors in this war."

"I know it. I was merely jesting."

He slipped into the underbrush and disappeared. Harry confessed to himself once more that he liked Shepard, but he felt more strongly than ever that it had become a personal duel between them, and they would meet yet again in violence.

That night he had little to do. It was a typical May night in Virginia, clear and beautiful with an air that would have been a tonic to the nerves, had it not been for the bitter smoke and odors that yet lingered from the battle of the Wilderness.

Before dawn the scouts brought in a rumor that there was a heavy movement of Federal troops, although they did not know its meaning. It might portend another flank march by Grant, but a mist that had begun to rise after midnight hid much from them. The mist deepened into a fog, which made it harder for the Southern leaders to learn the meaning of the Northern movement.

Just as the dawn was beginning to show a little through the fog, Hancock and Burnside, with many more generals, led a tremendous attack upon the Southern right center. They had come so silently through the thickets that for once the Southern leaders were surprised. The Union veterans, rushing forward in dense columns, stormed and took the breastworks with the bayonet.

Many of the Southern troops, sound asleep, awoke to find themselves in the enemy's hands. Others, having no time to fire them, fought with clubbed rifles.

Harry, dozing, was awakened by the terrific uproar. Even before the dawn had fairly come the battle was raging on a long front. The center of Lee's army was broken, and the Union troops were pouring into the gap. Grant had already taken many guns and thousands of prisoners, and the bulldog of Shiloh and Vicksburg and Chattanooga was hurrying fresh divisions into the combat to extend and insure his victory. Through the forests swelled the deep Northern cry of triumph.

Harry had never before seen the Southern army in such danger, and he looked at General Lee, who had now mounted Traveller. The turmoil and confusion in front of them was frightful and indescribable. The Union troops had occupied an entire Confederate salient, and their generals, feeling that the moment was theirs, led them on, reckless of life, and swept everything before them.

Harry never took his eyes from Lee. The rising sun shot golden beams through the smoke and disclosed him clearly. His face was calm and his voice did not shake as he issued his orders with rapidity and precision. The lion at bay was never more the lion.

A new line of battle was formed, and the fugitives formed up with it. Then the Southern troops, uttering once more the fierce rebel yell, charged directly upon their enemy and under the eye of the great chief whom they almost worshiped.

Now Harry for the first time saw his general show excitement. Lee galloped to the head of one of the Virginia regiments, and ranging his horse beside the colors snatched off his hat and pointed it at the enemy. It was a picture which with all the hero worship of youth he never forgot. It did not even grow dim in his memory — the great leader on horseback, his hat in his hand, his eyes fiery, his face flushed, his hand pointing the way to victory or death.

It was an occasion, too, when the personal presence of a leader meant everything. Every man knew Lee and tremendous rolling cheers greeted his arrival, cheers that could be heard above the thunder of cannon and rifles. It infused new courage into them and they gathered themselves for the rush upon their victorious foe.

Gordon of Georgia, spurring through the smoke, seized Lee's horse by the bridle. He did not mean to have their commander-in-chief sacrificed in a charge.

"This is no place for you, General Lee!" he cried. "Go to the rear!"

Lee did not yet turn, and Gordon shouted:

"These men are Virginians and Georgians who have never failed. Go back, I entreat you!"

Then Gordon turned to the troops and cried, as he rose on his toes in his stirrups:

"Men, you will not fail now!"

Back came the answering shout:

"No! No!" and the whole mass of troops burst into one thunderous, echoing cry:

"Lee to the rear! Lee to the rear! Lee to the rear!"

Nor would they move until Lee turned and rode back. Then, led by Gordon, they charged straight upon their foe, who met them with an equal valor. All day long the battle of Spottsylvania, equal in fierceness and desperation to that of the Wilderness, swayed to and fro. To Harry as he remembered them they were much alike. Charge and defense, defense and charge. Here they gained a little, and there they lost a little. Now they were stumbling through sanguinary thickets, and then they rushed across little streams that ran red.

The firing was rapid and furious to an extraordinary degree. The air rained shell and bullets. Areas of forest between the two armies were mowed down. More than one large tree was cut through entirely by rifle bullets. Other trees here, as in the Wilderness, caught fire and flamed high.

Midnight put an end to the battle, with neither gaining the victory and both claiming it. Harry had lost another horse, killed under him, and now he walked almost dazed over the terrible field of Spottsylvania, where nearly thirty thousand men had fallen, and nothing had yet been decided.

Yet in Harry's heart the fear of the grim and silent Grant was growing. The Northern general had fought within a few days two battles, each the equal of Waterloo, and Harry felt sure that he was preparing for a third. The combat of the giants was not over, and with an anxious soul he waited the next dawn. They remained some days longer in the Wilderness, or the country adjacent to it, and there was much skirmishing and firing of heavy artillery, but the third great pitched battle did not come quite as soon as Harry expected. Even Grant, appalled by the slaughter, hesitated and began to maneuver again by the flank to get past Lee. Then the fighting between the skirmishers and heavy detached parties became continuous.

During the days that immediately followed Harry was much with Sherburne. The brave colonel was one of Stuart's most trusted officers. Despite the forests and thickets there was much work for the cavalry to do, while the two armies circled and circled, each seeking to get the advantage of the other.

Sheridan, they heard, was trying to curve about with his horsemen and reach Richmond, and Stuart, with his cavalry, including Sherburne's, was sent to intercept him, Harry riding by Sherburne's side. It was near the close of May, but the air was cool and pleasant, a delight to breathe after the awful Wilderness.

Stuart, despite his small numbers, was in his gayest spirits, and when he overtook the enemy at a little place called Yellow Tavern he attacked with all his customary fire and vigor. In the height of the charge, Harry saw him sink suddenly from his horse, shot through the body. He died not long afterward and the greatest and most brilliant horseman of the South passed away to join Jackson and so many who had gone before. Harry was one of the little group who carried the news to Lee, and he saw how deeply the great leader was affected. So many of his brave generals had fallen that he was like the head of a family, bereft.

Nevertheless the lion still at bay was great and terrible to strike. It was barely two weeks after Spottsylvania when Lee took up a strong position at Cold Harbor, and Grant, confident in his numbers and powerful artillery, attacked straightaway at dawn.

Harry was in front during that half-hour, the most terrible ever seen on the American continent, when Northern brigade after brigade charged to certain death. Lee's men, behind their earthworks, swept the field with a fire in which nothing could live. The charging columns fairly melted away before them and when the half-hour was over more than twelve thousand men in blue lay upon the red field.

Grant himself was appalled, and the North, which had begun to anticipate a quick and victorious end of the war, concealed its disappointment as best it could, and prepared for another campaign.

Grant and Lee, facing each other, went into trenches along the lines of Cold Harbor, and the hopes of the young Southern soldiers after the victory there rose anew. But Harry was not too sanguine, although he kept his thoughts to himself.

The officers of the Invincibles had recovered from their wounds, and Colonel Leonidas Talbot and Lieutenant-Colonel Hector St. Hilaire, sitting in a trench, resumed their game of chess.

Colonel Talbot took a pawn, the first man captured by either since early spring.

"That was quite a victory," he said.

"Not important! Not important, Leonidas!"

"And why not, Hector?"

"Because you've left the way to your king easier. I shall promptly move along that road."

"As Grant moved through the Wilderness."

"Don't depreciate Grant, Leonidas. He never stops pounding. We've fought two great battles with him in the Wilderness and a third at Cold Harbor, but he's still out there facing us. Can't you see the Yankees with your glasses, Harry?"

"Yes, sir, quite clearly. They're about to fire a shot from a big gun in a wood. There it goes!"

The deep note of the cannon came to them, passed on, and then rolled back in echoes like a threat.